ACCOUNTING: The Language of Business

NINTH EDITION • TWENTIETH ANNIVERSARY EDITION
Copyright © 1974, 1975, 1977, 1979, 1982, 1984, 1987, 1990, 1994

Roman L. Weil, Ph.D., CPA, CMA
University of Chicago

Patricia C. O'Brien, Ph.D.
University of Michigan

In Collaboration With

Michael M. Maher, Ph.D., CPA
University of California, Davis

Clyde P. Stickney, DBA, CPA
Dartmouth College

THOMAS HORTON AND DAUGHTERS
26662 S. New Town Drive • Sun Lakes, Arizona 85248

For Our Children

Thomas Horton and Daughters

ISBN 0-913878-51-0

Library of Congress Cataloging in Publication Data

Weil, Roman L
    Accounting: the language of business, ninth edition

1. Accounting-Terminology. 2. Accounting.

I. O'Brien Patricia C.   joint author.

III. Title.

HF5621.D28   657.03   94-5974

Typography by Greg Swann Typography & Graphics
Printed by Bookcrafters, Inc.

Preface

Accounting is the language of business. We hope this book will assist the student in becoming familiar with the language required to understand business communications. The first edition appeared in 1974. Since that time feedback from readers about the contents of the book has enabled us to refine the presentation—adding here, deleting there—to suit the wishes of teacher and students as well as those earning a living in business. Although some of the material here will seem too advanced for the beginner, we think the book has something cost-effective for all interested in business.

WE ARE PROFIT-ORIENTED and are eager to learn from you how we can make the book more successful. We will pay the first person who makes a given suggestion incorporated in subsequent editions. Such suggestions might include typographical errors ($1), additional cross references ($1), errors of fact or substance ($5), and additional terms with their explanation ($5).

This edition contains the following sections.

Glossary. Accounting's vocabulary comprises many words that have other meanings in ordinary usage. Understanding the concepts and using accounting reports require that the reader know how to interpret the words used and their special meaning. Students of accounting and readers of accounting reports will find the tasks easier the sooner they learn, for example, the difference between the meanings of *revenue* and *receipt*, between *fund* and *reserve*. The Glossary defines these and some 1,400 other terms. A glossary is not a dictionary, so that we have given definitions of terms only as accounting uses them.

Students and readers of financial reports will not encounter all the terms in the Glossary. We have tried to include, however, the terms found in textbooks, problems, financial reports, financial periodicals, and newspapers.

The Glossary defines many words and phrases in terms of other entries in the Glossary. Terms in a given definition themselves explained elsewhere are *italicized*. Many of the entries in the Glossary are multiple-word phrases because much of the specialized terminology of accounting depends upon such phrases. We have tried to anticipate the most likely phrase that will occur to the reader and have used that phrase in the Glossary. Nevertheless, we probably have failed in some cases to put the explanation by the word or phrase that occurs to you. As Jim Schindler (our co-author before his death) used to say, "If you can't find what you're looking for under one listing, keep looking under others."

Words and phrases are alphabetized using the word-by-word principle. Thus, the following terms appear in the order shown: *account, account form, account payable, accountancy, accounting, accounting standards, accounts receivable turnover*.

A few words in accounting, for example *cost* and *expense*, mean different things to different people. We believe that the more precise the meaning of the words used, the easier is the understanding of accounting. Consequently, we give the restricted definition, for example, of *cost* that we think enhances the user's ability to understand. We also give the variants in meaning often used in practice. Further, certain terms used widely in the accounting profession, for example, *prepaid expenses* seem to us to be oxymorons given our preference for restricted and unambiguous definitions.

General Electric Company's Annual Report. GE's annual report is consistently among the best published. We reproduce GE's annual report issued in 1994 along with our own comments which should help in understanding it, and, we hope, other financial statements as well.

Penn Central Transportation Company's Balance Sheet Just Before Its Bankruptcy. One widely-known bankruptcies was that of Penn Central. We reproduce Penn Central's balance sheet so that the reader can see the limitations of analyzing the stockholders' equity section of the balance sheet in forecasting bankruptcy. The annual report shows retained earnings of almost half a billion dollars and stockholders' equity of almost $2 billion. Yet soon after the report appeared, the company petitioned for bankruptcy because it could not meet its obligations.

Accounting Magic. This example shows how generally accepted accounting principles allow such a range of accounting treatments that two firms, exactly alike in all respects except for their accounting methods, report drastically different incomes.

Pronouncements Governing Generally Accepted Accounting Principles. We include a list of pronouncements governing generally accepted accounting principles and their dates of issuance.

    We gratefully acknowledge the permission of The Dryden Press to reproduce material from our *Financial Accounting* and *Managerial Accounting* texts they publish. Gregg Swann and Eli Worman designed the book and planned the layout. We thank them for their help.

Table of Contents

Glossary

The definitions of many words and phrases in the Glossary use other Glossary terms. We *italicize* terms in a given definition (definiens) that themselves (or variants thereof) appear elsewhere under their own listings (as definienda). The cross references generally take one of two forms:

[1] **absorption costing.** See *full absorption costing.*

[2] **ABC.** *Activity-based costing.*

Form [1] refers you to another term for discussion of this **boldfaced** term (definiendum). Form [2] tells you that this **boldfaced** term (definiendum) is synonymous with the *italicized* term, which you can consult for discussion if necessary.

A

AAA. *American Accounting Association.*

Abacus. A scholarly journal containing articles on theoretical aspects of accounting. Published twice a year by the Sydney University Press, Sydney, Australia.

abatement. A complete or partial cancellation of a levy imposed by a government unit.

ABC. *Activity-based costing.*

abnormal spoilage. Actual spoilage exceeding that expected when operations are normally efficient. Usual practice treats this cost as an *expense* of the period rather than as a *product cost.* Contrast with *normal spoilage.*

aboriginal cost. In public utility accounting, the *acquisition cost* of an *asset* incurred by the first *entity* devoting that asset to public use. Most public utility regulation is based on aboriginal cost. If it were not, then public utilities could exchange assets among themselves at ever-increasing prices in order to raise the rate base and, then, prices based thereon.

absorbed overhead. *Overhead costs* allocated to individual products at some *overhead rate.* Also called *applied overhead.*

absorption costing. See *full absorption costing.*

Abstracts of the EITF. See *Emerging Issues Task Force.*

Accelerated Cost Recovery System. ACRS. A form of accelerated depreciation that Congress enacted in 1981 and amended in 1986. The system provides percentages of the asset's cost that a firm depreciates each year for tax purposes. ACRS ignores salvage value. We do not generally use these amounts for *financial accounting.*

accelerated depreciation. Any method of calculating *depreciation* charges where the charges become progressively smaller each period. Examples are *double-declining-balance* and *sum-of-the-years'-digits* methods.

acceptance. A written promise to pay that is equivalent to a *promissory note.*

account. Any device for accumulating additions and subtractions relating to a single *asset, liability,* or *owners' equity* item, including *revenues* and *expenses.*

account analysis method. A method of separating *fixed* from *variable costs* involving the classification of the various *product cost accounts.* For example, we classify *direct materials* as variable and *depreciation* on a factory building as fixed.

account form. The form of *balance sheet* where *assets* are shown on the left and *equities* are shown on the right. Contrast with *report form.* See also *T-account.*

account payable. A *liability* representing an amount owed to a *creditor,* usually arising from purchase of *merchandise* or materials and supplies, not necessarily due or past due. Normally, a *current* liability.

account receivable. A claim against a *debtor* usually arising from sales or services rendered, not necessarily due or past due. Normally, a *current asset.*

accountability center. *Responsibility center.*

accountancy. The British word for *accounting*. In the United States, it means the theory and practice of accounting.

accountant's comments. Canada. A written communication issued by a public accountant at the conclusion of a review engagement. It consists of a description of the work performed and a statement that, under the terms of the engagement, the accountant has not performed an audit and consequently expresses no opinion. (Compare *auditor's report; denial of opinion.*)

Accountants' Index. A publication of the *AICPA* that indexes, in detail, the accounting literature of the period.

accountant's opinion. *Auditor's report.*

accountant's report. *Auditor's report.*

accounting. A system conveying information about a specific *entity.* The information is in financial terms and appears only if it is reasonably precise. The *AICPA* defines accounting as a service activity whose "function is to provide quantitative information, primarily financial in nature, about economic entities that is intended to be useful in making economic decisions."

accounting changes. As defined by *APB Opinion No. 20,* a change in (a) an *accounting principle* (such as a switch from *FIFO* to *LIFO* or from *sum-of-the-years'-digits* to *straight-line depreciation),* (b) an accounting estimate (such as estimated useful lives or salvage value of depreciable assets and estimates of *warranty* costs or *uncollectible accounts),* and (c) the reporting *entity.* Changes of type (a) should be disclosed. The cumulative effect of the change on *retained earnings* at the start of the period during which the change was made should be included in reported earnings for the period of change. Changes of type (b) should be treated as affecting only the period of change and, if necessary, future periods. The reasons for changes of type (c) should be disclosed and, in statements reporting on operations of the period of the change, the effect of the change on all other periods reported on for comparative purposes should also be shown. In some cases (such as a change from *LIFO* to other inventory *flow assumptions* or in the method of accounting for long-term construction contracts), changes of type (a) are treated like changes of type (c). That is, for these changes all statements shown for prior periods must be restated to show the effect of adopting the change for those periods as well. See *all-inclusive concept* and *accounting errors.*

accounting conventions. Methods or procedures used in accounting. This term tends to be used when the method or procedure has not been given official authoritative sanction by a pronouncement of a group such as the *APB, EITF, FASB,* or *SEC.* Contrast with *accounting principles.*

accounting cycle. The sequence of accounting procedures starting with *journal entries* for various transactions and events and ending with the *financial statements* or, perhaps, the *post-closing trial balance.*

accounting deficiency. Canada. A failure to adhere to generally accepted *accounting principles* or to disclose essential information in *financial statements.*

accounting entity. See *entity.*

accounting equation. *Assets = Equities. Assets = Liabilities + Owners' Equity.*

accounting errors. Arithmetic errors and misapplications of *accounting principles* in previously published financial statements that are corrected in the current period with direct *debits* or *credits* to *retained earnings.* In this regard, they are treated like *prior-period adjustments,* but, technically, they are not classified by *APB Opinion No. 9* as prior-period adjustments. See *accounting changes* and contrast with changes in accounting estimates as described there.

accounting event. Any occurrence that is recorded in the accounting records.

Accounting Horizons. Quarterly journal of the *American Accounting Association.*

accounting methods. *Accounting principles.* Procedures for carrying out accounting principles.

accounting period. The time period between consecutive *balance sheets.* The time period for which *financial statements* that measure *flows,* such as the *income statement* and the *statement of cash flows,* are prepared. Should be clearly identified on the financial statements. See *interim statements.*

accounting policies. *Accounting principles* adopted by a specific *entity.*

accounting principles. The methods or procedures used in accounting for events reported in the *financial statements.* We tend to use this term when the method or procedure has received official authoritative sanction from a pronouncement of a group such as the *APB, EITF, FASB,* or *SEC.* Contrast with *accounting conventions* and *conceptual framework.*

Accounting Principles Board. See *APB.*

accounting procedures. See *accounting principles;* however, this term usually refers to the methods for implementing accounting principles.

accounting rate of return. Income for a period divided by average investment during the period. Based on income, rather than discounted cash flows and, hence, is a poor decision making aid or tool. See *ratio.*

Accounting Research Bulletin. ARB. The name of the official pronouncements of the former *Committee on Accounting Procedure* of the *AICPA.* Fifty-one bulletins were issued between 1939 and 1959. *ARB No. 43* restated and codified the parts of the first forty-two bulletins not dealing solely with definitions.

Accounting Research Study. ARS. One of a series of studies published by the Director of Accounting Research of the *AICPA* "designed to provide professional accountants and others interested in the development of accounting with a discussion and documentation of accounting problems." Fifteen such studies were published between 1961 and 1974.

The Accounting Review. Scholarly publication of the *American Accounting Association.*

Accounting Series Release. ASR. See *SEC.*

accounting standards. Same as *accounting principles.*

Accounting Standards Executive Committee. AcSEC. The senior technical committee of the *AICPA* authorized to speak for the AICPA in the areas of *financial accounting* and reporting as well as *cost accounting.*

accounting system. The procedures for collecting and summarizing financial data in a firm.

Accounting Terminology Bulletin. ATB. One of four releases of the Committee on Terminology of the *AICPA* issued in the period 1953-1957.

Accounting Trends and Techniques. An annual publication of the *AICPA* that surveys the reporting practices of 600 large corporations. It presents tabulations of specific practices, terminology, and disclosures along with illustrations taken from individual annual reports.

accounts receivable turnover. Net *sales on account* divided by average *accounts receivable.* See *ratio.*

accretion. See *amortization.* When a *book value* grows over time, such as a *bond* originally issued at a *discount,* the correct technical term is "accretion," not "amortization." Also, increase in economic worth through physical change, usually said of a natural resource such as an orchard, caused by natural growth. Contrast with *appreciation.*

accrual. Recognition of an *expense (or revenue)* and the related *liability (or asset)* that is caused by an *accounting event,* frequently by the passage of time, and that is not signaled by an explicit cash transaction. For example, the recognition of interest expense or revenue (or wages, salaries, or rent) at the end of a period even though no explicit cash transaction is made at that time. Cash flow follows accounting recognition; contrast with *deferral.*

accrual basis of accounting. The method of recognizing *revenues* as a firm sells *goods* (or delivers them) and as it renders *services,* independent of the time when it receives cash. This systems recognizes *expenses* in the period when it recognizes the related revenue independent of the time when it pays out cash. *SFAC No. 1* says "accrual accounting attempts to record the financial effects on an enterprise of transactions and other events and circumstances that have cash consequences for the enterprise in the periods in which those transactions, events, and circumstances occur rather than only in the periods in which cash is received or paid by the enterprise." Contrast with the *cash basis of accounting.* See *accrual* and *deferral.* We could more correctly call the basis "accrual/deferral" accounting.

accrue. See *accrued* and contrast with *incur.*

accrued. Said of a *revenue (expense)* that has been earned (recognized) even though the related *receivable (payable)* is not yet due or incurred. We prefer not to use this adjective as part of an account title. Thus, we prefer to use Interest Receivable (Payable) as the account title, rather than Accrued Interest Receivable (Payable). See *matching convention.* See *accrual.* Contrast with *incur.*

accrued depreciation. An incorrect term for *accumulated depreciation.* Acquiring an asset with cash, capitalizing it, and then amortizing its cost over periods of use is a process of *deferral* and allocation, not of *accrual.*

accrued payable. A *payable* usually resulting from the passage of time. For example, *salaries* and *interest* accrue as time passes. See *accrued.*

accrued receivable. A *receivable* usually resulting from the passage of time. See *accrued.*

accumulated benefit obligation. See *projected benefit obligation* for definition and contrast.

accumulated depreciation. A preferred title for the *contra-asset* account that shows the sum of *depreciation* charges on an asset since it was acquired. Other titles used are *allowance* for *depreciation* (acceptable term) and *reserve* for *depreciation* (unacceptable term).

accurate presentation. The qualitative accounting objective suggesting that information reported in financial statements should correspond as precisely as possible with the economic effects underlying transactions and events. See *fair presentation* and *full disclosure.*

acid test ratio. *Quick ratio.*

acquisition cost. Of an *asset,* the net *invoice* price plus all *expenditures* to place and ready the asset for its intended use. The other expenditures might include legal fees, transportation charges, and installation costs.

ACRS. *Accelerated Cost Recovery System.*

AcSEC. *Accounting Standards Executive Committee* of the *AICPA.*

activity accounting. *Responsibility accounting.*

activity-based costing. ABC. Method of assigning *indirect costs,* including non-manufacturing *overhead,* to products and services. ABC assumes that almost all overhead costs associate with activities within the firm and vary with respect to the *drivers* of those activities. Some practitioners suggest that ABC attempts to find the drivers for all indirect costs; these people note that in the long run, all costs are *variable,* so *fixed* indirect costs do not occur. The method first assigns costs to activities and then to products based on the products' usages of the activities.

activity-based depreciation. *Production method of depreciation.*

activity basis. *Costs* are *variable* or *fixed* (*incremental* or *unavoidable*) with respect to some activity, such as production of units (or the undertaking of some new project). Usage calls this activity the "activity basis."

activity center. Unit of the organization that performs a set of tasks.

activity variance. *Sales volume variance.*

actual cost (basis). *Acquisition* or *historical cost.* Also contrast with *standard cost.*

actual costing (system). Method of allocating costs to products using actual *direct materials,* actual *direct labor,* and actual *factory overhead.* Contrast with *normal costing* and *standard costing.*

actuarial. Usually said of computations or analyses that involve both *compound interest* and probabilities, such as the computation of the *present value* of a life-contingent *annuity.* Sometimes the term is used if only one of the two is involved.

actuarial accrued liability. A 1981 report of the Joint Committee on Pension Terminology (of various actuarial societies) stated that this term is the preferred one for *prior service cost.*

ad valorem. A method of levying a tax or duty on goods by using their estimated value as the tax base.

additional paid-in capital. An alternative acceptable title for the *capital contributed in excess of par (or stated) value account.*

additional processing cost. *Costs* incurred in processing *joint products* after the *splitoff point.*

adequate disclosure. *Fair presentation* of *financial statements* requires *disclosure* of *material* items. This *auditing standard* does not, however, require publicizing all information detrimental to a company. For example, the company may be threatened with a lawsuit and disclosure might seem to require a *debit* to a *loss* account and a *credit* to an *estimated liability.* But the mere making of this entry might adversely affect the actual outcome of the suit. Such entries need not be made although impending suits should be disclosed.

adjunct account. An *account* that accumulates additions to another account. For example, Premium on Bonds Payable is adjunct to the liability Bonds Payable; the effective liability is the sum of the two account balances at a given date. Contrast with *contra account.*

adjusted acquisition (historical) cost. Sometimes said of the *book value* of a *plant asset.* Also, cost adjusted to a *constant dollar* amount to reflect *general price level changes.*

adjusted bank balance of cash. The *balance* shown on the statement from the bank plus or minus amounts, such as for unrecorded deposits or outstanding checks, to reconcile the bank's balance with the correct cash balance. See *adjusted book balance of cash.*

adjusted basis. The *basis* used to compute gain or loss on disposition of an *asset* for tax purposes. See also *book value.*

adjusted book balance of cash. The *balance* shown in the firm's account for cash in bank plus or minus amounts, such as for *notes* collected by the bank or bank service charges, to reconcile the account balance with the correct cash balance. See *adjusted bank balance of cash.*

adjusted trial balance. *Trial balance* taken after *adjusting entries* but before *closing entries.* Contrast with *pre-* and *post-closing trial balances.* See *unadjusted trial balance* and *post-closing trial balance.* See also *work sheet.*

adjusting entry. An entry made at the end of an *accounting period* to record a *transaction* or other *accounting event,* which for some reason has not been recorded or has been improperly recorded during the accounting period. An entry to update the accounts. See *work sheet.*

adjustment. A change in an *account* produced by an *adjusting entry.* Sometimes accountants use the term to refer to the process of restating *financial statement* amounts to *constant dollars.*

administrative costs (expenses). *Costs (expenses)* incurred for the firm as a whole, in contrast with specific functions such as manufacturing or selling. Includes items such as salaries of top executives, general office rent, legal fees, and auditing fees.

admission of partner. Legally, when a new partner joins a *partnership,* the old partnership is dissolved and a new one comes into being. In practice, however, the old accounting records may be kept in use and the accounting entries reflect the manner in which the new partner joined the firm. If the new partner merely purchases the interest of another partner, the only accounting is to change the name for one capital account. If the new partner contributes *assets* and *liabilities* to the partnership, then the new assets must be recognized with debits and the liabilities and other source of capital, with credits. See *bonus method.*

ADR. See *asset depreciation range.*

advances from (by) customers. A preferred title for the *liability* account representing *receipts* of *cash* in advance of delivering the *goods* or rendering the *service* (that will cause *revenue* to be recognized). Sometimes called "deferred revenue" or "deferred income."

advances to affiliates. *Loans* by a parent company to a *subsidiary.* Frequently combined with "investment in subsidiary" as "investments and advances to subsidiary" and shown as a *noncurrent asset* on the parent's *balance sheet.* These advances are eliminated in *consolidated financial statements.*

advances to suppliers. A preferred term for the *asset account* representing *disbursements* of cash in advance of receiving *assets* or *services.*

adverse opinion. An *auditor's report* stating that the financial statements are not fair or are not in accord with *GAAP.*

affiliated company. Said of a company controlling or controlled by another company.

after closing. *Post-closing;* said of a *trial balance* at the end of the period.

after cost. Said of *expenditures* to be made subsequent to *revenue* recognition. For example, *expenditures* for *repairs* under warranty are after costs. Proper recognition of after costs involves a debit to expense at the time of the sale and a credit to an *estimated liability.* When the liability is discharged, the debit is to the estimated liability and the credit is to the assets consumed.

AG; Aktiengesellschaft. Germany. The form of a German company whose shares can trade on the stock exchange.

agency fund. An account for *assets* received by governmental units in the capacity of trustee or agent.

agency theory. A branch of economics relating the behavior of *principals* (such as owner non-managers or bosses) and their *agents* (such as non-owner managers or subordinates). The principal assigns responsibility and authority to the agent but the agent's own risks and preferences differ from those of the principal. The principal cannot observe all activities of the agent. Both the principal and the agent must consider the differing risks and preferences in designing incentive contracts.

agent. One authorized to transact business, including executing contracts, for another.

aging accounts receivable. The process of classifying *accounts receivable* by the time elapsed since the claim came into existence for the purpose of estimating the amount of uncollectible accounts receivable as of a given date. See *sales contra, estimated uncollectibles,* and *allowance for uncollectibles.*

aging schedule. A listing of *accounts receivable,* classified by age, used in *aging accounts receivable.*

AICPA. American Institute of Certified Public Accountants. The national organization that represents *CPAs.* See *AcSEC.* It oversees the writing and grading of the Uniform CPA Examination. Each state, however, sets its own requirements for becoming a CPA in that state. See *certified public accountant.*

all-capital earnings rate. *Rate of return on assets.*

all-current method. *Foreign currency translation* where all *financial statement* items are translated at the *current exchange rate.*

all-inclusive (income) concept. Under this concept, no distinction is drawn between *operating* and *nonoperating revenues* and *expenses;* thus, the only entries to retained earnings are for *net income* and *dividends.* Under this concept all *income, gains,* and *losses* are reported in the *income statement;* thus, events usually reported as *prior-period adjustments* and as *corrections of errors* are included in net income. This concept in its pure form is not the basis of *GAAP,* but *APB Opinions Nos. 9 and 30* move far in this direction. They do permit retained earnings entries for prior-period adjustments and correction of errors.

allocate. To spread a *cost* from one *account* to several accounts, to several products or activities, or to several periods.

allocation base. Accounting often assigns *joint costs* to *cost objectives* with some systematic method. The allocation base specifies the method. For example, a firm might assign the cost of a truck to periods based on miles driven during the period; the allocation base is miles. Or, the firm might assign the cost of a factory supervisor to a product based on *direct labor* hours; the allocation base is direct labor hours.

allocation of income taxes. See *deferred income tax.*

allowance. A balance sheet *contra account* generally used for *receivables* and depreciable assets. See *sales* (or *purchase*) *allowance* for another use of this term.

allowance for funds used during construction. One principle of public utility regulation and rate setting is that customers should pay the full costs of producing the services (e.g., electricity) that they use, nothing more and nothing less. Thus, an electric utility is even more careful than other businesses to capitalize into an *asset account* the full costs, but no more, of producing a new electric power generating plant. One of the costs of building a new plant is the *interest* cost on money tied up during construction. If *funds* are explicitly borrowed by an ordinary business, the journal entry for interest of $1,000 is typically:

Interest Expense	1,000	
Interest Payable		1,000
Interest expense for the period.		

If the firm is constructing a new plant, then another entry would be made capitalizing interest into the plant-under-construction account:

Construction Work in Progress	750	
Interest Expense.		750
Capitalize relevant portion of interest relating to construction work in progress into the asset account.		

The cost of the *plant asset* is increased; when the plant is used, *depreciation* is charged; the interest will become an expense through the depreciation process in the later periods of use, not currently as the interest is paid. Thus, the full cost of the electricity generated during a given period is reported as expense in that period. But suppose, as is common, that the electric utility does not explicitly borrow the funds, but uses some of its own funds, including funds raised from equity issues as well as from debt. Even though there is no explicit interest expense, there is the *opportunity cost* of the funds. Put another way, the cost of the plant under construction is not less in an economic sense just because the firm used its own cash, rather than borrowing. The public utility using its own funds, on which $750 of interest would be payable if the funds had been explicitly borrowed, will make the following entry:

Construction Work in Progress	750	
Allowance for Funds Used During Construction		750
Recognition of interest, an opportunity cost, on own funds used.		

The allowance account is a form of *revenue,* to appear on the income statement, and will be closed to Retained Earnings, increasing it. On the *funds statement,* it is an income or revenue item not producing funds and so must be subtracted from net income in deriving *funds provided by operations. SFAS No. 34* specifically prohibits nonutility companies from capitalizing the opportunity cost (interest) on own funds used into plant under construction.

allowance for uncollectibles (accounts receivable). A *contra* to Accounts Receivable that shows the estimated amount of *accounts receivable* that will not be collected. When such an allowance is used, the actual *write-off* of specific accounts receivable (*debit* allowance, *credit* specific account) does not affect *revenue* or *expense* at the time of the write-off. The revenue reduction is recognized when *bad debt expense* (or, preferred by your authors, a revenue contra account) is *debited* and the allowance is credited; the amount of the credit to the allowance may be based on a percentage of sales on account for a period of time or computed from *aging accounts receivable.* This contra account enables an estimate to be shown of the amount of receivables that will be collected without identifying specific uncollectible accounts. See *allowance method.*

allowance method. A method of attempting to *match* all *expenses* of a transaction with their associated *revenues.* Usually involves a debit to expense and a credit to an *estimated liability,* such as for estimated warranty expenditures, or a debit to a revenue (*contra*) account and a credit to an asset (*contra*) account, such as in some firms' accounting for uncollectible accounts. See *allowance for uncollectibles* for further explanation. When the allowance method is used for *sales discounts,* sales are recorded at *gross invoice* prices (not reduced by the amounts of discounts made available). An estimate of the amount of discounts to be taken is debited to a *revenue contra account* and *credited* to an allowance account, shown contra to *accounts receivable.*

American Accounting Association. AAA. An organization primarily for academic accountants, but open to all interested in accounting. It publishes *The Accounting Review.*

American Institute of Certified Public Accountants. See *AICPA.*

American Stock Exchange. AMEX. ASE. A public market where various corporate *securities* are traded.

AMEX. *American Stock Exchange.*

amortization. Strictly speaking, the process of liquidating or extinguishing ("bringing to death") a *debt* with a series of payments to the *creditor* (or to a *sinking fund*). From that usage has evolved a related use involving the accounting for the payments themselves: "amortization schedule" for a mortgage which is a table showing the allocation between *interest* and *principal.* The term has come to mean writing off ("liquidating") the cost of an asset. In this context it means the general process of *allocating acquisition cost* of an asset to either the periods of benefit as *expenses* or to *inventory* accounts as *product costs.* Called *depreciation* for *plant assets, depletion* for *wasting assets* (natural resources), and "amortization" for *intangibles. SFAC No. 6* refers to amortization as "the accounting process of reducing an amount by periodic payments or write-downs." The expressions "unamortized debt discount or premium" and "to amortize debt discount or premium" relate to *accruals,* not to *deferrals.* The expressions "amortization of long-term assets" and "to amortize long-term assets" refer to deferrals, not accruals. Contrast with *accretion.*

amortized cost. A measure required by *SFAS No. 115* for *debt securities held-to-maturity.* This amount results from applying the method described at *effective interest method.* The firm records the security at its initial cost and computes the *effective interest rate* for the security. Whenever the firm receives cash from the issuer of the security or whenever the firm reaches the end of one of its own *accounting periods* (that is, reaches the time for its own *adjusting entries),* it takes the following steps. It multiplies the amount currently recorded on the books by the effective interest rate (which remains constant over the time the firm holds the security). It debits that amount to the debt security account and credits the amount to Interest Revenue. If the firm receives cash, it debits Cash and credits the debt security account. The firm recomputes the book value of the debt security as the book value before these entries plus the increase for the interest revenue less the decrease for the cash received. The resulting amount is amortized cost.

analysis of variances. See *variance analysis.*

annual report. A report prepared once a year for shareholders and other interested parties. Includes a *balance sheet,* an *income statement,* a *statement of cash flows,* a reconciliation of changes in *owners' equity* accounts, a *summary of significant accounting principles,* other explanatory *notes,* the *auditor's report,* and comments from management about the year's events. See *10-K* and *financial statements.*

annuitant. One who receives an *annuity.*

annuity. A series of payments of equal amount, usually made at equally spaced time intervals.

annuity certain. An *annuity* payable for a definite number of periods. Contrast with *contingent annuity.*

annuity due. An *annuity* whose first payment is made at the start of period 1 (or at the end of period 0). Contrast with *annuity in arrears.*

annuity in advance. An *annuity due.*

annuity in arrears. An *ordinary annuity* whose first payment occurs at the end of the first period.

annuity method of depreciation. See *compound interest depreciation.*

antidilutive. Said of a *potentially dilutive security* that will increase *earnings per share* if it is *exercised* or *converted* into common stock. In computing *primary* and *fully diluted earnings per share,* antidilutive securities may not be assumed to be exercised or converted and, hence, do not increase reported earnings per share in a given period.

APB. Accounting Principles Board of the *AICPA.* It set *accounting principles* from 1959 through 1973, issuing 31 *APB Opinions* and 4 *APB Statements.* It was superseded by the *FASB.*

APB Opinion. The name given to pronouncements of the *APB* that make up much of *generally accepted accounting principles;* there are 31 *APB Opinions,* issued from 1962 through 1973.

APB Statement. The *APB* issued four *Statements* between 1962 and 1970. The *Statements* were approved by at least two thirds of the Board, but they are recommendations, not requirements. For example, *Statement No. 3* (1969) suggested the publication of *constant dollar financial statements* but did not require them.

APBs. An abbreviation used for *APB Opinions.*

applied cost. A *cost* that a firm has *allocated* to a department, product, or activity; it is not necessarily based on actual costs incurred.

applied overhead. *Overhead costs* charged to departments, products, or activities. Also called *absorbed overhead.*

appraisal. The process of obtaining a valuation for an *asset* or *liability* that involves expert opinion rather than evaluation of explicit market transactions.

appraisal method of depreciation. The periodic *depreciation* charge is the difference between the beginning and end-of-period appraised value of the *asset* if that difference is positive. If negative, there is no charge. Not based on *historical cost* nor, hence, generally accepted.

appreciation. An increase in economic worth caused by rising market prices for an *asset.* Contrast with *accretion.*

appropriated retained earnings. See *retained earnings, appropriated.*

appropriation. In governmental accounting, an *expenditure* authorized for a specified amount, purpose, and time.

appropriation account. In governmental accounting, an account set up to record specific authorizations to spend; it is credited with appropriation amounts. *Expenditures* during the period and *encumbrances* outstanding at the end of the period are closed (debited) to this account at the end of the period.

approximate net realizable value method. A method of assigning joint costs to *joint products* based on revenues minus *additional processing costs* of the end products.

ARB. *Accounting Research Bulletin.*

arbitrage. Strictly speaking, the simultaneous purchase in one market and sale in another of a *security* or commodity in hope of making a *profit* on price differences in the different markets. Often this term is loosely used when the item sold is somewhat different from the item purchased; for example, the sale of shares of *common stock* and the simultaneous purchase of a *convertible bond* that is convertible into identical common shares.

arm's length. Said of a transaction negotiated by unrelated parties, each acting in his or her own self-interest; the basis for a *fair market value* determination.

arrears. Said of *cumulative preferred stock dividends* that have not been declared up to the current date. See *annuity in arrears* for another context.

ARS. *Accounting Research Study.*

articles of incorporation. Document filed with state authorities by persons forming a corporation. When the document is returned with a certificate of incorporation, it becomes the corporation's *charter.*

articulate. Said of the relationship between any operating statement (for example, *income statement* or *statement of cash flows*) and *comparative balance sheets,* where the operating statement explains (or reconciles) the change in some major balance sheet category (for example, *retained earnings* or *working capital*).

ASE. *American Stock Exchange.*

ASR. *Accounting Series Release.*

assess. To value property for the purpose of property taxation; the assessment is computed by the taxing authority. To levy a charge on the owner of property for improvements thereto, such as for sewers or sidewalks.

assessed valuation. A dollar amount for real estate or other property used by a government as a basis for levying taxes. The amount may or may not bear some relation to *market value.*

asset. *SFAC No. 6* defines assets as "probable future economic benefits obtained or controlled by a particular entity as a result of past transactions.... An asset has three essential characteristics: (a) it embodies a probable future benefit that involves a capacity, singly or in combination with other assets, to contribute directly or indirectly to future net cash inflows, (b) a particular entity can obtain the benefit and control others' access to it, and (c) the transaction or other event giving rise to the entity's right to or control of the benefit has already occurred." A footnote points out that "probable" means that which we can reasonably expect or believe but that is not certain or proved. May be *tangible* or *intangible, short-term* (current) or *long-term* (noncurrent).

asset depreciation range. ADR. The range of *depreciable lives* allowed by the *Internal Revenue Service* for a specific depreciable *asset.*

asset turnover. Net sales divided by average assets. See *ratio.*

assignment of accounts receivable. Transfer of the legal ownership of an *account receivable* through its sale. Contrast with *pledging* accounts receivable where the receivables serve as *collateral* for a *loan.*

ATB. *Accounting Terminology Bulletin.*

at par. Said of a *bond* or *preferred stock* issued or selling at its *face amount.*

attachment. The laying claim to the *assets* of a borrower or debtor by a lender or creditor when the borrower has failed to pay debts on time.

attest. Rendering of an *opinion* by an auditor that the *financial statements* are fair. Common usage calls this procedure the "attest function" of the CPA. See *fair presentation.*

attestor. The *FASB* describes accounting's constituency as comprising preparers, attestors, and users. Attestors are independent *CPAs*, those who *audit financial statements* prepared by management for the benefit of users.

attribute measured. When making physical measurements, such as of a person, one needs to decide the units with which to measure, such as inches or centimeters or pounds or grams. One chooses the attribute height or weight independently of the measuring unit, English or metric. In conventional accounting the attribute measured is *historical cost* and the measuring unit is *nominal dollars.* Some theorists argue that accounting is more useful when the attribute measured is *current cost.* Others argue that accounting is more useful when the measuring unit is *constant dollars.* Some, including us, think both changes from conventional accounting should be made. The attribute historical cost can be measured in nominal dollars or in constant dollars. The attribute current cost can also be measured in nominal dollars or constant dollars. Choosing between the two attributes and the two measuring units implies four different accounting systems. Each of these four has its uses.

attribute(s) sampling. The use of sampling technique in which each item selected is assessed on the basis of whether it has a particular qualitative characteristic in order to ascertain the rate of occurrence of this characteristic in the population. See also *estimation sampling.* Compare *variables sampling.*

audit. Systematic inspection of accounting records involving analyses, tests, and *confirmations.* See *internal audit.*

audit committee. A committee of the board of directors of a *corporation* usually consisting of outside directors who nominate the independent auditors and discuss the auditors' work with them. If the auditors believe the shareholders should know about certain matters, the auditors first bring these matters to the attention of the audit committee.

Audit Guides. See *Industry Audit Guides.*

audit program. The procedures followed by the *auditor* in carrying out the *audit.*

audit trail. A reference accompanying an *entry,* or *posting,* to an underlying source record or document. A good audit trail is essential for efficiently checking the accuracy of accounting entries. See *cross-reference.*

Auditing Research Monograph. Publication series of the *AICPA.*

auditing standards. A set of ten standards promulgated by the *AICPA,* including three general standards, three standards of field work, and four standards of reporting. According to the AICPA, these standards "deal with the measures of the quality of the performance and the objectives to be attained," rather than with specific auditing procedures.

Auditing Standards Advisory Council. An *AICPA* committee.

Auditing Standards Board. Operating committee of the *AICPA* promulgating auditing rules.

auditor. One who checks the accuracy, fairness, and general acceptability of accounting records and statements and then *attests* to them.

auditor's opinion. *Auditor's report.*

auditor's report. The auditor's statement of the work done and an opinion of the *financial statements.* The auditor usually gives unqualified ("clean") opinions, but may qualify them, or the auditor may disclaim an opinion in the report. Often called the "accountant's report." See *adverse opinion.*

AudSEC. The former Auditing Standards Executive Committee of the *AICPA,* now functioning as the *Auditing Standards Board.*

authorized capital stock. The number of *shares* of stock that can be issued by a corporation; specified by the *articles of incorporation.*

available for sale, securities. *Marketable securities* a firm holds that are neither *trading securities* nor *held-to-maturity securities.* A classification important in *SFAS No. 115,* which requires the owner to carry marketable equity securities on the balance sheet at market value, not at cost. Under *SFAS No. 115,* the income statement reports *holding gains and losses* on trading securities, but not on securities available for sale. The required accounting *credits (debits)* holding gains (losses) on securities available for sale directly to an *owners' equity* account. On sale, the firm reports realized gain or loss as the difference between the selling price and original cost.

average. The arithmetic mean of a set of numbers; obtained by summing the items and dividing by the number of items.

average collection period of receivables. See *ratio.*

average-cost flow assumption. An *inventory flow assumption* where the cost of units equals the *weighted average* cost of the *beginning inventory* and purchases. See *inventory equation.*

average tax rate. The rate found by dividing *income tax expense* by *net income* before taxes. Contrast with *marginal tax rate, statutory tax rate.*

avoidable cost. A *cost* that ceases if a firm discontinues an activity. An *incremental* or *variable cost.* See *programmed cost.*

B

backflush costing. A method of *allocating indirect costs* and *overhead* to product used by companies which hope to have zero

or small *work-in-process inventory* at the end of the period. The method *debits* all *product costs* to *Cost of Goods Sold* (or *Finished Goods Inventory)* during the period. To the extent work in process actually exists at the end of the period, the method then debits Work-In-Process and *credits* Cost of Goods Sold (or Finished Goods Inventory). This method is "backflush" in the sense that costing systems usually allocate first to work in process and then forward to cost of goods sold or to finished goods.

backlog. Orders for which a firm has insufficient *inventory* on hand for current delivery and will fill in a later period.

backlog depreciation. In *current cost accounting,* a problem arising for the *accumulated depreciation* on *plant assets.* Consider an *asset* costing $10,000 with a 10-year life depreciated with the *straight-line method.* Assume that a similar asset has a current cost of $10,000 at the end of the first year but $12,000 at the end of the second year. Assume that the depreciation charge is based on the average current cost during the year, $10,000 for the first year and $11,000 for the second. The depreciation charge for the first year is $1,000 and for the second is $1,100 (= .10 x $11,000), so the *accumulated depreciation account* is $2,100 after 2 years. Note that at the end of the second year, 20 percent of the asset's future benefits have been used, so the accounting records based on current costs must show a *net book value* of $9,600 (= .80 x $12,000), which would result if accumulated depreciation of $2,400 were subtracted from a current cost of $12,000. But the sum of the depreciation charges has been only $2,100. The *journal entry* to increase the accumulated depreciation account requires a *credit* to that account of $300. The question arises, what account do we debit? That is the problem of backlog depreciation. Some theorists would *debit* an *income* account and others would *debit* a *balance sheet owners' equity* account without reducing current-period earnings. The answer to the question of what to do with the debit is closely tied to the problem of how *holding gains* are recorded. When the asset account is debited for $2,000 to increase the recorded amount from $10,000 to $12,000, a holding gain or $2,000 must be recorded with a credit. Many theorists believe that whatever account is credited for the holding gains is the same account that should be debited for backlog depreciation. Sometimes called "catch-up depreciation."

bad debt. An *uncollectible account receivable;* see *bad debt expense* and *sales contra, estimated uncollectibles.*

bad debt expense. The name for an *account debited* in both the *allowance method* for *uncollectibles* and the *direct write-off method.* Under the allowance method, some prefer to treat the account as a revenue contra, not as an expense and give it an appropriate title.

bad debt recovery. Collection, perhaps partial, of a specific account receivable previously written off as uncollectible. If the *allowance method* is used, the *credit* is usually to the *allowance* account. If the *direct write-off method* is used, the credit is to a *revenue account.*

bailout period. In a *capital budgeting* context, the total time that must elapse before net accumulated cash inflows from a project, including potential *salvage value* of assets at various times, equal or exceed the accumulated cash outflows. Contrast with *payback period,* which assumes completion of the project and uses terminal salvage value. Bailout is superior to payback because bailout takes into account, at least to some degree, the *present value* of the cash flows after termination date being considered. The potential salvage value at any time includes some estimate of the flows that can occur after that time.

balance. As a noun, the sum of *debit* entries minus the sum of *credit* entries in an *account*. If positive, we call the difference a debit balance; if negative, a credit balance. As a verb, to find the difference described above.

balance sheet. Statement of financial position that shows Total *Assets* = Total *Liabilities* + *Owners' Equity*. The *balance sheet accounts* compromising Total Assets are usually classified under the headings (1) *current assets,* (2) *investments,* (3) *property, plant, and equipment,* or (4) *intangible assets.* The balance sheet accounts compromising Total Liabilities are usually classified under the heading current liabilities or long-term liabilities.

balance sheet account. An account that can appear on a balance sheet. A *permanent account;* contrast with *temporary account.*

balloon. Most *mortgage* and *installment loans* require relatively equal periodic payments. Sometimes, the loan requires relatively equal periodic payments with a large final payment. Usage calls the large final payment a "balloon" payment and the loan with them a "balloon" loan. Although a *coupon bond* meets this definition, usage seldom if ever, applies this term to bond loans.

bank balance. The amount of the balance in a checking account shown on the *bank statement.* Compare with *adjusted bank balance* and see *bank reconciliation schedule.*

bank prime rate. See *prime rate.*

bank reconciliation schedule. A schedule that shows how the difference between the book balance of the cash in bank account and the bank's statement can be explained. Takes into account the amount of such items as checks issued that have not cleared or deposits that have not been recorded by the bank as well as errors made by the bank or the firm.

bank statement. A statement sent by the bank to a checking account customer showing deposits, checks cleared, and service charges for a period, usually one month.

bankrupt. Said of a company whose *liabilities* exceed its *assets* where a legal petition has been filed and accepted under the bankruptcy law. A bankrupt firm is usually, but need not be, *insolvent.*

base stock method. A method of inventory valuation that assumes that there is a minimum normal or base stock of goods that must be kept on hand at all times for effective continuity of operations. This base quantity is valued at *acquisition cost* of the inventory on hand in the earliest period when inventory was on hand. The method is not allowable for income tax purposes and is no longer used, but is generally considered to be the forerunner of the *LIFO* method.

basic accounting equation. *Accounting equation.*

basic cost-flow equation. *Cost-flow equation.*

basis. *Acquisition cost,* or some substitute therefore, of an *asset* or *liability* used in computing gain or loss on disposition or retirement. *Attribute measured.* This term is used in both *financial* and *tax reporting,* but the basis of a given item need not be the same for both purposes.

basket purchase. Purchase of a group of *assets* (and *liabilities*) for a single price; *costs* must be assigned to each of the items so that the individual items can be recorded in the *accounts.*

bear. One who believes that security prices will fall. A "bear market" refers to a time when stock prices are generally declining. Contrast with *bull.*

bearer bond. See *registered bond* for contrast and definition.

beginning inventory. Valuation of *inventory* on hand at the beginning of the *accounting period.*

behavioral congruence. *Goal congruence.*

betterment. An *improvement,* usually *capitalized.*

BGB. See *GbR.*

bid. An offer to purchase, or the amount of the offer.

big bath. A *write-off* of a substantial amount of costs previously treated as *assets.* Usually caused when a corporation drops a line of business that required a large investment but that proved to be unprofitable. Sometimes used to describe a situation where a corporation takes a large write-off in one period in order to free later periods of gradual write-offs of those amounts. In this sense it frequently occurs when there is a change in top management.

Big Six. The six largest U.S. *public accounting (CPA)* partnerships; in alphabetical order: Arthur Andersen & Co.; Coopers & Lybrand; Deloitte & Touche; Ernst & Young; KPMG Peat Marwick; and Price Waterhouse.

bill. An *invoice* of charges and *terms of sale* for *goods* and *services.* Also, a piece of currency.

bill of materials. A specification of the quantities of *direct materials* a firm expects to use to produce a given job or quantity of output.

blocked currency. Currency whose holder by law cannot withdraw from the issuing country or exchange for the currency of another country.

board of directors. The governing body of a corporation elected by the shareholders.

bond. A certificate to show evidence of debt. The *par value* is the *principal* or face amount of the bond payable at maturity. The *coupon rate* is the amount of interest payable in one year divided by the principal amount. Coupon bonds have attached to them coupons that can be redeemed at stated dates for interest payments. Normally, bonds carry semiannual coupons.

bond conversion. The act of exchanging *convertible bonds* for *preferred* or *common stock.*

bond discount. From the standpoint of the issuer of a *bond* at the issue date, the excess of the *par value* of a bond over its initial sales price; at later dates the excess of par over the sum of the following two amounts: initial issue price plus the portion of discount already *amortized.* From the standpoint of a bondholder, the difference between par value and selling price when the bond sells below par.

bond indenture. The contract between an issuer of *bonds* and the bondholders.

bond premium. Exactly parallel to *bond discount* except that the issue price (or current selling price) is higher than *par value.*

bond ratings. Ratings of corporate and *municipal bond* issues by Moody's Investors Service and by Standard & Poor's Corporation, based on the issuer's existing *debt* level, its previous record of payment, the *coupon rate* on the bonds, and the safety of the *assets* or *revenues* that are committed to paying off *principal* and *interest.* Moody's top rating is Aaa; Standard & Poor's is AAA.

bond redemption. Retirement of *bonds.*

bond refunding. To incur *debt,* usually through the issue of new *bonds,* intending to use the proceeds to retire an *outstanding* bond issue.

bond sinking fund. See *sinking fund.*

bond table. A table showing the current price of a *bond* as a function of the *coupon rate,* years to *maturity,* and effective *yield to maturity* (or *effective rate).*

bonus. Premium over normal *wage* or *salary,* paid usually for meritorious performance.

bonus method. When a new partner is admitted to a *partnership,* and the new partner is to be credited with *capital* in excess proportion to the amount of *tangible* assets he or she contributes, two methods may be used to recognize this excess, say $10,000. First, $10,000 may be transferred from the old partners to the new one. This is the bonus method. Second, goodwill in the amount of $10,000 may be recognized as an asset with the credit to the new partner's capital account. This is the *goodwill method.* (Notice that the new partner's percentage of total ownership is not the same under the two methods.) If the new partner is to be credited with capital in smaller proportion than the amount of contribution, then there will be bonus or goodwill for the old partners.

book. As a verb, to record a transaction. As a noun, usually plural, the *journals* and *ledgers.* As an adjective, see *book value.*

book cost. *Book value.*

book inventory. An *inventory* amount that results, not from physical count, but from the amount of beginning inventory plus *invoice* amounts of net purchases less invoice amounts of *requisitions* or withdrawals; implies a *perpetual* method.

book of original entry. A *journal.*

book value. The amount shown in the books or in the *accounts* for an *asset, liability,* or *owners' equity* item. Generally used to refer to the *net* amount of an *asset* or group of assets shown in the account that records the asset and reductions, such as for *amortization,* in its cost. Of a firm, the excess of total assets over total liabilities. *Net assets.*

book value per share of common stock. Common *shareholders' equity* divided by the number of shares of *common stock outstanding.* See *ratio.*

bookkeeping. The process of analyzing and recording transactions in the accounting records.

boot. The additional money paid (or received) along with a used item in a trade-in or exchange transaction for another item. See *trade-in transaction.*

borrower. See *loan.*

branch. A sales office or other unit of an enterprise physically separated from the home office of the enterprise but not organized as a legally separate *subsidiary.* Writers seldom use this term to refer to manufacturing units.

branch accounting. An accounting procedure that enables the financial position and operations of each *branch* to be reported separately but later combined for published statements.

breakeven analysis. See *breakeven chart.*

breakeven chart. Two kinds of breakeven charts are shown here. The charts are based on the information for a month shown below. Revenue is $30 per unit.

Cost Classification	Variable Cost, Per Unit	Fixed Cost, Per Month
Manufacturing costs:		
Direct material	$ 4	—
Direct labor	9	—
Overhead	4	$3,060
Total manufacturing costs	$17	$3,060
Selling, general and administrative costs	5	1,740
Total costs	$22	$4,800

The cost-volume-profit graph presents the relationship of changes in volume to the amount of *profit,* or *income.* On such a graph, total *revenue* and total *costs* for each volume level are indicated and profit or loss at any volume can be read directly from the chart. The profit-volume graph does not show revenues and costs but more readily indicates profit (or loss) at various output levels. Two caveats should be kept in mind about these graphs. Although the curve depicting *variable cost* and total cost is shown as being a straight line for its entire length, it is likely that at low or high levels of output, variable cost would probably differ from $22 per unit. The variable cost figure was probably established by studies of operations at some broad central area of production, called the *relevant range.* For low (or high) levels of activity, the chart may not be applicable. For this reason, the total cost and profit-loss curves are sometimes shown as dotted lines at lower (or higher) volume levels. Second, this chart is simplified because it assumes a single product firm. For a multiproduct firm, the horizontal axis would have to be stated in dollars rather than in physical units of output. Breakeven charts for multiproduct firms necessarily assume that constant proportions of the several products are sold and changes in this mixture as well as in costs or selling prices would invalidate such a chart.

A. Cost-Volume-Profit Graph

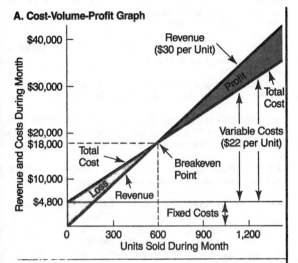

B. Profit-Volume Graph

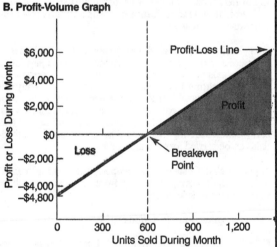

breakeven point. The volume of sales required so that total *revenues* and total *costs* are equal. May be expressed in units (*fixed costs/contribution per unit*) or in sales dollars [selling price per unit x (fixed costs/contribution per unit)].

budget. A financial plan that a firm uses to estimate the results of future operations. Frequently used to help control future operations. In governmental operations, budgets often become the law.

budgetary accounts. In governmental accounting, the accounts that reflect estimated operations and financial condition, as affected by estimated *revenues, appropriations,* and *encumbrances.* In contrast to *proprietary accounts* that record the transactions.

budgetary control. Management of governmental (non-governmental) unit in accordance with an official (approved) *budget* in order to keep total expenditures within authorized (planned) limits.

budgeted cost. See *standard cost* for definition and contrast.

budgeted statements. *Pro forma statements* prepared before the event or period occurs.

bull. One who believes that security prices will rise. A "bull market" refers to a time when stock prices are generally rising. Contrast with *bear.*

burden. See *overhead costs.*

burn rate. A new business usually begins life with cash-absorbing operating losses, but with a limited amount of cash. The "burn rate" measures how long the new business can survive before operating losses must stop or a new infusion of cash will be necessary. The measurement is ordinarily stated in terms of months.

business combination. As defined in *APB Opinion No. 16,* the bringing together into a single accounting *entity* of two or more incorporated or unincorporated businesses. The *merger* will be accounted for either with the *purchase method* or the *pooling-of-interests method.* See *conglomerate.*

business entity. *Entity. Accounting entity.*

bylaws. The rules adopted by the shareholders of a corporation that specify the general methods for carrying out the functions of the corporation.

by-product. A *joint product* whose sales value is so small relative to the sales value of the other joint product(s) that it does not receive normal accounting treatment. The costs assigned to by-products reduce the costs of the main product(s). Accounting allocates by-products a share of joint costs such that the expected gain or loss upon their sale is zero. Thus, by-products appear in the *accounts* at *net realizable value.*

C

CA. *Chartered accountant.*

call. An option to buy *shares* of a publicly-traded corporation at a fixed price during a fixed time span. Contrast with *put.*

call premium. See *callable bond.*

call price. See *callable bond.*

callable bond. A *bond* for which the issuer reserves the right to pay a specific amount, the call price, to retire the obligation before *maturity* date. If the issuer agrees to pay more than the *face amount* of the bond when called, the excess of the payment over the face amount is the "call premium."

Canadian Institute of Chartered Accountants. The national organization that represents *chartered accountants* in Canada.

cancelable lease. See *lease*.

capacity. Stated in units of product, the amount that a firm can produce per unit of time. Stated in units of input, such as *direct labor* hours, the amount of input that a firm can use in production per unit of time. A firm uses this measure of output or input in allocating *fixed costs* if the amounts producible are normal, rather than maximum, amounts.

capacity cost. A *fixed cost* incurred to provide a firm with the capacity to produce or to sell. Consists of *standby costs* and *enabling costs*. Contrast with *programmed costs*.

capacity variance. *Production volume variance*.

capital. *Owners' equity* in a business. Often used, equally correctly, to mean the total assets of a business. Sometimes used to mean *capital assets*.

capital asset. Properly used, a designation for income tax purposes that describes property held by a taxpayer, except *cash*, inventoriable *assets*, goods held primarily for sale, most depreciable property, *real estate, receivables*, certain *intangibles*, and a few other items. Sometimes this term is imprecisely used to describe *plant* and *equipment*, which are clearly not capital assets under the income tax definition. Writers often use the term to refer to an *investment* in *securities*.

capital budget. Plan of proposed outlays for acquiring long-term *assets* and the means of *financing* the acquisition.

capital budgeting. The process of choosing *investment* projects for an enterprise by considering the *present value* of cash flows and deciding how to raise the funds the investment requires.

capital consumption allowance. The term used for *depreciation expense* in national income accounting and the reporting of funds in the economy.

capital contributed in excess of par (or stated) value. A preferred title for the account that shows the amount received by the issuer for *capital stock* in excess of *par (or stated) value*.

capital expenditure (outlay). An *expenditure* to acquire long-term *assets*.

capital gain. The excess of proceeds over *cost*, or other *basis*, from the sale of a *capital asset* as defined by the Internal Revenue Code. If the capital asset has been held for a sufficiently long time before sale, then the tax on the gain is computed at a rate lower than is used for other gains and ordinary income.

capital lease. A *lease* treated by the *lessee* as both the borrowing of funds and the acquisition of an *asset* to be *amortized*. Both the *liability* and the asset are recognized on the balance sheet. Expenses consist of *interest* on the *debt* and *amortization* of the asset. The *lessor* treats the lease as the sale of the asset in return for a series of future cash receipts. Contrast with *operating lease*.

capital loss. A negative capital gain; see *capital gain*.

capital rationing. In a *capital budgeting* context, the imposing of constraints on the amounts of total capital expenditures in each period.

capital stock. The ownership shares of a corporation. Consists of all classes of *common* and *preferred stock*.

capital structure. The composition of a corporation's equities; the relative proportions of *short-term debt, long-term debt,* and *owners' equity*.

capital surplus. An inferior term for *capital contributed in excess of par (or stated) value*.

capitalization of a corporation. A term used by investment analysts to indicate *shareholders' equity* plus *bonds outstanding*.

capitalization of earnings. The process of estimating the economic worth of a firm by computing the *net present value* of the predicted *net income* (not *cash flows*) of the firm for the future.

capitalization rate. An *interest rate* used to convert a series of payments or receipts or earnings into a single *present value*.

capitalize. To record an *expenditure* that may benefit a future period as an *asset* rather than to treat the expenditure as an *expense* of the period of its occurrence. Whether or not expenditures for advertising or for research and development should be capitalized is controversial, but *SFAS No. 2* requires expensing of *R&D* costs. We believe expenditures should be capitalized if they lead to future benefits and thus meet the criterion to be an asset.

carryback, carryforward, carryover. The use of losses or tax credits in one period to reduce income taxes payable in other periods. There are two common kinds of carrybacks: for net operating losses and for *capital losses*. They are applied against taxable income. In general, carrybacks are for three years with the earliest year first. Operating losses can be carried forward for fifteen years. Corporate capital loss carryforwards are for five years. The capital loss for individuals can be carried forward indefinitely.

carrying cost. Costs (such as property taxes and insurance) of holding, or storing, *inventory* from the time of purchase until the time of sale or use.

carrying value (amount). *Book value*.

CASB. Cost Accounting Standards Board. A board authorized by the U.S. Congress to "promulgate cost-accounting standards designed to achieve uniformity and consistency in the cost-accounting principles followed by defense contractors and subcontractors under federal contracts." The *principles* the CASB promulgated since 1970 have considerable weight in practice where the *FASB* has not established a standard. Congress allowed the CASB to go out of existence in 1980 but reinstated it in 1990.

cash. Currency and coins, negotiable checks, and balances in bank accounts. For the *statement of cash flows*, "cash" also includes *marketable securities* held as *current assets*.

cash basis of accounting. In contrast to the *accrual basis of accounting*, a system of accounting in which a firm recognizes *revenues* when it receives *cash* and recognizes *expenses* as it makes *disbursements*. The firm makes no attempt to match *revenues* and *expenses* in measuring *income*. See *modified cash basis*.

cash budget. A schedule of expected cash *receipts* and *disbursements.*

cash collection basis. The *installment method* for recognizing *revenue.* Not to be confused with the *cash basis of accounting.*

cash conversion cycle. *Cash cycle.*

cash cycle. The period of time that elapses during which *cash* is converted into *inventories,* inventories are converted into *accounts receivable,* and receivables are converted back into cash. Sometimes called *earnings cycle.*

cash disbursements journal. A specialized *journal* used to record *expenditures* by *cash* and by *check.* If a *check register* is also used, a cash disbursements journal records only expenditures of currency and coins.

cash discount. A reduction in sales or purchase price allowed for prompt payment.

cash dividend. See *dividend.*

cash equivalent. According to *SFAS No. 95,* "short-term, highly liquid investments that are both readily convertible to known amounts of cash [and] so near their maturity that they present insignificant risk of changes in value because of changes in interest rates.... Examples of items commonly considered to be cash equivalents are Treasury bills, commercial paper, [and] money market funds... ."

cash equivalent value. A term used to describe the amount for which an *asset* could be sold. Sometimes called *market value* or *fair market price (value).*

cash flow. Cash *receipts* minus *disbursements* from a given *asset,* or group of assets, for a given period. Financial analysts sometimes use this term to mean *net income + depreciation + depletion + amortization.* See also *operating cash flow* and *free cash flow.*

cash flow statement. *Statement of cash flows.*

cash provided by operations. An important subtotal in the *statement of cash flows.* This amount is the total of revenues producing *cash* less *expenses* requiring cash. Often, the amount is shown as *net income* plus expenses not requiring cash (such as depreciation charges) minus revenues not producing cash (such as revenues recognized under the *equity method* of accounting for a long-term investment). The statement of cash flows maintains the same distinctions between *continuing operations, discontinued operations,* and *income* or *loss* from *extraordinary items* as does the *income statement.*

cash receipts journal. A specialized *journal* used to record all *receipts* of *cash.*

cash (surrender) value of life insurance. An amount equal, not to the face value of the policy to be paid in the event of death, but to the amount that the owner could realize by immediately canceling the policy and returning it to the insurance company for cash. If a firm owns a life insurance policy, the policy is reported as an asset at an amount equal to this value.

cash yield. See *yield.*

cashier's check. A bank's own *check* drawn on itself and signed by the cashier or other authorized official. It is a direct obligation of the bank. Compare with *certified check.*

catch-up depreciation. *Backlog depreciation.*

CCA. *Current cost accounting; current value accounting.*

central corporate expenses. General *overhead expenses* incurred in running the corporate headquarters and related supporting activities of a corporation. Accounting treats these expenses as *period expenses.* Contrast with *manufacturing overhead.* A major problem in *line of business reporting* is the treatment of these expenses.

central processing unit (CPU). The component of a computer system carrying out the arithmetic, logic and data transfer.

certificate. The document that is the physical embodiment of a *bond* or a *share of stock.* A term sometimes used for the *auditor's report.*

certified management accountant. *CMA.*

certificate of deposit. Federal law constrains the *rate of interest* that banks can pay. Under current law banks are allowed to pay a rate higher than the one allowed on a *time deposit* if the depositor promises to leave funds on deposit for several months or more. When the bank receives such funds, it issues a certificate of deposit. The depositor can withdraw the funds before maturity if a penalty is paid.

certified check. The *check* of a depositor drawn on a bank on the face of which the bank has inserted the words "accepted" or "certified" with the date and signature of a bank official. The check then becomes an obligation of the bank. Compare with *cashier's check.*

certified financial statement. A financial statement attested to by an independent *auditor* who is a *CPA.*

certified internal auditor. See *CIA.*

certified public accountant. *CPA.* An accountant who has satisfied the statutory and administrative requirements of his or her jurisdiction to be registered or licensed as a public accountant. In addition to passing the Uniform CPA Examination administered by the *AICPA,* the CPA must meet certain educational, experience, and moral requirements that differ from jurisdiction to jurisdiction. The jurisdictions are the 50 states, the District of Columbia, Guam, Puerto Rico, and the Virgin Islands.

CGA. Canada. Certified General Accountant. An accountant who has satisfied the experience, education, and examination requirements of the Certified General Accountants' Association.

chain discount. A series of *discount* percentages; for example, if a chain discount of 10 and 5 percent is quoted, then the actual, or *invoice,* price is the nominal, or list, price times .90 times .95, or 85.5 percent of invoice price.

change fund. Coins and currency issued to cashiers, delivery drivers, and so on.

changes, accounting. See *accounting changes.*

changes in financial position. See *statement of cash flows.*

charge. As a noun, a *debit* to an account; as a verb, to debit.

charge off. To treat as a *loss* or *expense* an amount originally recorded as an *asset;* use of this term implies that the charge is not in accord with original expectations.

chart of accounts. A list of names and numbers, systematically organized, of *accounts.*

charter. Document issued by a state government authorizing the creation of a corporation.

chartered accountant. CA. The title used in Australia, Canada, and the United Kingdom for an accountant who has satisfied the requirements of the institute of his or her jurisdiction to be qualified to serve as a *public accountant.* In Canada, each provincial institute or order has the right to administer the examination and set the standards of performance and ethics for Chartered Accountants in its province. For a number of years, however, the provincial organizations have pooled their rights to qualify new members through the Inter-provincial Education Committee and the result is that there are nationally set and graded examinations given in English and French. Deviation from the pass/fail grade awarded by the Board of Examiners (a subcommittee of the Inter-provincial Education Committee) is rare.

check. You know what a check is. The Federal Reserve Board defines a check as "a *draft* or order upon a bank or banking house purporting to be drawn upon a deposit of funds for the payment at all events of a certain sum of money to a certain person therein named or to him or his order or to bearer and payable instantly on demand." It must contain the phrase "pay to the order of." The amount shown on the check's face must be clearly readable and it must have the signature of the drawer. Checks need not be dated, although they usually are. The *balance* in the *cash account* is usually reduced when a check is issued, not later when it clears the bank and reduces cash in bank. See *remittance advice.*

check register. A *journal* to record *checks* issued.

CIA. Certified Internal Auditor. One who has satisfied certain requirements of the *Institute of Internal Auditors* including experience, ethics, education, and passing examinations.

CICA. *Canadian Institute of Chartered Accountants.*

CIF. Cost, insurance, and freight; a term used in contracts along with the name of a given port to indicate that the quoted price includes insurance, handling, and freight charges up to delivery by the seller at the given port.

circulating capital. *Working capital.*

clean opinion. See *auditor's report.*

clean surplus concept. The notion that the only entries to the *retained earnings* account are to record *net income* and *dividends.* See *comprehensive income.* Contrast with *current operating performance concept.* This concept, with minor

exceptions, is now controlling in *GAAP.* (See *APB Opinions Nos.* 9 and 30.)

clearing account. An account containing amounts to be transferred to another account(s) before the end of the *accounting period.* Examples are the *income summary* account (whose balance is transferred to *retained earnings)* and the purchases account (whose balance is transferred to *inventory* or to *cost of goods sold).*

close. As a verb, to transfer the *balance* of a *temporary* or *contra* or *adjunct* account to the main account to which it relates; for example, to transfer *revenue* and *expense* accounts directly, or through the *income summary* account, to an *owners' equity* account, or to transfer *purchase discounts* to purchases.

closed account. An *account* with equal *debits* and *credits,* usually as a result of a *closing entry.* See *ruling an account.*

closing entries. The *entries* that accomplish the transfer of balances in *temporary accounts* to the related *balance sheet accounts.* See *work sheet.*

closing inventory. *Ending inventory.*

CMA. Certified Management Accountant certificate. Awarded by the *Institute of Certified Management Accountants* of the *Institute of Management Accountants* to those who pass a set of examinations and meet certain experience and continuing education requirements.

CoCoA. *Continuously contemporary accounting.*

coding of accounts. The numbering of *accounts,* as for a *chart of accounts,* which is necessary for computerized accounting.

coinsurance. Insurance policies that protect against hazards such as fire or water damage often specify that the owner of the property may not collect the full amount of insurance for a loss unless the insurance policy covers at least some specified "coinsurance" percentage, usually about 80 percent, of the *replacement cost* of the property. Coinsurance clauses induce the owner to carry full, or nearly full, coverage.

COLA. Cost-of-living adjustment. See *indexation.*

collateral. *Assets* pledged by a *borrower* that will be given up if the *loan* is not paid.

collectible. Capable of being converted into *cash;* now, if due; later, otherwise.

collusion. Cooperative effort by employees to commit fraud or other unethical act.

combination. See *business combination.*

comfort letter. A letter in which an auditor conveys negative assurances as to unaudited financial statements in a prospectus or draft financial statements included in a preliminary prospectus.

commercial paper. *Short-term notes* issued by corporate borrowers.

commission. Remuneration, usually expressed as a percentage, to employees based upon an activity rate, such as sales.

committed costs. *Capacity costs.*

Committee on Accounting Procedure. CAP. Predecessor of the *APB*. The *AICPA's* principles-promulgating body from 1939 through 1959. Its 51 pronouncements are *Accounting Research Bulletins.*

common cost. *Cost* resulting from use of *raw materials,* a facility (for example, plant or machines), or a service (for example, fire insurance) that benefits several products or departments and that a firm must allocate to those products or departments. Common costs result when two or more departments produce multiple products together although the departments could produce them separately; *joint costs* occur when two or more departments must produce multiple products together. Many writers use common costs and joint costs synonymously. See *joint costs, indirect costs,* and *overhead.* See *sterilized allocation.*

common dollar accounting. *Constant dollar accounting.*

common monetary measuring unit. For U.S. corporations, the dollar. See also *stable monetary unit assumption* and *constant dollar accounting.*

common shares. *Shares* representing the class of owners who have residual claims on the *assets* and *earnings* of a *corporation* after all *debt* and *preferred shareholders'* claims have been met.

common stock equivalent. A *security* whose primary value arises from its ability to be exchanged for *common shares;* includes *stock options, warrants,* and also *convertible bonds* or *convertible preferred stock* whose *effective interest rate* at the time of issue is less than two-thirds the average Aa corporate bond yield. See *bond ratings.*

common size statement. A *percentage statement* usually based on total *assets* or *net sales* or *revenues.*

company-wide control. See *control system.*

comparative (financial) statements. *Financial statements* showing information for the same company for different times, usually two successive years. Nearly all published financial statements are in this form. Contrast with *historical summary.*

compensating balance. When a bank lends funds to a customer, it often requires that the customer keep on deposit in his or her checking account an amount equal to some percentage – say, 20 percent – of the loan. The amount required to be left on deposit is the compensating balance. Such amounts effectively increase the *interest rate.* The amounts of such balances must be disclosed in *notes* to the *financial statements.*

completed contract method. Recognizing *revenues* and *expenses* for a job or order only when it is finished, except that when a loss on the contract is expected, revenues and expenses are recognized in the period when the loss is first forecast. This term is generally used only for long-term contracts. It is otherwise equivalent to the *sales basis* of *revenue recognition.*

completed sales basis. See *sales basis of revenue recognition.*

compliance audit. Objectively obtaining and evaluating evidence regarding assertions, actions, and events to ascertain the degree of correspondence between them and established performance criteria.

compliance procedure. An *audit* procedure used to gain evidence as to whether the prescribed internal controls are operating effectively.

composite cost of capital. See *cost of capital.*

composite depreciation. *Group depreciation* of dissimilar items.

composite life method. *Group depreciation* when the items are of unlike kind. The term may be used when a single item, such as a crane, which consists of separate units with differing service lives, such as the chassis, the motor, the lifting mechanism, and so on, is depreciated as a whole rather than treating each of the components separately.

compound entry. A *journal entry* with more than one *debit* or more than one *credit,* or both. See *trade-in transaction* for an example.

compound interest. *Interest* calculated on *principal* plus previously undistributed interest.

compound interest depreciation. A method designed to hold the *rate of return* on an asset constant. First find the *internal rate of return* on the cash inflows and outflows of the asset. The periodic depreciation charge is the cash flow for the period less the internal rate of return multiplied by the asset's book value at the beginning of the period. When the cash flows from the asset are constant over time, usage sometimes refers to the method as the "annuity method" of depreciation.

compounding period. The time period for which a firm calculates *interest.* At the end of the period, the borrower may pay interest to the lender or may add the interest (that is, convert it) to principal for the next interest-earning period, which is usually a year or some portion of a year.

comprehensive budget. *Master budget.*

comprehensive income. Defined in *SFAC No. 3* as "the change in equity (net assets) of an entity during a period from transactions and other events and circumstances from nonowner sources. It includes all changes in equity during a period except those resulting from investments by owners and distributions to owners." In this definition, "equity" means *owners' equity.*

comptroller. Same meaning and pronunciation as *controller.*

conceptual framework. A coherent system of interrelated objectives and fundamentals, promulgated by the *FASB* primarily through its *SFAC* publications, expected to lead to consistent standards for *financial accounting* and reporting.

confidence level. The measure of probability that the actual characteristics of the population lie within the stated precision of the estimate derived from a sampling process. A sample estimate may be expressed in the following terms: "Based on the sample, we are 95% sure [confidence level] that the true population value is within the range of X to Y [precision]". See *precision.*

confirmation. A formal memorandum delivered by the customers or suppliers of a company to its independent *auditor* verifying the amounts shown as receivable or payable. The confirmation document is originally sent by the auditor to the customer. If the auditor asks that the document be returned whether the *balance* is correct or incorrect, then usage calls it a "positive confirmation." If the auditor asks that the document be returned only if there is an error, then usage calls it a "negative confirmation."

conglomerate. *Holding company.* This term is used when the owned companies are in dissimilar lines of business.

conservatism. A *reporting objective* that calls for anticipation of all *losses* and *expenses* but defers recognition of *gains* or *profits* until they are *realized* in *arm's-length* transactions. In the absence of certainty, report events to minimize cumulative income. Conservatism does not mean reporting low income in every *accounting period.* Over long enough time spans, income is cash-in less cash-out. If a (conservative) reporting method shows low income in early periods, it must show higher income in some later period.

consignee. See *on consignment.*

consignment. See *on consignment.*

consignor. See *on consignment.*

consistency. Treatment of like *transactions* in the same way in consecutive periods so that financial statements will be more comparable than otherwise. The reporting policy implying that procedures, once adopted, should be followed from period to period by a reporting *entity.* See *accounting changes* for the treatment of inconsistencies.

consol. A *bond* that never matures; a *perpetuity* in the form of a bond. Originally issued by Great Britain after the Napoleonic wars to consolidate debt issues of that period. The term arose as an abbreviation for "consolidated annuities."

consolidated financial statements. Statements issued by legally separate companies that show financial position and income as they would appear if the companies were one economic *entity.*

constant dollar. A hypothetical unit of *general purchasing power,* denoted "C$" by the *FASB.*

constant dollar accounting. Accounting where items are measured in *constant dollars.* See *historical cost/constant dollar accounting* and *current cost/constant dollar accounting.*

constant dollar date. The time at which the *general purchasing power* of one *constant dollar* is exactly equal to the *general purchasing power* of one *nominal dollar;* that is, the date when C$1 = $1. When the constant dollar date is mid-period, then the nominal amounts of *revenues* and *expenses* spread evenly throughout the period are equal to their constant dollar amounts, but end-of-period *balance sheet* amounts measured in constant mid-period dollars differ from their nominal dollar amounts. When the constant dollar date is at the end of the period, then the constant dollar and nominal dollar amounts on a balance sheet for that date are identical.

constrained share company. Canada. A public company whose *charter* specifies that at least a certain prescribed percentage of the shares must be beneficially owned by persons who are Canadian citizens or who are corporations resident in Canada.

constructive receipt. An item is included in taxable income when the taxpayer can control funds whether or not cash has been received. For example, *interest* added to *principal* in a savings account is deemed by the *IRS* to be constructively received.

Consumer Price Index. CPI. A *price index* computed and issued monthly by the Bureau of Labor Statistics of the U.S. Department of Labor. The index attempts to track the price level of a group of goods and services purchased by the average consumer. The CPI is used in *constant dollar accounting.* Contrast with *GNP Implicit Price Deflator.*

contingency. A potential *liability;* if a specified event were to occur, such as losing a lawsuit, a liability would be recognized. The contingency is merely disclosed in notes, rather than shown in the balance sheet. *SFAS No. 5* requires treatment as a contingency until the outcome is "probable" and the amount of payment can be reasonably estimated, perhaps within a range. When the outcome becomes probable (the future event is "likely" to occur) and the amount can be reasonably estimated (using the lower end of a range if only a range can be estimated), then the liability is recognized in the accounts, rather than being disclosed in the notes. A *material* contingency may lead to a qualified, "*subject to,*" auditor's opinion. *Gain* contingencies are not recorded in the accounts, but are merely disclosed in notes.

contingent annuity. An *annuity* whose number of payments depends upon the outcome of an event whose timing is uncertain at the time the annuity is set up; for example, an annuity payable until death of the *annuitant.* Contrast with *annuity certain.*

contingent issue (securities). Securities issuable to specific individuals upon the occurrence of some event, such as the firm's attaining a specified level of earnings.

contingent liability. *Contingency.* Avoid this term because it refers to something that is not a *liability* on the *balance sheet.*

continuing appropriation. A governmental *appropriation* automatically renewed without further legislative action until it is altered or revoked or expended.

continuing operations. See *income from continuing operations.*

continuity of operations. The assumption in accounting that the business *entity* will continue to operate long enough for current plans to be carried out. The *going-concern assumption.*

continuous budget. A *budget* that perpetually adds a period in the future as the period just ended is dropped.

continuous compounding. *Compound interest* where the *compounding period* is every instant of time. See *e* for the computation of the equivalent annual or periodic rate.

continuous inventory method. The *perpetual inventory* method.

Continuously Contemporary Accounting. CoCoA. A name coined by the Australian theorist, Raymond J. Chambers, to indicate a combination of *current value accounting* where amounts are measured in *constant dollars* and based on *exit values*.

contra account. An *account*, such as *accumulated depreciation*, that accumulates subtractions from another account, such as machinery. Contrast with *adjunct account*.

contributed capital. The sum of the balances in *capital stock* accounts plus *capital contributed in excess of par (or stated) value* accounts. Contrast with *donated capital*.

contributed surplus. An inferior term for *capital contributed in excess of par value*.

contribution approach. Method of preparing *income statements* that separates *variable costs* from *fixed costs* in order to emphasize the importance of cost behavior patterns for purposes of planning and control.

contribution margin. *Revenue* from *sales* less all variable *expenses*. Contrast with *gross margin*.

contribution margin ratio. *Contribution margin* divided by *net sales;* usually measured from the price and cost of a single unit. Sometimes measured in total for companies with multiple products.

contribution per unit. Selling price less *variable costs* per unit.

contributory. Said of a *pension plan* where employees, as well as employers, make payments to a pension *fund*. Note that the provisions for *vesting* are applicable only to the employer's payments. Whatever the degree of vesting of the employer's payments, the employee typically gets back all of his or her payments, with interest, in case of death, or other cessation of employment, before retirement.

control (controlling) account. A summary *account* with totals equal to those of entries and balances that appear in individual accounts in a *subsidiary ledger*. Accounts Receivable is a control account backed up with an account for each customer. The balance in a control account should not be changed unless a corresponding change is made in one of the subsidiary accounts.

control system. A device top management uses to ensure that lower-level management carries out its plans or to safeguard assets. Control designed for a single function within the firm is "operational control;" control designed for autonomous segments within the firm that generally have responsibility for both revenues and costs is "divisional control;" control designed for activities of the firm as a whole is "company-wide control." Systems designed for safeguarding *assets* are "internal control" systems.

controllable cost. A *cost* influenced by the way a firm carries out operations. For example, marketing executives control advertising costs. These costs are *fixed* or *variable*. See *programmed costs* and *managed costs*.

controlled company. A company, a majority of whose voting shares is held by an individual or corporation. Effective control can sometimes be exercised when less than 50 percent of the shares is owned.

controller. The title often used for the chief accountant of an organization. Often spelled *comptroller*.

conversion. The act of exchanging a convertible security for another security.

conversion audit. An examination of change-over procedures, and new accounting procedures and files, that takes place when a significant change in the accounting system (e.g. a change from a manual to a computerized system or a change of computers) has occurred.

conversion cost. *Direct labor* costs plus factory *overhead* costs incurred in producing a product. That is, the cost to convert raw materials to finished products. *Manufacturing cost*.

conversion period. *Compounding period*. Also, period during which a *convertible bond* or *convertible preferred stock* can be converted into *common stock*.

convertible bond. A *bond* that may be converted into a specified number of shares of *capital stock* during the *conversion period*.

convertible preferred stock. *Preferred shares* that may be converted into a specified number of shares of *common stock*.

co-operative. An incorporated organization formed for the benefit of its members (owners), who are either producers or consumers, in order to acquire for them profits or savings which otherwise accrue to middlemen. Members exercise control on the basis of one vote per member.

co-product. A product sharing production facilities with another product. For example, if an apparel manufacturer produces shirts and jeans on the same line, these are co-products. Distinguish co-products from *joint products* and *by-products* that, by their very nature a firm must produce together, such as the various grades of wood a lumber factory produces.

copyright. Exclusive right granted by the government to an individual author, composer, playwright, and the like for the life of the individual plus 50 years. If the copyright is granted to a firm, then the right extends 75 years after the original publication. The *economic life* of a copyright may be considerably less than the legal life as, for example, the copyright of this book.

corner. The control of a quantity of shares or a commodity that is sufficient in a free market to enable the holder effectively to control the market price.

corporation. A legal entity authorized by a state to operate under the rules of the entity's *charter*.

correcting entry. An *adjusting entry* where an improperly recorded *transaction* is properly recorded. Not to be confused with entries that correct *accounting errors*.

correction of errors. See *accounting errors*.

cost. The sacrifice, measured by the *price* paid or required to be paid, to acquire *goods* or *services*. See *acquisition cost* and *replacement cost*. Terminology often uses "cost" when referring to the valuation of a good or service acquired. When writers use the word in this sense, a cost is an *asset*. When the benefits of the acquisition (the goods or services acquired) expire, the cost becomes an *expense* or *loss.* Some writers, however, use cost and expense as synonyms. Contrast with *expense.* The word "cost" appears in more than 50 phrases, each with sometimes subtle distinctions in meaning, used in accounting. See *cost terminology* for elaboration.

cost accounting. Classifying, summarizing, recording, reporting, and allocating current or predicted *costs.* A subset of *managerial accounting.*

Cost Accounting Standards Board. See *CASB.*

cost accumulation. Bringing together, usually in a single *account,* all *costs* of a specified activity. Contrast with *cost allocation.*

cost allocation. Assigning *costs* to individual products or time periods. Contrast with *cost accumulation.*

cost-based transfer price. A *transfer price* based on *historical costs.*

cost behavior. The functional relation between changes in activity and changes in *cost.* For example, *fixed* versus *variable costs; linear* versus *curvilinear cost.*

cost/benefit criterion. Some measure of *costs* compared to some measure of *benefits* for a proposed undertaking. If the costs exceed the benefits, then the analyst judges undertaking not worthwhile. This criterion will not yield good decisions unless the analyst estimates all costs and benefits flowing from the undertaking.

cost center. A unit of activity for which a firm accumulates *expenditures* and *expenses.*

cost driver. A factor that causes an activity's costs. See *activity basis.*

cost effective. Among alternatives, the one whose benefit, or payoff, per unit of cost is highest. Sometimes said of an action whose expected benefits exceed expected costs whether or not other alternatives exist with larger benefit/cost ratios.

cost estimation. The process of measuring the functional relation between changes in activity levels and changes in cost.

cost flow assumption. See *flow assumption.*

cost flow equation. Beginning Balance + Transfers In = Transfers Out + Ending Balance; BB + TI = TO + EB.

cost flows. Costs passing through various classifications within an entity. See *flow of costs* for a diagram.

cost method (for investments). Accounting for an investment in the *capital stock* or *bonds* of another company where the investment is shown at *acquisition cost,* and only *dividends* declared or *interest receivable* is treated as *revenue.*

cost method (for treasury stock). The method of showing *treasury stock* in a *contra account* to all other items of *shareholders' equity* in an amount equal to that paid to reacquire the stock.

cost objective. Any activity for which management desires a separate measurement of *costs.* Examples include departments, products, and territories.

cost of capital. *Opportunity cost* of funds invested in a business. The rate of return rational owners require an asset to earn before they will devote that asset to a particular purpose. Sometimes measured as the average rate per year a company must pay for its *equities.* In efficient capital markets, the *discount rate* that equates the expected *present value* of all future cash flows to common shareholders with the market value of common stock at a given time.
    Analysts often measure the cost of capital by taking a *weighted average* of the firm's *debt* and various *equity securities.* We sometimes call the measurement so derived the "composite cost of capital," and some analysts confuse this measurement of the cost of capital with the cost of capital itself. For example, if the equities of a firm include substantial amounts for the *deferred income tax liability,* the composite cost of capital will underestimate the true cost of capital, the required rate of return on a firm's assets, because the deferred income tax liability has no explicit cost.

cost of goods manufactured. The sum of all costs allocated to products completed during a period, including materials, labor, and *overhead.*

cost of goods purchased. Net purchase price of goods acquired plus costs of storage and delivery to the place where the items can be productively used.

cost of goods sold. Inventoriable *costs* that firms *expense* because they sold the units; equals *beginning inventory* plus *cost of goods purchased* or *manufactured* minus *ending inventory.*

cost of sales. Generally refers to *cost of goods sold;* occasionally, to *selling expenses.*

cost or market, whichever is lower. See *lower of cost or market.*

cost percentage. One less *markup percentage. Cost* of *goods available for sale* divided by selling prices of goods available for sale (when FIFO is used). With *LIFO, cost of purchases* divided by selling price of purchases. See *markup* for further detail on inclusions in calculation of cost percentage.

cost pool. *Indirect cost pool.* Groupings or aggregations of costs, usually for subsequent analysis.

cost principle. The *principle* that requires reporting *assets* at *historical* or *acquisition cost,* less accumulated *amortization.* This principle is based on the assumption that cost is equal to *fair market value* at the date of acquisition and subsequent changes are not likely to be significant.

cost-recovery-first method. A method of *revenue* recognition that *credits inventory* as collections are received until all costs are recovered. Only after costs are completely recovered is *income* recognized. To be used in financial reporting only when the total amount of collections is highly uncertain. Can never be used in income tax reporting. Contrast with the *installment method* where *constant* proportions of each collection are credited both to cost and to income.

cost sheet. Statement that shows all the elements comprising the total cost of an item.

cost terminology. The word "cost" appears in many accounting terms. The accompanying exhibit classifies some of these terms according to the distinctions between the terms in accounting usage. Joel Dean was, to our knowledge, the first to attempt such distinctions; we have used some of his ideas here. We discuss some of the terms in more detail under their own listings.

cost-to-cost. The *percentage-of-completion method* where the estimate of completion is the ratio of costs incurred to date divided by total costs expected to be incurred for the entire project.

cost-volume-profit analysis. A study of the sensitivity of *profits* to changes in units sold (or produced), or costs or prices.

cost-volume-profit graph (chart). A graph that shows the relation between *fixed costs, contribution per unit, breakeven point,* and *sales.* See *breakeven chart.*

costing. The process of calculating the cost of activities, products, or services. The British word for *cost accounting.*

coupon. That portion of a *bond* document redeemable at a specified date for *interest* payments. Its physical form is much like a ticket; each coupon is dated and is deposited at a bank, just like a check, for collection or is mailed to the issuer's agent for collection.

coupon rate. Of a *bond,* the amount of annual coupons divided by par value. Contrast with *effective rate.*

covenant. A promise with legal validity. A loan covenant specifies the terms under which the lender can force the borrower to repay funds otherwise not yet due. For example, a *bond* covenant might say that the *principal* of a bond issue falls due on December 31, 2010, unless the firm's *debt-equity ratio* falls below 40 percent, when the amount becomes immediately due.

CPA. See *certified public accountant.* The *AICPA* suggests that no periods be shown in the abbreviation.

CPI. *Consumer price index.*

CPP. Current purchasing power; usually used as an adjective modifying the word "accounting" to mean the accounting that produces *constant dollar financial statements.*

Cr. Abbreviation for *credit.*

creative accounting. Selection of *accounting principles* and interpretation of transactions or events designed to manipulate, typically to increase but sometimes merely to smooth, reported *income from continuing operations.* Many attempts at creative accounting involve premature *revenue recognition.* One form of *fraudulent financial reporting.*

credit. As a noun, an entry on the right-hand side of an *account.* As a verb, to make an entry on the right-hand side of an account. Records increases in *liabilities, owners' equity, revenues,* and *gains;* records decreases in *assets* and *expenses.* See *debit and credit conventions.* Also the ability or right to buy or borrow in return for a promise to pay later.

credit bureau. An organization which gathers and evaluates data on the ability of a person to meet financial obligations and sells this information to its clients.

credit loss. The amount of *accounts receivable* that is, or is expected to become, *uncollectible.*

credit memorandum. A document used by a seller to inform a buyer that the buyer's *account receivable* is being credited (reduced) because of *errors, returns,* or *allowances.* Also, the document provided by a bank to a depositor to indicate that the depositor's balance is being increased because of some event other than a deposit, such as the collection by the bank of the depositor's *note receivable.*

creditor. One who lends.

Critical Path Method. A method of *network analysis* in which normal duration time is estimated for each activity within a project. The critical path identifies the shortest completion period based on the most time-consuming sequence of activities from the beginning to the end of the network. Compare *PERT.*

cross-reference (index). A number placed by each *account* in a *journal entry* indicating the *ledger* account to which the entry is posted and placing in the ledger the page number of the journal where the entry was made. Used to link the *debit* and *credit* parts of an entry in the ledger accounts back to the original entry in the journal. See *audit trail.*

cross-section analysis. Analysis of *financial statements* of various firms for a single period of time; contrast with *time-series analysis* where accountants analyze statements of a given firm for several periods of time.

Crown corporation. Canada and the United Kingdom. A corporation that is ultimately accountable through a Minister of the Crown to Parliament or a legislature for the conduct of its affairs.

cum div. (dividend). The condition of shares whose quoted market price includes a declared but unpaid dividend. This condition pertains between the declaration date of the dividend and the record date. Compare *ex div. (dividend).*

cum rights. The condition of securities whose quoted market price includes the right to purchase new securities. (Compare *ex rights.*)

cumulative dividend. Preferred stock *dividends* that, if not paid, accrue as a commitment that must be paid before dividends to common shareholders can be declared.

cumulative preferred shares. *Preferred* shares with *cumulative dividend* rights.

current assets. *Cash* and other *assets* that a firm expects to turn into cash, sell, or exchange within the normal operating cycle of the firm or one year, whichever is longer. One year is the usual period for classifying asset balances on the balance sheet. Current assets include *cash, marketable securities, receivables, inventory,* and *current prepayments.*

current cost. *Cost* stated in terms of current values (of *productive capacity*) rather than in terms of *acquisition cost.* See *net realizable value, current selling price.*

Cost Terminology: Distinctions among Terms Containing the Word "Cost"

Terms (Synonyms Given in Parentheses)			Distinctions and Comments
			1. The following pairs of terms distinguish the basis measured in accounting.
Historical Cost (Acquisition Cost)	vs.	Current Cost	A distinction used in financial accounting. Current cost can be used more specifically to mean replacement cost, net realizable value, or present value of cash flows. "Current cost" is often used narrowly to mean replacement cost.
Historical Cost (Actual Cost)	vs.	Standard Cost	The distinction between historical and standard costs arises in product costing for inventory valuation. Some systems record actual costs while others record the standard costs.
			2. The following pairs of terms denote various distinctions among historical costs. For each pair of terms, the sum of the two kinds of costs equals total historical cost used in financial reporting.
Variable Cost (Constant Cost)	vs.	Fixed Cost	Distinction used in breakeven analysis and in designing cost accounting systems, particularly for product costing. See (4), below, for a further subdivision of fixed costs and (5), below, for an economic distinction closely paralleling this one.
Traceable Cost (Joint Cost)	vs.	Common Cost	Distinction arises in allocating manufacturing costs to product. Common costs are allocated to product, but the allocations are more-or-less arbitrary. The distinction also arises in segment reporting and in separating manufacturing from nonmanufacturing costs.
Direct Cost	vs.	Indirect Cost	Distinction arises in designing cost accounting systems and in product costing. Direct costs can be traced directly to a cost object, (e.g., a product, a responsibility center) whereas indirect costs cannot.
Out-of-Pocket Cost (Outlay Cost; Cash Cost)	vs.	Book Cost	Virtually all costs recorded in financial statements require a cash outlay at one time or another. The distinction here separates expenditures to occur in the future from those already made and is used in making decisions. Book costs, such as for depreciation, reduce income without requiring a future outlay of cash. The cash has already been spent. See future v. past costs in (5), below.
Incremental Cost (Marginal Cost; Differential Cost)	vs.	Unavoidable Cost (Inescapable Cost; Sunk Cost)	Distinction used in making decisions. Incremental costs will be incurred (or saved) if a decision is made to go ahead (or to stop) some activity, but some activity, but not otherwise. Unavoidable costs will be reported in financial statements whether the decision is made to go ahead or not, because cash has already been spent or committed. Not all unavoidable costs are book costs, as, for example, a salary promised but not yet earned, that will be paid even if a no-go decision is made.
			The economist restricts the term marginal cost to the cost of producing one more unit. Thus the next unit has a marginal cost; the next week's output has an incremental cost. If a firm produces and sells a new product, the related new costs would properly be called incremental, not marginal. If a factory is closed, the costs saved are incremental, not marginal.
Escapable Cost (Unavoidable Cost)	vs.	Inescapable Cost	Same distinction as incremental v. sunk costs, but this pair is used only when the decision maker is considering stopping something ceasing to produce a product, closing a factory, or the like. See next pair.
Avoidable Cost	vs.	Unavoidable Cost	A distinction sometimes used in discussing the merits of variable and absorption costing. Avoidable costs are treated as product cost and unavoidable costs are treated as period expenses under variable costing.

Terms (Synonyms Given in Parentheses)			Distinctions and Comments
Controllable Cost	vs.	Uncontrollable	The distinction here is used in assigning responsibility and in setting bonus Costincentive plans. All costs can be affected by someone in the entity; those who design incentive schemes attempt to hold a person responsible for a cost only if that person can influence the amount of the cost.
			3. In each of the following pairs, used in historical cost accounting, the word "cost" appears in one of the terms where "expense" is meant.
Expired Cost	vs.	Unexpired Cost	The distinction is between *expense* and *asset*.
Product Cost	vs.	Period Cost	The terms distinguish product cost from period expense. When a given asset is used, is its cost converted into work in process and then into finished goods on the balance sheet until the goods are sold, or is it an expense shown on this period's income statement? Product costs appear on the income statement as part of cost of goods sold in the period when the goods are sold. Period expenses appear on the income statement with an appropriate caption for the item in the period when the cost is incurred or recognized.

4. The following subdivisions of fixed (historical) costs are used in analyzing operations. The relation between the components of fixed costs is:

$$\underbrace{\text{Fixed Costs}} = \underbrace{\text{Capacity Costs}} + \underbrace{\text{Programmed Costs}}$$

| Semifixed + Fixed
Costs Portions
+ of
"Pure" Semivariable
Fixed Costs Costs | Standby + Enabling
Costs Costs | |

Capacity Cost	vs.	Programmed Cost	Capacity costs give a firm the capability to produce or to sell. Programmed costs, such as for advertising or research and development, may not be essential, but once a decision to incur them is made, they become fixed costs.
Standby Cost	vs.	Enabling Cost	Standby costs will be incurred whether capacity, once acquired, is used or not, such as property taxes and depreciation on a factory. Enabling costs, such as for security force, can be avoided if the capacity is unused.
Semifixed Cost	vs.	Semivariable Cost	A cost fixed over a wide range but that can change at various levels is a semifixed cost or "step cost." An example is the cost of rail lines from the factory to the main rail line where fixed cost depends on whether there are one or two parallel lines, but are independent of the number of trains run per day. Semivariable costs combine a strictly fixed component cost plus a variable component. Telephone charges usually have a fixed monthly component plus a charge related to usage.
			5. The following pairs of terms distinguish among economic uses or decision making uses or regulatory uses of cost terms.
Fully Absorbed Cost vs.		Variable Cost (Direct Cost)	Fully absorbed costs refer to costs where fixed costs have been allocated to units or departments as required by generally accepted accounting principles. Variable costs, in contrast, may be more relevant for making decisions, such as in setting prices.
Fully Absorbed Cost vs.		Full Cost	In full costing, all costs, manufacturing costs as well as central corporate express (including financing expenses) are allocated to product or divisions. In full absorption costing, only manufacturing costs are allocated to product. Only in full costing will revenues, expenses, and income summed over all products or divisions equal corporate revenues, expenses, and income.

Cost Terminology: Distinctions among Terms Containing the Word "Cost"

Terms (Synonyms Given in Parentheses)			Distinctions and Comments
Opportunity Cost	vs.	Outlay Cost (Out-of-pocket Cost)	Opportunity cost refers to the economic benefit foregone by using a resource for one purpose instead of for another. The outlay cost of the resource will be recorded in financial records. The distinction arises because a resource is already in the possession of the entity with a recorded historical cost. Its economic value to the firm, opportunity cost, generally differs from the historical cost; it can be either larger or smaller.
Future Cost	vs.	Past Cost	Effective decision making analyzes only present and future outlay costs, or out-of-pocket costs. Opportunity costs are relevant for profit maximizing; past costs are used in financial reporting.
Short-Run Cost	vs.	Long-Run Cost	Short-run costs vary as output is varied for a given configuration of plant and equipment. Long-run costs can be incurred to change that configuration. This pair of terms is the economic analog of the accounting pair, see (2) above, variable and fixed costs. The analogy is not perfect because some short-run costs are fixed, such as property taxes on the factory, from the point of view of break-even analysis.
Imputed Cost	vs.	Book Cost	In a regulatory setting some costs, for example the cost of owners' equity capital, are calculated and used for various purposes; these are imputed costs. Imputed costs are not recorded in the historical costs accounting records for financial reporting. Book costs are recorded.
Average Cost	vs.	Marginal Cost	The economic distinction equivalent to fully absorbed cost of product and direct cost of product. Average cost is total cost divided by number of units. Marginal cost is the cost to produce the next unit (or the last unit).
Incremental Cost	vs.	Variable Cost	Whether a cost changes or remains fixed depends on the activity basis being considered. Typically, but not invariably, costs are said to be variable or fixed with respect to an activity basis such as changes in production levels. Typically, but not invariably, costs are said to be incremental or not with respect to an activity basis such as the undertaking of some new venture. For example, consider the decision to undertake the production of food processors, rather than food blenders, which the manufacturer has been making. To produce processors requires the acquisition of a new machine tool. The cost of the new machine tool is incremental with respect to a decision to produce food processors instead of food blenders, but, once acquired, becomes a fixed cost of producing food processors. If costs of direct labor hours are going to be incurred for the production of food processors or food blenders, whichever is produced (in a scenario when not both are to be produced), such costs are variable with respect to production measured in units, but not incremental with respect to the decision to produce processors rather than blenders. This distinction is often blurred in practice, so a careful understanding of the activity basis being considered is necessary for understanding of the concepts being used in a particular application.

current cost accounting. The *FASB's* term for *financial statements* where the *attribute measured* is *current cost*.

current cost/nominal dollar accounting. Accounting based on *current cost* valuations measured in *nominal dollars*. Components of *income* include an *operating margin* and *holding gains and losses*.

current exchange rate. The rate at which one unit of currency can be converted into another at the end of the *accounting period* being reported on or, for *revenues, expenses, gains,* and *losses,* the date of recognition of the transaction.

current exit value. *Exit value.*

current fund. In governmental accounting, a synonym for *general fund.*

current funds. *Cash* and other assets readily convertible into cash. In governmental accounting, funds spent for operating purposes during the current period. Includes *general, special revenue, debt service,* and *enterprise funds.*

current (gross) margin. See *operating margin (based on current costs).*

current liability. A debt or other obligation that a firm must discharge within a short time, usually the *earnings cycle* or one year, normally by expending *current assets.*

current (gross) margin. See *operating margin (based on current costs).*

current operating performance concept. The notion that reported *income* for a period ought to reflect only ordinary, normal, and recurring operations of that period. A consequence is that *extraordinary* and nonrecurring items are entered directly in the Retained Earnings account. Contrast with *clean surplus concept.* This concept is no longer acceptable. (See *APB Opinion Nos. 9* and *30.)*

current ratio. Sum of *current assets* divided by sum of *current liabilities.* See *ratio.*

current realizable value. *Realizable value.*

current replacement cost. Of an *asset,* the amount currently required to acquire an identical asset (in the same condition and with the same service potential) or an asset capable of rendering the same service at a current *fair market price.* If these two amounts differ, the lower is usually used. Contrast with *reproduction cost.*

current selling price. The amount for which an *asset* could be sold as of a given time in an *arm's-length* transaction, rather than in a forced sale.

current service costs. *Service costs* of a *pension plan.*

current value accounting. The form of accounting where all assets are shown at *current replacement cost (entry value)* or *current selling price* or *net realizable value (exit value),* and all *liabilities* are shown at *present value.* Entry and exit values may be quite different from each other, so there is no general agreement on the precise meaning of current value accounting.

current yield. Of a *bond,* the annual amount of *interest coupons* divided by current market price of the bond. Contrast with *yield to maturity.*

currently attainable standard cost. *Normal standard cost.*

curvilinear (variable) cost. A continuous, but not necessarily linear (straight-line), functional relation between activity levels and *costs.*

customers' ledger. The *ledger* that shows *accounts receivable* of individual customers. It is the *subsidiary ledger* for the *controlling account,* Accounts Receivable.

cutoff rate. *Hurdle rate.*

D

data bank. An organized file of information, such as customer name and address file, used in and kept up to date by a processing system.

data base. A comprehensive collection of interrelated information stored together in computerized form to serve several applications.

data base management system. Generalized software programs used to handle physical storage and manipulation of data bases.

days of average inventory on hand. See *ratio.*

days of grace. The days allowed by law or contract for payment of a debt after its due date.

DCF. *Discounted cash flow.*

DDB. *Double-declining-balance depreciation.*

debenture bond. A *bond* not secured with *collateral.*

debit. As a noun, an entry on the left hand side of an *account.* As a verb, to make an entry on the left hand side of an account. Records increases in *assets* and *expenses;* records decreases in *liabilities, owners' equity,* and *revenues.* See *debit and credit conventions.*

debit and credit conventions. The equality of the two sides of the *accounting equation* is maintained by recording equal amounts of *debits* and *credits* for each *transaction.* The conventional use of the *T-account* form and the rules for debit and credit in *balance sheet accounts* are summarized as follows.

Any Asset Account

Opening Balance Increase + Dr. Ending Balance	Decrease − Cr.

Any Liability Account

Decrease – Dr.	Opening Balance Increase + Cr. Ending Balance

Any Owners' Equity Account

Decrease – Dr.	Opening Balance Increase + Cr. Ending Balance

Revenue and expense accounts belong to the owners' equity group. The relationship and the rules for debit and credit in these accounts can be expressed as follows.

Any Owners' Equity Account

Decrease – Dr. Expenses		Increase + Cr. Revenues	
Dr.	Cr.	Dr.	Cr.
+	–	–	+
*			*

* Normal balance prior to closing

debit memorandum. A document used by a seller to inform a buyer that the seller is debiting (increasing) the amount of the buyer's *account receivable*. Also, the document provided by a bank to a depositor to indicate that the depositor's *balance* is being decreased because of some event other than payment for a *check*, such as monthly service charges or the printing of checks.

debt. An amount owed. The general name for *notes, bonds, mortgages,* and the like that are evidence of amounts owed and have definite payment dates.

debt-equity ratio. Total *liabilities* divided by total equities. See *ratio*. Sometimes the denominator is merely total shareholders' equity. Sometimes the numerator is restricted to *long-term debt*.

debt capital. *Noncurrent liabilities*. See *debt financing* and contrast with *equity financing*.

debt financing. Raising *funds* by issuing *bonds, mortgages,* or *notes*. Contrast with *equity financing. Leverage*.

debt guarantee. See *guarantee*.

debt ratio. *Debt-equity ratio*.

debt service fund. In governmental accounting, a *fund* established to account for payment of *interest* and *principal* on all

general-obligation *debt* other than that payable from special *assessments*.

debt service requirement. The amount of cash required for payments of *interest*, current maturities of *principal* on outstanding *debt*, and payments to *sinking funds* (corporations) or to the *debt service fund* (governmental).

debtor. One who borrows.

decentralized decision making. A firm gives a manager of a business unit responsibility for that unit's *revenues* and *costs*, freeing the manager to make decisions about prices, sources of supply, and the like, as though the unit were a separate business that the manager owns. See *responsibility accounting* and *transfer price*.

declaration date. Time when a *dividend* is declared by the *board of directors*.

declining balance depreciation. The method of calculating the periodic *depreciation* charge by multiplying the *book value* at the start of the period by a constant percentage. In pure declining-balance depreciation the constant percentage is $1 - \sqrt[n]{s/c}$, where n is the *depreciable life*, s is *salvage value*, and c is *acquisition cost*. See *double-declining balance depreciation*.

deep discount bonds. Said of *bonds* selling much below (exactly how much is not clear) *par value*.

defalcation. Embezzlement.

default. Failure to pay *interest* or *principal* on a *debt* when due.

defeasance. *Interest rates* have increased over the past several decades. Consequently, the *market value* of *debt* outstanding is substantially less than its *book value* for many firms. In *historical cost accounting* for debt retirements, retiring debt with a *cash* payment less than the book value of the debt results in a gain (generally, an *extraordinary item*). Many firms would like to retire the outstanding debt issues and report the gain. Two factors impede doing so: (1) the gain can be a taxable event generating adverse *income tax* consequences; and (2) the transactions costs in retiring all of the debt can be large, in part because not all debt holders can easily be located or persuaded to sell back their bonds to the issuer. The process of "defeasance" is the economic equivalent to retiring a debt issue that saves the issuer from adverse tax consequences and actually having to locate and retire the bonds. The process works as follows. The debt issuing firm turns over to an independent trustee, such as bank, amounts of cash or low risk government bonds sufficient to make all debt service payments on the outstanding debt, including bond retirements, in return for the trustee's commitment to make all debt service payments. The debt issuer effectively retires the outstanding debt. It debits the liability account, credits Cash or Marketable Securities, as appropriate, and credits Extraordinary Gain on Debt Retirement. The trustee is free to retire debt or make debt service payments, whichever it chooses. For income tax purposes, however, the firm's debt is still outstanding. The firm will have taxable interest *deductions* for its still outstanding debt and taxable interest *revenue* on the investments held by the trustee for debt service. In law, the term "defeasance" means "a rendering null and void." This process renders the outstanding debt economically null and void, without causing a taxable event.

defensive interval. A financial *ratio* equal to the number of days of normal cash *expenditures* covered by *quick assets*. It is defined as

Quick Assets
———————————————
(All Expenses Except Amortization and Others Not Using Funds/365)

The denominator of the ratio is the cash expenditure per day. This ratio has been found useful in predicting *bankruptcy*.

deferral. The accounting process concerned with past *cash receipts* and *payments;* in contrast to *accrual.* Recognizing a liability resulting from a current cash receipt (as for magazines to be delivered) or recognizing an asset from a current cash payment (or for prepaid insurance or a long-term depreciable asset).

deferral method. See *flow-through method* (of accounting for the *investment credit)* for definition and contrast.

deferred annuity. An *annuity* whose first payment is made sometime after the end of the first period.

deferred asset. *Deferred charge.*

deferred charge. *Expenditure* not recognized as an *expense* of the period when made but carried forward as an *asset* to be *written-off* in future periods, such as for advance rent payments or insurance premiums. See *deferral.*

deferred cost. *Deferred charge.*

deferred credit. Sometimes used to indicate *advances from customers.*

deferred debit. *Deferred charge.*

deferred expense. *Deferred charge.*

deferred gross margin. *Unrealized gross margin.*

deferred income. *Advances from customers.*

deferred income tax (liability). An *indeterminate term liability* that arises when the pretax income shown on the tax return is less than what it would have been had the same *accounting principles* and *cost basis* for *assets* and *liabilities* been used in tax returns as used for financial reporting. *SFAS No. 109* requires that the firm debit income tax *expense* and credit deferred income tax with the amount of the taxes delayed by using different accounting principles in tax returns from those used in financial reports. See *temporary difference, timing difference,* and *permanent difference.* See *installment sales.* If, as a result of temporary differences, cumulative taxable income exceeds cumulative reported income before taxes, the deferred income tax account will have a *debit* balance and will be reported as a *deferred charge.*

deferred revenue. Sometimes used to indicate *advances from customers.*

deferred tax. See *deferred income tax.*

deficit. A *debit balance* in the Retained Earnings account; presented on the balance sheet in a *contra account* to shareholders' equity. Sometimes used to mean negative *net income* for a period.

defined-benefit plan. A *pension plan* where the employer promises specific dollar amounts to each eligible employee; the amounts usually depend on a formula which takes into account such things as the employee's earnings, years of employment, and age. The employer's cash contributions and pension expense are adjusted in relation to *actuarial* experience in the eligible employee group and investment performance of the pension *fund.* Sometimes called a "fixed-benefit" pension plan. Contrast with *money purchase plan.*

defined contribution plan. A *money purchase (pension) plan* or other arrangement, based on formula or discretion, where the employer makes cash contributions to eligible individual employee *accounts* under the terms of a written plan document. Profit-sharing pension plans are of this type.

deflation. A period of declining *general price changes*.

demand deposit. *Funds* in a *checking account* at a bank.

demand loan. See *term loan* for definition and contrast.

denial of opinion. Canada. The statement that an *auditor,* for reasons arising in the *audit,* is unable to express an opinion whether the *financial statement*s provide *fair presentation.*

denominator volume. Capacity measured in the number of units the firm expects to produce this period; when divided into *budgeted fixed costs,* results in fixed costs applied per unit of product.

department(al) allocation. First, accumulate *costs* in *cost pools* for each department. Then, using separate rates, or sets of rates, for each department, allocate from each cost pool to products produced in that department.

dependent variable. See *regression analysis.*

depletion. Exhaustion or *amortization* of a *wasting asset,* or *natural resource.* Also see *percentage depletion.*

depletion allowance. See *percentage depletion.*

deposit method (of revenue recognition). This method of *revenue* recognition does not differ from the *completed sale* or *completed contract method.* In some contexts such as retail land sales, the customer must make substantial payments while still having the right to back out of the deal and receive a refund. When there is uncertainty about whether the deal will be completed but a cash collection is made by the seller, the seller must *credit* deposits, a *liability account,* rather than *revenue.* (In this regard, the accounting differs from the completed contract method where the account credited is offset against the *work-in-process inventory* account.) When the *sale* becomes complete, a revenue account is credited and the deposit account is *debited.*

deposit, sinking fund. Payments made to a *sinking fund.*

deposits (by customers). A *liability* arising upon receipt of *cash* (as in a bank, or in a grocery store when the customer pays cash for soda pop bottles to be repaid when the bottles are returned).

deposits in transit. Deposits made by a firm but not yet reflected on the *bank statement*.

depreciable cost. That part of the *cost* of an asset, usually *acquisition cost* less *salvage value*, that is to be charged off over the life of the asset through the process of *depreciation*.

depreciable life. For an *asset*, the time period or units of activity (such as miles driven for a truck) over which *depreciable cost* is to be allocated. For tax returns, depreciable life may be shorter than estimated *service life*.

depreciation. *Amortization of plant assets;* the process of allocating the cost of an asset to the periods of benefit – the *depreciable life*. Classified as a *production cost* or a *period expense*, depending on the asset and whether the firm uses *full absorption* or *variable costing*. Depreciation methods described in this glossary include the *annuity method, appraisal method, composite method, compound interest method, production method, replacement method, retirement method, straight line method, sinking fund method, and sum-of-the-years'-digits method.*

depreciation reserve. An inferior term for *accumulated depreciation*. See *reserve*. Do not confuse with a replacement *fund*.

Descartes' rule of signs. In a *capital budgeting* context, the rule says that a series of cash flows will have a nonnegative number of *internal rates of return*. The number equals the number of variations in the sign of the cash flow series or is less than that number by an even integer. Consider the following series of cash flows, the first occurring now and the others at subsequent yearly intervals: –100, –100, +50, +175, –50, +100. The internal rates of return are the numbers for *r* that satisfy the equation

$$-100 - \frac{100}{(1+r)} + \frac{50}{(1+r)^2} + \frac{175}{(1+r)^3} - \frac{50}{(1+r)^4} + \frac{100}{(1+r)^5} = 0$$

The series of cash flows has three variations in sign: a change from minus to plus, a change from plus to minus, and a change from minus to plus. The rule says that this series must have either one or three internal rates of return; in fact, it has only one, about 12 percent. But also see *reinvestment rate*.

detective controls. *Internal controls* designed to detect, or maximize the chance of detection of, errors and other irregularities. Compare *preventive controls*.

determination. See *determine*.

determine. Accountants and those who describe the accounting process often use (in our opinion, overuse) the verb "determine" and the noun "determination." A leading dictionary associates the following meanings with the verb "determine": settle, decide, conclude, ascertain, cause, affect, control, impel, terminate, and decide upon. In addition, accounting writers can mean any one of the following: measure, allocate, report, calculate, compute, observe, choose, and legislate. In accounting, there are two distinct sets of meanings – those encompassed by the synonym "cause or legislate" and those encompassed by the synonym "measure." The first set of uses conveys the active notion of causing something to happen and the second set of uses conveys the more passive notion of observing something that someone else has caused to happen. An accountant who speaks of cost or income "determination" generally means measurement or observation, not causation; management and economic conditions cause costs and income to be what they are. One who speaks of accounting principles "determination" can mean choosing or applying (as in "determining depreciation charges" from an allowable set) or causing to be acceptable (as in the *FASB* "determining" the accounting for *leases)*. In the long run, income is cash in less cash out, so management and economic conditions "determine" (cause) income to be what it is. In the short run, reported income is a function of accounting principles chosen and applied, so the accountant "determines" (measures) income. A question such as "Who determines income?" has, therefore, no unambiguous answer. The meaning of "an accountant determining acceptable accounting principles" is also vague. Does the clause mean merely choosing one from the set of generally acceptable principles, or does it mean using professional judgment to decide that some of the generally accepted principles are not correct under the current circumstances? We try never to use "determine" unless we mean "cause." Otherwise we use "measure," "report," "calculate," "compute," or whatever specific verb seems appropriate. We suggest that careful writers will always "determine" to use the most specific verb to convey meaning. "Determine" is seldom the best choice of words to describe a process where those who make decisions often differ from those who apply technique.

development stage enterprise. As defined in *SFAS No. 7,* a firm whose planned principal *operations* have not commenced or, having commenced, have not generated significant *revenue*. Such enterprises should be so identified, but no special *accounting principles* apply to them.

differentiable cost. If a total cost curve is smooth (in mathematical terms, differentiable), then we say that the curve graphing the derivative of the total cost curve shows differentiable costs, the cost increments associated with infinitesimal changes in volume.

differential. An adjective used to describe the change (increase or decrease) in a *cost, expense, investment, cash flow, revenue, profit,* and the like as the firm produces or sells one or more additional (or fewer) units or undertakes (or ceases) an activity.

differential analysis. Analysis of *differential costs, revenues, profits, investment, cash flow,* and the like.

differential cost. See *differential*.

dilution. A potential reduction in *earnings per share* or *book value* per share by the potential *conversion* of securities or by the potential exercise of *warrants* or *options*.

dilutive. Said of a *security* that would reduce *earnings per share* if it were exchanged for *common stock*.

dipping into LIFO layers. See *LIFO inventory layer*.

direct access. Access to computer storage where information can be located directly, regardless of its position in the storage file. Compare *sequential access*.

direct cost. Cost of *direct material* and *direct labor* incurred in producing a product. See *prime cost*. In some accounting literature, writers use this term to mean the same thing as *variable cost*.

direct costing. Another, less-preferred, term for *variable costing*.

direct-financing (capital) lease. See *sales-type (capital) lease* for definition and contrast.

direct labor (material) cost. Cost of labor (material) applied and assigned directly to a product; contrast with *indirect labor (material)*.

direct labor variance. Difference between actual and *standard direct labor* allowed.

direct method. See *statement of cash flows*.

direct posting. A method of bookkeeping where *entries* are made directly in *ledger accounts*, without the use of a *journal*.

direct write-off method. See *write-off method*.

disbursement. Payment by *cash* or by *check*. See *expenditure*.

DISC. Domestic International Sales Corporation. A U.S. *corporation*, usually a *subsidiary*, whose *income* is primarily attributable to exports. *Income tax* on 50 percent of a DISC's income is usually deferred for a long period. Generally, this results in a lower overall corporate tax for the *parent* than would otherwise be incurred.

disclaimer of opinion. An *auditor's report* stating that an opinion cannot be given on the *financial statements*. Usually results from *material* restrictions on the scope of the audit or from material uncertainties about the accounts which cannot be resolved at the time of the audit.

disclosure. The showing of facts in *financial statements, notes* thereto, or the *auditor's report*.

discontinued operations. See *income from discontinued operations*.

discount. In the context of *compound interest, bonds* and *notes*, the difference between *face* or *future value* and *present value* of a payment. In the context of *sales* and *purchases*, a reduction in price granted for prompt payment. See also *chain discount, quantity discount*, and *trade discount*.

discount factor. The reciprocal of one plus the *discount rate*. If the discount rate is 10 percent per period, the discount factor for three periods is $1/(1.10)^3 = (1.10)^3 = 0.75131$.

discount rate. *Interest rate* used to convert future payments to *present values*.

discounted bailout period. In a *capital budgeting* context, the total time that must elapse before discounted value of net accumulated cash flows from a project, including potential *salvage value* at various times of assets, equals or exceeds the *present value* of net accumulated cash outflows. Contrast with *discounted payback period*.

discounted cash flow. DCF. Using either the *net present value* or the *internal rate of return* in an analysis to measure the value of future expected cash *expenditures* and *receipts* at a common date. In discounted cash flow analysis, choosing the alternative with the largest *internal rate of return* may yield wrong answers given *mutually exclusive projects* with differing amounts of initial investment for two of the projects. Consider, to take an unrealistic example to illustrate the point, a project involving an initial investment of $1, with an *IRR* of 60 percent and another project involving an initial investment of $1 million with an IRR of 40 percent. Under most conditions, most firms will prefer the second project to the first, but choosing the project with the larger IRR will lead to undertaking the first, not the second. Usage calls this shortcoming of choosing between alternatives based on the magnitude of the internal rate or return, rather than based on the magnitude of the *net present value* of the cash flows, the "scale effect."

discounted payback period. The shortest amount of time which must elapse before the discounted present value of cash inflows from a project, excluding potential *salvage value* equals the discounted *present value* of the cash outflows.

discounting a note. See *note receivable discounted* and *factoring*.

discounts lapsed (lost). The sum of *discounts* offered for prompt payment that were not taken (or allowed) because of expiration of the discount period. See *terms of sale*.

discovery sampling. Acceptance sampling whereby an entire population is accepted if and only if the sample contains no disparities.

discovery value accounting. See *reserve recognition accounting*.

discretionary costs. *Programmed costs*.

Discussion Memorandum. A neutral discussion of all the issues concerning an accounting problem of current concern to the *FASB*. The publication of such a document usually implies that the FASB is considering issuing an *SFAS* or *SFAC* on this particular problem. The discussion memorandum brings together material about the particular problem to facilitate interaction and comment by those interested in the matter. A public hearing follows before the FASB will issue an *Exposure Draft*.

dishonored note. A *promissory note* whose maker does not repay the loan at *maturity* for a *term loan*, or on demand, for a *demand loan*.

disintermediation. Federal law regulates the maximum *interest rate* that both banks and savings and loan associations can pay for *time deposits*. When free-market interest rates exceed the regulated interest ceiling for such time deposits, some depositors withdraw their funds and invest them elsewhere at a higher interest rate. This process is known as "disintermediation."

distributable income. The portion of conventional accounting net income that can be distributed to owners (usually in the form of *dividends)* without impairing the physical capacity of the firm to continue operations at current levels. Pretax distributable income is conventional pretax income less the excess of *current cost* of goods sold and *depreciation* charges based on the replacement cost of *productive capacity* over cost of goods sold and depreciation on an *acquisition cost basis.* Contrast with *sustainable income.* See *inventory profit.*

distributable surplus. Canada and the United Kingdom. The statutory designation to describe the portion of the proceeds of the issue of shares without *par value* not allocated to share capital.

distributed processing. Processing in a complex computer information network, in which data relevant only to individual locations is processed locally, while information required elsewhere is transmitted either to the central computer or to local computer for further processing.

distribution expense. *Expense* of selling, advertising, and delivery activities.

dividend. A distribution of assets generated from *earnings* to owners of a corporation; it may be paid in cash (cash dividend), with stock (stock dividend), with property, or with other securities (dividend in kind). Dividends, except stock dividends, become a legal liability of the corporation when they are declared. Hence, the owner of stock ordinarily recognizes *revenue* when a dividend, other than a stock dividend, is declared. See also *liquidating dividend* and *stock dividend.*

dividend yield. *Dividends* declared for the year divided by market price of the stock as of a given time of the year.

dividends in arrears. Dividends on *cumulative preferred stock* that have not been declared in accordance with the preferred stock contract. Such arrearages must usually be cleared before dividends on *common stock* can be declared.

dividends in kind. See *dividend.*

division. A more or less self-contained business unit which is part of a larger family of business units under common control.

divisional control. See *control system.*

divisional reporting. *Line-of-business reporting.*

dollar sign rules. In presenting accounting statements or schedules, place a dollar sign beside the first figure in each column and beside any figure below a horizontal line drawn under the preceding figure.

dollar-value LIFO method. A form of *LIFO* inventory accounting with inventory quantities (*layers*) measured in dollar, rather than physical, terms. Adjustments to account for changing prices are made by use of specific price indexes appropriate for the kinds of items in the inventory.

Domestic International Sales Corporation. See *DISC.*

donated capital. A *shareholders' equity* account credited when contributions, such as land or buildings, are freely given to the company. Do not confuse with *contributed capital.*

double entry. The system of recording transactions that maintains the equality of the accounting equation; each entry results in recording equal amounts of *debits* and *credits.*

double-declining-balance depreciation. DDB. *Declining-balance depreciation,* which see, where the constant percentage used to multiply by book value in computing the depreciation charge for the year is $2/n$ and n is the *depreciable life* in periods. *Salvage value* is omitted from the depreciable amount. Thus if the asset cost \$100 and has a depreciable life of 5 years, the depreciation in the first year would be \$40 = $2/5$ x \$100, in the second would be \$24 = $2/5$ x (\$100 − \$40), and in the third year would be \$14.40 = $2/5$ x (\$100 − \$40 − \$24). By the fourth year, the remaining undepreciated cost could be depreciated under the straight line method at \$10.80 = $1/2$ x (\$100 − \$40 − \$24 −\$14.40) per year for tax purposes.

double T-account. *T-account* with an extra horizontal line showing a change in the account balance to be explained by the subsequent entries into the account, such as:

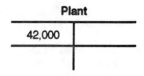

This account shows an increase in the asset account, plant, of \$42,000 to be explained. Such accounts are useful in preparing the *statement of cash flows;* they are not a part of the formal record-keeping process.

double taxation. The taxing authority (U.S. or state) taxes corporate income as earned (first tax) and then the same taxing authority taxes the aftertax income, when distributed to owners as dividends, again as personal income tax (second tax).

doubtful accounts. *Accounts receivable* estimated to be *uncollectible.*

Dr. The abbreviation for *debit.*

draft. A written order by the first party, called the drawer, instructing a second party, called the drawee (such as a bank) to pay a third party, called the payee. See also *check, cashier's check, certified check, NOW account, sight draft,* and *trade acceptance.*

drawee. See *draft.*

drawer. See *draft.*

drawing account. A *temporary account* used in *sole proprietorships* and *partnerships* to record payments to owners or partners during a period. At the end of the period, the drawing account is closed by crediting it and debiting the owner's or partner's share of income or, perhaps, his or her capital account.

drawings. Payments made to a *sole proprietor* or to a *partner* during a period. See *drawing account.*

driver. A cause of costs incurred. Examples include order processing, issuing an engineering change order, changing the production schedule, and stopping production to change machine settings. The notion arises primarily in product costing, particularly *activity-based costing.*

drop ship. Ordinarily a manufacturer sends goods to a distributor who sends the goods to its customer. If the distributor asks the manufacturer to send an order directly to the customer, usage calls the shipment a "drop shipment" and refers to the goods as "drop shipped."

dry-hole accounting. See *reserve recognition accounting* for definition and contrast.

dual transactions assumption (fiction). In presenting the *statement of cash flows,* some transactions not involving *cash* accounts are reported as though cash was generated and then used. For example, the issue of *capital stock* in return for the *asset,* land, is reported in the statement of cash flows as though stock were issued for *cash* and cash were used to acquire land. Other examples of transactions that require the dual transaction fiction are the issue of the *mortgage* in return for a non-current asset and the issue of stock to bondholders on *conversion* of their *convertible bonds.*

dual transfer prices. The *transfer price charged* to the buying *division* differs from that *credited* to the selling division. Such prices make sense when the selling division has excess capacity and, as usual, the *fair market value* exceeds the *incremental cost* to produce the goods or services being transferred.

duality. The axiom of *double entry* record keeping that every *transaction* is broken down into equal *debit* and *credit* amounts.

E

e. The base of natural logarithms; 2.71828.... If *interest* compounds continuously during a period at stated rate of *r* per period, then the effective *interest rate* is equivalent to interest compounded once per period at rate *i* where $i = e^r - 1$. Tables of e^r are widely available. If 12 percent annual interest is compounded continuously, the effective annual rate is $e^{.12} - 1 = 12.75$ percent. Interest compounded continuously at rate *r* for *d* days is $e^{rd/365} - 1$. For example, interest compounded for 92 days at 12 percent is $e^{.12 \times 92/365} - 1 = 3.07$ percent.

earned surplus. A term once used, but no longer considered proper, for *retained earnings.*

earnings. *Income,* or sometimes *profit.*

earnings cycle. The period of time that elapses for a given firm, or the series of transactions, during which *cash* is converted into *goods* and *services,* goods and services are sold to customers, and customers pay for their purchases with cash. *Cash cycle.*

earnings per share (of common stock). *Net income* to common shareholders (net income minus *preferred dividends)* divided by the average number of *common shares* outstanding; see also *primary earnings per share* and *fully diluted earnings per share.* See *ratio.*

earnings per share (of preferred stock). *Net income* divided by the average number of *preferred shares* outstanding during the period. This ratio indicates how well income covers or protects the preferred dividends; it does not indicate a legal share of *earnings.* See *ratio.*

earnings, retained. See *retained earnings.*

earnings statement. *Income statement.*

earn-out. An agreement between two merging firms under which the amount of payment by the acquiring firm to the acquired firm's shareholders depends on the future earnings of the acquired firm or, perhaps, of the *consolidated entity.*

easement. The acquired right or privilege of one person to use, or have access to, certain property of another. For example, a public utility's right to lay pipes or lines under property of another and to service those facilities.

economic depreciation. Decline in *current cost* of an *asset* during a period.

economic entity. See *entity.*

economic life. The time span over which the benefits of an *asset* are expected to be received. The economic life of a *patent, copyright,* or *franchise* may be less than the legal life. *Service life.*

economic order quantity. In mathematical *inventory* analysis, the optimal amount of stock to order when demand reduces inventory to a level called the "reorder point." If *A* represents the *incremental cost* of placing a single order, *D* represents the total demand for a period of time in units, and *H* represents the incremental holding cost during the period per unit of inventory, then the economic order quantity $Q = \sqrt{2AD/H}$. Usage sometimes calls *Q* the "optimal lot size."

ED. *Exposure Draft.*

EDP. Abbreviation for *electronic data processing.*

effective interest method. A systematic method for computing *interest expense* (or *revenue)* that makes the interest expense for each period divided by the amount of the net *liability (asset)* at the beginning of the period equal to the *yield rate* on the bond at the time of issue (acquisition). Interest for a period is yield rate (at time of issue) multiplied by the net liability (asset) at the start of the period. The *amortization* of discount or premium is the *plug* to give equal *debits* and *credits.* (Interest expense is a debit and the amount of coupon payments is a credit.)

effective (interest) rate. Of a bond, the *internal rate of return* or *yield to maturity* at the time of issue. Contrast with *coupon rate.* If the bond is issued for a price below *par,* the effective rate is higher than the coupon rate; if it is issued for a price greater than par, then the effective rate is lower than the coupon rate. In the context of *compound interest,* when the *compounding period* on a *loan* is different from one year, such as a nominal interest rate of 12 percent compounded monthly. The effective interest is the single rate that one could use at the end of the year to multiply the *principal* at the beginning of the year and give the same amount as results from compounding interest each period during the year. For example, if 12 percent per year is compounded monthly, the effective annual interest rate is 12.683 percent. That is, if you compound $100 each month at 1 percent per month, the $100 will grow to $112.68 at the end of the year. In general, if the nominal rate is *r* percent per year and is compounded *m* times per year, then the effective rate is $(1 + r/m)^m - 1$.

efficiency variance. A term used for the *quantity variance* for materials or labor or *variable overhead* in a *standard costing system.*

efficient market hypothesis. The supposition in finance that securities' prices reflect all available information and react nearly instantaneously and in an unbiased fashion to new information.

EITF. *Emerging Issues Task Force.*

eligible. Under income tax legislation, a term which restricts or otherwise alters the meaning of another tax or accounting term, generally to signify that the related assets or operations are entitled to specified tax treatment.

eliminations. *Work sheet* entries to prepare *consolidated statements* that are made to avoid duplicating the amounts of *assets, liabilities, owners' equity, revenues,* and *expenses* of the consolidated *entity* when the accounts of the *parent* and *subsidiaries* are summed.

Emerging Issues Task Force. EITF. A group convened by the *FASB* to deal more rapidly with accounting issues than the FASB's due process procedures can allow. The task force comprises about 20 members from public accounting, industry, and several trade associations. It meets every six weeks. Meetings are chaired by the FASB's director of research. Several FASB board members usually attend and participate. The chief accountant of the *SEC* has indicated that the SEC will require that published financial statements follow guidelines set by a consensus of the EITF. The EITF requires that nearly all of its members agree on a position before that position is given the label of "consensus." Such positions appear in *Abstracts of the EITF,* published by the FASB. Since 1984, the EITF has become one of the promulgators of *GAAP.*

employee stock option. See *stock option.*

Employee Stock Ownership Trust (or Plan). See *ESOT.*

employer, employee payroll taxes. See *payroll.*

enabling costs. A type of *capacity cost* that a firm will stop incurring if it shuts down operations completely but will incur in full if it carries out operations at any level. Costs of a security force or of a quality control inspector for an assembly line might be examples. Contrast with *standby costs.*

encumbrance. In governmental accounting, an anticipated *expenditure,* or *funds* restricted for anticipated expenditure, such as for outstanding purchase orders. *Appropriations* less expenditures less outstanding encumbrances yields unencumbered balance.

ending inventory. The *cost* of *inventory* on hand at the end of the *accounting period,* often called "closing inventory." The dollar amount of inventory is carried to the subsequent period.

endorsee. See *endorser.*

endorsement. See *draft.* The *payee* signs the draft and transfers it to a fourth party, such as the payee's bank.

endorser. The *payee* of a *note* or *draft* signs it, after writing "Pay to the order of X," transfers the note to person X, and presumably receives some benefit, such as cash, in return. Usage calls the payee who signs over the note the "endorser" and person X the "endorsee." The endorsee then has the rights of the payee and may in turn become an endorser by endorsing the note to another endorsee.

engineering method (of cost estimation). To estimate unit cost of product from study of the materials, labor, and *overhead* components of the production process.

enterprise. Any business organization, usually defining the accounting *entity.*

enterprise fund. A *fund* established by a governmental unit to account for acquisition, operation, and maintenance of governmental services that are supposed to be self-supporting from user charges, such as for water or airports.

entity. A person, *partnership, corporation,* or other organization. The *accounting entity* for which accounting statements are prepared may not be the same as the entity defined by law. For example, a *sole proprietorship* is an accounting entity but the individual's combined business and personal assets are the legal entity in most jurisdictions. Several affiliated corporations may be separate legal entities while *consolidated financial statements* are prepared for the group of companies operating as a single economic entity.

entity theory. The view of the corporation that emphasizes the form of the *accounting equation* that says *assets = equities.* Contrast with *proprietorship theory.* The entity theory is less concerned with a distinct line between *liabilities* and *shareholders' equity* than is the proprietorship theory. Rather, all equities are provided to the corporation by outsiders who merely have claims of differing legal standings. The entity theory implies using a *multiple-step* income statement.

entry value. The *current cost* of acquiring an asset or service at a *fair market price. Replacement cost.*

EOQ. *Economic order quantity.*

EPS. *Earnings per share.*

EPVI. *Excess present value index.*

equalization reserve. An inferior title for the allowance or *estimated liability* account when the firm uses the *allowance method* for such things as maintenance expenses. Periodically, the accounting will debit maintenance *expense* and credit the allowance. As the firm makes *expenditures* for maintenance, it will debit the allowance and credit cash or the other asset used in maintenance.

equities. *Liabilities* plus *owners' equity.* See *equity.*

equity. A claim to *assets;* a source of assets. *SFAC No. 3* defines equity as "the residual interest in the assets of an entity that remains after deducting its liabilities." Usage may be changing so that "equity" will exclude liabilities. We prefer to keep the broader definition, including liabilities, because there is no other single word that serves this useful purpose.

equity financing. Raising *funds* by issuance of *capital stock.* Contrast with *debt financing.*

equity method. A method of accounting for an *investment* in the stock of another company in which the proportionate share of the earnings of the other company is debited to the investment account and credited to a *revenue* account as earned. When *dividends* are received, *cash* is debited and the investment account is credited. Used in reporting when the investor owns sufficient shares of stock of an unconsolidated company to exercise significant control over the actions of that company. One of the few instances where revenue is recognized without a change in *working capital.*

equity ratio. *Shareholders' equity* divided by total *assets.* See *ratio.*

equivalent production. *Equivalent units.*

equivalent units (of work). The number of units of completed output that would require the same costs as a firm would actually incur for production of completed and partially completed units during a period. Used primarily in *process costing* calculations to measure in uniform terms the output of a continuous process.

ERISA. Employee Retirement Income Security Act of 1974. The federal law that sets most *pension plan* requirements.

error accounting. See *accounting errors.*

escalator clause. A clause inserted in a purchase or rental contract which permits, under specified conditions, upward adjustments of price or allowances.

escapable cost. *Avoidable costs.*

ESOP. Employee Stock Ownership Plan. See *ESOT.*

ESOT. Employee Stock Ownership Trust. A trust *fund* created by a corporate employer that can provide certain tax benefits to the corporate employer while providing for employee stock ownership. The corporate employer can contribute up to 25 percent of its payroll per year to the trust. The contributions are *deductions* from otherwise taxable income for federal *income tax* purposes. The assets of the trust must be used for the benefit of employees – for example, to fund death or retirement benefits. The assets of the trust are usually the *common stock*, sometimes nonvoting, of the corporate employer. For an example of the potential *tax shelter,* consider the case of a corporation with $1 million of *debt* outstanding, which it wishes to retire, and an annual payroll of $2 million. The corporation sells $1 million of common stock to the ESOT. The ESOT borrows $1 million with the loan guaranteed by, and therefore a *contingency* of, the corporation. The corporation uses the $1 million proceeds of the stock issue to retire its outstanding debt. (The debt of the corporation has been replaced with the debt of the ESOT.) The corporation can contribute $500,000 (= .25 x $2 million payroll) to the ESOT each year and treat the contribution as a deduction for tax purposes. After a little more than two years, the ESOT has received sufficient funds to retire its loan. The corporation has effectively repaid its original $1 million debt with pretax dollars. Assuming an income tax rate of 40 percent, it has saved $400,000 (= .40 x $1 million) of aftertax dollars *if* the $500,000 expense for the contribution to the ESOT for the pension benefits of employees

would have been made, in one form or another, anyway. Observe that the corporation could use the proceeds ($1 million in the example) of the stock issued to the ESOT for any of several different purposes: financing expansion, replacing plant assets, or acquiring another company. Basically this same form of pretax dollar financing through pensions is almost available with any corporate pension plan, but with one important exception. The trustees of an ordinary pension trust must invest the assets prudently, and if they do not, they are personally liable to employees. Current judgment about prudent investment requires diversification – pension trust assets should be invested in a wide variety of investment opportunities. (Not more than 10 percent of a pension trust's assets can ordinarily be invested in the parent's common stock.) Thus the ordinary pension trust cannot, in practice, invest all, or even most, of its assets in the parent corporation's stock. This constraint does not apply to the investments of an ESOT. All ESOT assets may be invested in the parent company's stock. The ESOT also provides a means for closely held corporations to achieve wider ownership of shares without *going public.* The laws enabling ESOT's provide for independent professional appraisal of shares not traded in public markets and for transactions between the corporation and the ESOT or between the ESOT and the employees to be based on the appraised values of the shares.

estate planning. The arrangement of an individual's affairs to facilitate the passage of assets to beneficiaries and to minimize taxes upon death.

estimated expenses. See *after cost.*

estimated liability. The preferred terminology for estimated costs to be incurred for such uncertain things as repairs under *warranty.* An estimated liability appears on the *balance sheet.* Contrast with *contingency.*

estimated revenue. A term used in governmental accounting to designate revenue expected to accrue during a period whether or not it will be collected during the period. A *budgetary account* is usually established at the beginning of the budget period.

estimated salvage value. Synonymous with *salvage value* of an *asset* before its retirement.

estimates, changes in. See *accounting changes.*

estimation sampling. The use of sampling technique whereby a qualitative or quantitative characteristic of the population is inferred from the occurrence of that characteristic in the sample drawn. See *attribute(s) sampling; variables sampling.*

EURL; Entreprise unipersonnelle à responsabilité limitée. France. Similar to *SARL*, but has only one shareholder.

ex rights. The condition of securities whose quoted market price no longer includes the right to purchase new securities, such rights having expired or been retained by the vendor. Compare *cum rights.*

except for. Qualification in *auditor's report,* usually caused by a change, approved by the auditor, from one acceptable accounting principle or procedure to another.

excess present value. In a *capital budgeting* context, *present value* of (anticipated net cash inflows minus cash outflows including initial cash outflow) for a project.

excess present value index. *Present value* of future *cash* inflows divided by initial cash outlay.

exchange. The generic term for a transaction (or more technically, a reciprocal transfer) between one entity and another. In another context, the name for a market, such as the New York Stock Exchange.

exchange gain or loss. The phrase used by the *FASB* for *foreign exchange gain or loss.*

exchange rate. The *price* of one country's currency in terms of another country's currency. For example, the British pound sterling might be worth $1.60 at a given time. The exchange rate would be stated as "one pound is worth one dollar and sixty cents" or "one dollar is worth £.625 (= £1/$1.60)."

excise tax. Tax on the manufacture, sale, or consumption of a commodity.

ex-dividend. Said of a stock at the time when the declared *dividend* becomes the property of the person who owned the stock on the *record date.* The payment date follows the ex-dividend date.

executory contract. A mere exchange of promises. An agreement providing for payment by a payor to a payee upon the performance of an act or service by the payee, such as a labor contract. Obligations under such contracts generally are not recognized as *liabilities.*

exemption. A term used for various amounts subtracted from gross income in computing taxable income. Usage does not call all such subtractions "exemptions." See *tax deduction.*

exercise. When owners of an *option* or *warrant* purchase the security that the option entitles them to purchase, they have exercised the option or warrant.

exercise price. See *option.*

exit value. The proceeds that would be received if assets were disposed of in an *arm's-length transaction. Current selling price. Net realizable value.*

expected value. The mean or arithmetic *average* of a statistical distribution or series of numbers.

expected value of (perfect) information. Expected *net benefits* from an undertaking with (perfect) information minus expected net benefits of the undertaking without (perfect) information.

expendable fund. In governmental accounting, a *fund* whose resources, *principal,* and earnings may be distributed.

expenditure. Payment of *cash* for goods or services received. Payment may be made either at the time the goods or services are received or at a later time. Virtually synonymous with *disbursement* except that disbursement is a broader term and includes all payments for goods or services. Contrast with *expense.*

expense. As a noun, a decrease in *owners' equity* caused by using up *assets* in producing *revenue* or carrying out other activities that comprise a part of the entity's *operations.* A "gone" asset or *net asset;* an expired cost. The amount is the *cost* of the assets used. Do not confuse with *expenditure* or *disbursement,* which may occur before, when, or after the firm recognizes the related expense. Use the word "cost" to refer to an item that still has service potential and is an asset. Use the word "expense" after the firm has used the asset's service potential. As a verb, to designate a past or current expenditure as a current expense.

expense account. An *account* to accumulate *expenses;* such accounts are closed at the end of the accounting period. A *temporary owners' equity* account. Also used to describe a listing of expenses by an employee submitted to the employer for reimbursement.

experience rating. A term used in insurance, particularly unemployment insurance, to denote changes from ordinary rates to reflect extraordinarily large or small amounts of claims over time by the insured.

expired cost. An *expense* or a *loss.*

Exposure Draft. ED. A preliminary statement of the *FASB* (or *APB* between 1962 and 1973) that shows the contents of a pronouncement the board is considering making effective.

external reporting. Reporting to shareholders and the public, as opposed to internal reporting for management's benefit. See *financial accounting* and contrast with *managerial accounting.*

extraordinary item. A *material expense* or *revenue* item characterized both by its unusual nature and infrequency of occurrence that appears along with its income tax effects separately from ordinary income and *income from discontinued operations* on the *income statement.* Accountants would probably classify a *loss* from an earthquake as an extraordinary item. Accountants treat gain (or loss) on retirement of *bonds* as an extraordinary item under the terms of *SFAS No. 4.*

F

FASAC. *Financial Accounting Standards Advisory Council.*

face amount (value). The nominal amount due at *maturity* from a *bond* or *note* not including contractual interest that may also be due on the same date. Good usage calls the corresponding amount of a stock certificate the *par* or *stated value,* whichever is applicable.

factoring. The process of buying *notes* or *accounts receivable* at a *discount* from the holder to whom the debt is owed; from the holder's point of view, the selling of such notes or accounts. When the transaction involves a single note, usage calls the process "discounting a note."

factory. Used synonymously with *manufacturing* as an adjective.

factory burden. *Manufacturing overhead.*

factory cost. *Manufacturing cost.*

factory expense. *Manufacturing overhead. Expense* is a poor term in this context because the item is a *product cost.*

factory overhead. Usually an item of *manufacturing cost* other than *direct labor* or *direct materials.*

fair market price (value). Price (value) negotiated at *arm's length* between a willing buyer and a willing seller, each acting rationally in his or her own self interest. May be estimated in the absence of a monetary transaction.

fair presentation (fairness). When the *auditor's report* says that the *financial statements* "present fairly... ," the auditor means that the accounting alternatives used by the entity are all in accordance with *GAAP.* In recent years, however, courts are finding that conformity with *generally accepted accounting principles* may be insufficient grounds for an opinion that the statements are fair. *SAS No. 5* requires that the auditor judge the accounting principles used "appropriate in the circumstances" before attesting to fair presentation.

FASB. Financial Accounting Standards Board. An independent board responsible, since 1973, for establishing *generally accepted accounting principles.* Its official pronouncements are *"Statements of Financial Accounting Concepts"* *("SFAC")*, *"Statements of Financial Accounting Standards"* *("SFAS")*, and *"Interpretations."* See also *Discussion Memorandum* and *Technical Bulletin.*

FASB Interpretation. An official statement of the *FASB* interpreting the meaning of *Accounting Research Bulletins, APB Opinions,* and *Statements of Financial Accounting Standards.*

FASB Technical Bulletin. See *Technical Bulletin.*

favorable variance. An excess of actual *revenues* over expected revenues. An excess of *standard cost* over actual cost.

federal income tax. *Income tax* levied by the U.S. government on individuals and corporations.

Federal Insurance Contributions Act. See *FICA.*

Federal Unemployment Tax Act. See *FUTA.*

feedback. The process of informing employees about how their actual performance compares with the expected or desired level of performance in the hope that the information will reinforce desired behavior and reduce unproductive behavior.

FEI. *Financial Executives Institute.*

FICA. Federal Insurance Contributions Act. The law that sets *"Social Security" taxes* and benefits.

fiduciary. Someone responsible for the custody or administration of property belonging to another, such as an executor (of an estate), agent, receiver (in *bankruptcy),* or trustee (of a trust).

FIFO. First-in, first-out; the *inventory flow assumption* which firms use to compute *ending inventory* cost from most recent purchases and *cost of goods sold* from oldest purchases including beginning inventory. See *LISH.* Contrast with *LIFO.*

finance. As a verb, to supply with *funds* through the *issue* of stocks, bonds, notes, or mortgages, or through the retention of earnings.

financial accounting. The accounting for *assets, equities, revenues,* and *expenses* of a business. Primarily concerned with the historical reporting of the *financial position* and operations of an *entity* to external users on a regular, periodic basis. Contrast with *managerial accounting.*

Financial Accounting Foundation. The independent foundation (committee) that raises funds to support the *FASB* and *GASB.*

Financial Accounting Standards Advisory Council. **FASAC.** A committee of academics, preparers, attestors, and uses giving advice to the *FASB* on matters of strategy and emerging issues. The Council spends much of each meeting being informed about current developments in standard setting by the FASB Staff.

Financial Accounting Standards Board. *FASB.*

Financial Executives Institute. An organization of financial executives, such as chief accountants, *controllers,* and treasurers, of large businesses.

financial expense. An *expense* incurred in raising or managing *funds.*

financial flexibility. As defined by *SFAC No. 5,* "the ability of an entity to take effective actions to alter amounts and timing of cash flows so it can respond to unexpected needs and opportunities."

financial forecast. See *financial projection* for definition and contrast.

financial leverage. See *leverage.*

financial projection. An estimate of *financial position,* results of *operations,* and changes in cash flows for one or more future periods based on a set of assumptions. If the assumptions are not necessarily the most likely outcomes, then *GAAS* call the estimate a "projection." If the assumptions represent the most probable outcomes, then *GAAS* call the estimate a "forecast." "Most probable" means that management has evaluated the assumptions and that they are management's judgment of the most likely set of conditions and most likely outcomes.

financial position (condition). Statement of the *assets* and *equities* of a firm displayed as a *balance sheet.*

financial ratio. See *ratio.*

financial reporting objectives. *FASB Statement of Financial Accounting Concepts No. 1* sets out the broad objectives of financial reporting that are intended to guide the development of specific *accounting standards.*

Financial Reporting Release. Series of releases, issued by the SEC since 1982. Replaces the *Accounting Series Releases.* See *SEC.*

financial statements. The *balance sheet, income statement, statement of retained earnings, statement of cash flows,* statement of changes in *owners' equity accounts,* and *notes* thereto.

financial structure. *Capital structure.*

financial year. The term for *fiscal year* in Australia and Britain.

financing activities. Obtaining resources from (a) owners and providing them with a return on and a return of their *investment* and (b) *creditors* and repaying amounts borrowed (or otherwise settling the obligation). See *statement of cash flows.*

financing lease. *Capital lease.*

finished goods (inventory account). Manufactured product ready for sale; a *current asset (inventory) account.*

firm. Informally, any business entity. (Strictly speaking, a firm is a *partnership.*)

first in, first out. See *FIFO.*

fiscal year. A period of 12 consecutive months chosen by a business as the *accounting period* for *annual reports.* May or may not be a *natural business year* or a calendar year.

FISH. An acronym, conceived by George H. Sorter, for *first in, still here.* FISH is the same cost flow assumption as *LIFO.* Many readers of accounting statements find it easier to think about inventory questions in terms of items still on hand. Think of LIFO in connection with *cost of goods sold* but of FISH in connection with *ending inventory.* See *LISH.*

fixed assets. *Plant assets.*

fixed assets turnover. *Sales* divided by average total *fixed assets.*

fixed benefit plan. A *defined-benefit (pension) plan.*

fixed budget. A plan that provides for specified amounts of *expenditures* and *receipts* that do not vary with activity levels. Sometimes called a "static budget." Contrast with *flexible budget.*

fixed charges earned (coverage) ratio. *Income* before *interest expense* and *income tax expense* divided by interest expense.

fixed cost (expense). An *expenditure* or *expense* that does not vary with volume of activity, at least in the short run. See *capacity costs,* which include *enabling costs* and *standby costs,* and *programmed costs* for various subdivisions of fixed costs. See *cost terminology.*

fixed interval sampling. A method of choosing a sample in which the first item is selected from the population randomly, with the remaining sample items drawn at equally spaced intervals. Compare *variable interval sampling.*

fixed liability. *Long-term* liability.

fixed manufacturing overhead applied. The portion of *fixed manufacturing overhead cost* allocated to units produced during a period.

fixed overhead variance. Difference between *actual fixed manufacturing costs* and fixed manufacturing costs applied to production in a *standard costing system.*

flexible budget. *Budget* that projects receipts and expenditures as a function of activity levels. Contrast with *fixed budget.*

flexible budget allowance. With respect to manufacturing overhead, the total cost that a firm should have incurred at the level of activity actually experienced during the period.

float. *Checks* whose amounts have been *added* to the depositor's bank account, but not yet subtracted from the *drawer's* bank account.

flow. The change in the amount of an item over time. Contrast with *stock.*

flow assumption. When a *withdrawal* is made from *inventory,* the cost of the withdrawal must be computed by a flow assumption if *specific identification* of units is not used. The usual flow assumptions are *FIFO, LIFO,* and *weighted average.*

flow of costs. *Costs* passing through various classifications within an *entity.* See the accompanying diagram for a summary of *product* and *period cost* flows.

flow-through method. Accounting for the *investment credit* to show all income statement benefits of the credit in the year of acquisition, rather than spreading them over the life of the asset acquired, called the "deferral method." The *APB* preferred the deferral method in *Opinion No. 2* (1962) but accepted the flow-through method in *Opinion No. 4* (1964). The term is also used in connection with *depreciation* accounting where *straight-line method* is used for financial reporting and an *accelerated* method for tax reporting. Followers of the flow-through method would not recognize a *deferred tax liability. APB Opinion No. 11* prohibits the use of the flow-through approach in financial reporting although it has been used by some regulatory commissions.

FOB. Free on board some location (for example, FOB shipping point; FOB destination); the *invoice* price includes delivery at seller's expense to that location. Title to goods usually passes from seller to buyer at the FOB location.

folio. A page number or other identifying reference used in posting to indicate the source of entry.

footing. Adding a column of figures.

footnotes. More detailed information than that provided in the *income statement, balance sheet, statement of retained earnings,* and *statement of cash flows;* these are considered an integral part of the statements and are covered by the *auditor's report.* Sometimes called "notes."

forecast. See *financial projection* for definition and contrast.

foreclosure. The borrower fails to make a required payment on a *mortgage;* the lender takes possession of the property for his or her own use or sale. Assume that the lender sells the property but the proceeds of sale are insufficient to cover the outstanding balance on the loan at the time of foreclosure. Under the terms of most mortgages, the lender becomes an unsecured creditor of the borrower for the still-unrecovered balance of the loan.

foreign currency. For *financial statements* prepared in a given currency, any other currency.

foreign currency translation. Reporting in the currency used in financial statements the amounts denominated or measured in a different currency.

foreign exchange gain or loss. Gain or loss from holding *net* foreign *monetary items* during a period when the *exchange rate* changes.

Foreign Sales Corporation. See *FSC.*

forfeited share. A share to which a subscriber has lost title because of nonpayment of a *call.*

Form 10-K. See *10-K.*

Form 20-F. See *20-F.*

forward exchange contract. An agreement to exchange at a specified future date currencies of different countries at a specified rate called the "forward rate".

forward price. The price of a commodity for delivery at a specified future date. Compare *spot price.*

franchise. A privilege granted or sold, such as to use a name or to sell products or services.

fraudulent financial reporting. Intentional or reckless conduct that results in materially misleading *financial statements.* See *creative accounting.*

free cash flow. Financial statement analysts use this term to mean *cash flow + interest expense + income tax expense.*

free on board. *FOB.*

freight-in. The *cost* of freight or shipping incurred in acquiring *inventory,* preferably treated as a part of the cost of *inventory.* Often shown temporarily in an *adjunct account* that is closed at the end of the period with other purchase accounts to the inventory account by the acquirer.

freight-out. The *cost* of freight or shipping incurred in selling *inventory,* treated by the seller as a selling *expense* in the period of sale.

Flow of Costs (and Sales Revenue)

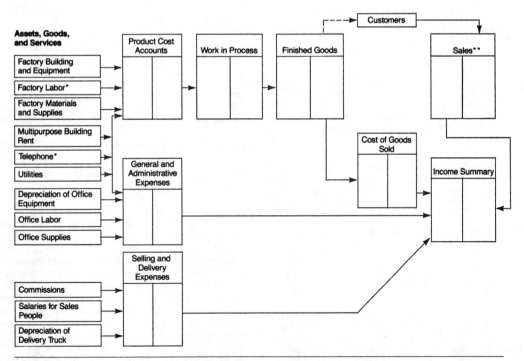

*The credit in the entry to record these items is usually to a payable; for all others, the credit is usually to an asset, or to an asset contra account.

**When sales to customers are recorded, the Sales account is credited. The debit is usually to Cash or Accounts Receivable.

FSC. Foreign Sales Corporation. A foreign *corporation* engaging in certain export activities, some of whose *income* is exempt from U.S. federal *income tax*. A U.S. corporation need pay no income taxes on *dividends* distributed by an FSC out of *earnings* attributable to certain foreign income.

full absorption costing. The method of *costing* which assigns all types of manufacturing costs (*direct material, direct labor, fixed* and *variable overhead*) to units produced; required by *GAAP*. Also called "absorption costing." Contrast with *variable costing.*

full costing. full costs. The total cost of producing and selling a unit. Full cost per unit equals *full absorption cost* per unit plus *marketing, administrative, interest,* and other *central corporate expenses,* per unit. The sum of full costs for all units equals total costs of the firm. Often used in *long-term* profitability and pricing decisions.

full disclosure. The reporting policy requiring that all significant or *material* information is to be presented in the financial statements. See *fair presentation.*

fully diluted earnings per share. Smallest *earnings per share* figure on *common stock* that can be obtained by computing an earnings per share for all possible combinations of assumed *exercise* or *conversion* of *potentially dilutive securities.* Must be reported on the *income statement* if it is less than 97 percent of earnings available to common shareholders divided by the average number of common shares outstanding during the period.

fully vested. Said of a *pension plan* when an employee (or his or her estate) has rights to all the benefits purchased with the employer's contributions to the plan even if the employee is not employed by this employer at the time of death or retirement.

function. In governmental accounting, said of a group of related activities for accomplishing a service or regulatory program for which the governmental unit is responsible. In mathematics, a rule for associating a number, called the dependent variable, with another number (or numbers), called independent variable(s).

functional classification. *Income statement* reporting form in which *expenses* are reported by functions, that is, cost of goods sold, administrative expenses, financing expenses, selling expenses; contrast with *natural classification.*

functional currency. Currency in which an entity carries out its principal economic activity.

fund. An *asset* or group of assets set aside for a specific purpose. See also *fund accounting.*

fund accounting. The accounting for resources, obligations, and *capital* balances, usually of a not-for-profit or governmental *entity,* which have been segregated into *accounts* representing logical groupings based on legal, donor, or administrative restrictions or requirements. The groupings are described as "funds." The accounts of each fund are *self-balancing,* and from them one can prepare a *balance sheet* and an operating statement for each fund. See *fund* and *fund balance.*

fund balance. In governmental accounting, the excess of assets of a *fund* over its liabilities and reserves; the not-for-profit equivalent of *owners' equity.*

funded. Said of a *pension plan* or other obligation when *funds* have been set aside for meeting the obligation when it becomes due. The federal law for pension plans requires that all *normal costs* be funded as recognized. In addition, *prior service cost* of pension plans must be funded over 30 or over 40 years, depending on the circumstances.

funding. Replacing *short-term* liabilities with *long-term* debt.

funds. Generally *working capital;* current assets less current liabilities. Sometimes used to refer to *cash* or to cash and *marketable securities.*

funds provided by operations. See *cash provided by operations.*

funds statement. An informal name often used for the *statement of cash flows.*

funny money. Said of securities such as *convertible preferred stock, convertible bonds, options,* and *warrants* that have aspects of *common stock* equity but that did not reduce reported *earnings per share* prior to the issuance of *APB Opinions No. 9* in 1966 and *No. 15* in 1969.

FUTA. Federal Unemployment Tax Act which provides for taxes to be collected at the federal level, to help subsidize the individual states' administration of their unemployment compensation programs.

future value. Value at a specified future date of a sum increased at a specified *interest rate.*

G

GAAP. *Generally accepted accounting principles.* A plural noun.

GAAS. *Generally accepted auditing standards.* A plural noun. Not to be confused with *GAS.*

gain. Increase in *owners' equity* caused by a transaction not part of a firm's typical, day-to-day operations and not part of owners' *investment* or *withdrawals.* The term "gain" (or "*loss*") is distinguished in two separate ways from related terms. First, gains (and losses) are generally used for nonoperating, incidental, peripheral, or nonroutine transactions: gain on sale of land in contrast to *gross margin* on *sale* of *inventory.* Second, gains and losses are *net* concepts, not gross concepts: gain or loss results from subtracting some measure of *cost* from the measure of inflow. *Revenues* and *expenses,* on the other hand, are gross concepts; their difference is a net concept. Gain is nonroutine and net, *profit* or *margin* is routine and net; revenue is routine and gross. Loss is net but can be either routine ("loss on sale of inventory") or not ("loss on disposal of segment of business").

gain contingency. See *contingency.*

GAS. *Goods available for sale.* Not to be confused with *GAAS.*

GASB. Governmental Accounting Standards Board. An independent body responsible, since 1984, for establishing accounting standards for state and local government units. It is part of the *Financial Accounting Foundation,* parallel to the *FASB,* and currently consists of five members.

GbR; Gesellschaft des bürgerlichen Rechtes. Germany. A *partnership* whose members agree to share in specific aspects of their own separate business pursuits, such as an office. This partnership has no legal form and is not a separate accounting *entity.*

gearing. British term for *financial leverage.*

gearing adjustment. Consider a firm, part of whose assets are *noncurrent liabilities* and who has experience *holding gains* on its *assets* during a period. All of the increase in wealth caused by the holding gains belongs to the owners; none typically belongs to the lenders. Some British accounting authorities believe that published *income statements* should show the part of the holding gain financed with debt in *income* for the period. Usage calls that part the "gearing adjustment."

general debt. Debt of a governmental unit legally payable from general revenues and backed by the full faith and credit of the governmental unit.

general expenses. *Operating expenses* other than those specifically assigned to cost of goods sold, selling, and administration.

general fixed asset (group of accounts). Accounts showing those long-term assets of a governmental unit not accounted for in *enterprise, trust,* or intragovernmental service funds.

general fund. Assets and liabilities of a nonprofit entity not specifically earmarked for other purposes; the primary operating fund of a governmental unit.

general journal. The formal record where transactions, or summaries of similar transactions, are recorded in *journal entry* form as they occur. Use of the adjective "general" usually implies only two columns for cash amounts or that there are also various *special journals,* such as a *check register* or *sales journal,* in use.

general ledger. The name for the formal *ledger* containing all of the financial statement accounts. It has equal debits and credits as evidenced by the *trial balance.* Some of the accounts in the general ledger may be *controlling accounts,* supported by details contained in *subsidiary ledgers.*

general partner. Member of *partnership* personally liable for all debts of the partnership; contrast with *limited partner.*

general price index. A measure of the aggregate prices of a wide range of goods and services in the economy at one time relative to the prices during a base period. See *consumer price index* and *GNP Implicit Price Deflator.* Contrast with *specific price index.*

general price level-adjusted statements. See *constant dollar accounting.*

general price level changes. Changes in the aggregate prices of a wide range of goods and services in the economy. These price changes are measured using a *general price index.* Contrast with *specific price changes.*

general purchasing power. The command of the dollar over a wide range of goods and services in the economy. The general purchasing power of the dollar is inversely related to changes in a general price index. See *general price index.*

general purchasing power accounting. See *constant dollar accounting.*

generally accepted accounting principles. GAAP. As previously defined by the *APB* and now by the *FASB,* the conventions, rules, and procedures necessary to define accepted accounting practice at a particular time; includes both broad guidelines and relatively detailed practices and procedures.

generally accepted auditing standards. GAAS. The standards, as opposed to particular procedures, promulgated by the *AICPA* (in *Statements on Auditing Standards)* that concern "the auditor's professional quantities" and "the judgment exercised by him in the performance of his examination and in his report." Currently, there are ten such standards: three general ones (concerned with proficiency, independence, and degree of care to be exercised), three standards of field work, and four standards of reporting. The first standard of reporting requires that the *auditor's report* state whether or not the *financial statements* are prepared in accordance with *generally accepted accounting principles.* Thus the typical auditor's report says that the examination was conducted in accordance with generally accepted auditing standards and that the statements are prepared in accordance with generally accepted accounting principles. See *auditor's report.*

geographic segment. A single operation or a group of operations located in a particular geographic area that generate revenue, incur costs, and have assets employed in or associated with generating such revenue.

GIE; Groupement d'intérêt économique. France. A joint venture, normally used for exports and research and development pooling.

GmbH; Gesellschaft mit beschränkter Haftung. Germany. A private company with unlimited number of shareholders. Transfer of ownership can take place only with the consent of other shareholders. Contrast with *AG.*

GNP Implicit Price Deflator (Index). A *price index* issued quarterly by the Office of Business Economics of the U.S. Department of Commerce. This index attempts to trace the price level of all *goods and services* comprising the *gross national product.* Contrast with *consumer price index.*

goal congruence. All members of an organization have incentives to perform for a common interest, such as *shareholder* wealth maximization for a *corporation.*

going-concern assumption. For accounting purposes, accountants assume a business will remain in operation long enough to carry out all its current plans. This assumption partially justifies the *acquisition cost* basis, rather than a *liquidation* or *exit value,* basis of accounting.

going public. Said of a business when its *shares* become widely traded, rather than being closely held by relatively few shareholders. Issuing shares to the general investing public.

goods. Items of merchandise, supplies, raw materials, or finished goods. Sometimes the meaning of "goods" is extended to include all *tangible* items, as in the phrase "goods and services."

goods available for sale. The sum of *beginning inventory* plus all acquisitions of merchandise or finished goods during an *accounting period.*

goods in process. *Work in process.*

goodwill. The excess of cost of an acquired firm (or operating unit) over the current *fair market value* of the separately identifiable *net assets* of the acquired unit. Before goodwill is recognized, all identifiable assets, whether or not on the books of the acquired unit, must be given a *fair market value.* For example, a firm has developed a *patent* which is not recognized on its books because of *SFAS No. 2.* If another company acquires the firm, the acquirer will recognize the patent at an amount equal to its estimated fair market value before computing goodwill. Informally, the term is used to indicate the value of good customer relations, high employee morale, a well-respected business name, and so on, that are expected to result in greater than that normal earning power.

goodwill method. A method of accounting for the *admission* of a new partner to a *partnership* when the new partner is to be credited with a portion of capital different from the value of the *tangible* assets contributed as a fraction of tangible assets on the partnership. See *bonus method* for a description and contrast.

Governmental Accounting Standards Advisory Council. A group that consults with the *GASB* on agenda, technical issues, and the assignment of priorities to projects. It comprises more than a dozen members representing various areas of expertise.

Governmental Accounting Standards Board. *GASB.*

GPL. General price level; usually used as an adjective modifying the word "accounting" to mean *constant dollar accounting.*

GPLA. General price level-adjusted accounting; *constant dollar accounting.*

GPP. General purchasing power; usually used as an adjective modifying the word "accounting" to mean *constant dollar accounting.*

graded vesting. Said of a *pension plan* where not all employee benefits are currently *vested.* By law, the benefits must become vested according to one of several formulas as time passes.

grandfather clause. An exemption in new accounting *pronouncements* exempting transactions that occurred before a given date from the new accounting treatment. For example, *APB Opinion No. 17,* adopted in 1970, exempted *goodwill*

acquired before 1970 from required *amortization.* The term "grandfather" appears in the title to *SFAS No. 10.*

gross. Not adjusted or reduced by deductions or subtractions. Contrast with *net.*

gross margin. *Net sales* minus *cost of goods sold.*

gross margin percent. $100 \times (1 - cost\ of\ goods\ sold/net\ sales) = 100 \times (gross\ margin/net\ sales).$

gross national product. GNP. The market value within a nation for a year of all goods and services produced as measured by final sales of goods and services to individuals, corporations, and governments plus the excess of exports over imports.

gross price method (of recording purchase or sales discounts). The *purchase* (or *sale)* is recorded at its *invoice price,* not deducting the amounts of *discounts* available. Discounts taken are recorded in a *contra* account to purchases (or sales). Information on discounts lapsed is not made available, and for this reason, most firms prefer the *net price method* of recording purchase discounts.

gross profit. *Gross margin.*

gross profit method. A method of estimating *ending inventory* amounts. *Cost of goods sold* is measured as some fraction of sales; the *inventory equation* is then used to value *ending inventory.*

gross profit ratio. *Gross margin* divided by *net sales.*

gross sales. All *sales* at *invoice* prices, not reduced by *discounts, allowances, returns,* or other adjustments.

group depreciation. A method of calculating *depreciation* charges where similar assets are combined, rather than depreciated separately. No gain or loss is recognized on retirement of items from the group until the last item in the group is sold or retired. See *composite life method.*

guarantee. A promise to answer for payment of debt or performance of some obligation if the person liable for the debt or obligation fails to perform. A guarantee is a *contingency* of the *entity* making the promise. Often, writers use the words "guarantee" and "warranty" to mean the same thing. In precise usage, however, "guarantee" means promise to fulfill the promise of some person to perform a contractual obligation such as to pay a sum of money, whereas "warranty" refers to promises about pieces of machinery or other products. See *warranty.*

H

half-year convention. An assumption used in *tax accounting* under *ACRS,* and sometimes in *financial accounting,* that *depreciable assets* were acquired at mid-year of the year of acquisition. When this convention is used, the *depreciation charge* for the year is computed as one-half the charge that would be used if the assets had been acquired at the beginning of the year.

hardware. The physical equipment or devices forming a computer and peripheral equipment.

hash total. A control used to establish accuracy of data processing, whereby a total of data is made by adding values which would not normally be added together (e.g. the sum of a list of part numbers) and subsequently compared to a computer-generated total of the same values.

Hasselback. An annual directory of accounting faculty at colleges and universities, which gives information about the faculty's training and fields of specialization. James R. Hasselback of Florida State University has compiled the directory since the 1970s; Prentice-Hall distributes it.

held-to-maturity securities. *Marketable debt securities* a firm expects to, and has the ability to, hold to *maturity.* A classification important in *SFAS No. 115,* which generally requires the owner to carry marketable securities on the balance sheet at market value, not at cost. Under *SFAS No. 115,* the firm may show held-to-maturity debt securities at *amortized cost.* If the firm lacks either the expectation or the intent to hold the debt security to its maturity, then the firm will show that security at market value as a security *available for sale.*

hidden reserve. The term refers to an amount by which *owners' equity* has been understated, perhaps deliberately. The understatement arises from an undervaluation of *assets* or overvaluation of *liabilities.* By undervaluing assets on this period's *balance sheet, net income* in some future period can be made to look artificially high by disposing of the asset: actual *revenues* less artificially low cost of assets sold yields artificially high net income. There is no *account* that has this title.

hire-purchase agreement. A lease containing a purchase option.

historical cost. *Acquisition cost; original cost; a sunk cost.*

historical cost/constant dollar accounting. Accounting based on *historical cost* valuations measured in *constant dollars.* *Nonmonetary items* are restated to reflect changes in the *general purchasing power* of the dollar since the time the specific *assets* were acquired or *liabilities* were incurred. A *gain* or *loss* is recognized on *monetary items* as they are held over time periods when the general purchasing power of the dollar changes.

historical exchange rate. The rate at which one currency converts into another at the date a transaction took place. Contrast with *current exchange rate.*

historical summary. A part of the *annual report* to shareholders that shows important items, such as *net income, revenues, expenses, asset* and *equity* totals, *earnings per share,* and the like, for five or ten periods including the current one. Usually not as much detail is shown in the historical summary as in *comparative statements,* which typically report as much detail for the two preceding years as for the current year. Annual reports may contain both comparative statements and a historical summary.

holdback. A portion of the progress payments called for under the terms of a contract which the customer need not pay until the contractor has fulfilled the contract or satisfied financial obligations to subcontractors.

holding company. A company that confines its activities to owning *stock* in, and supervising management of, other companies. A holding company usually owns a controlling interest in, that is more than 50 percent of the voting stock of, the companies whose stock it holds. Contrast with *mutual fund.* See *conglomerate.* In British usage, the term refers to any company with controlling interest in another company.

holding gain or loss. Difference between end-of-period price and beginning-of-period price of an asset held during the period. Realized holding gains and losses are not ordinarily separately reported in financial statements. Unrealized gains are not usually reflected in income at all. Some unrealized losses, such as on inventory or marketable securities, are reflected in income or *owners' equity* as the losses occur; see *lower of cost or market.* See *inventory profit* for further refinement, including *gains* on *assets* sold during the period.

holding gain or loss net of inflation. Increase or decrease in the *current cost* of an asset while it is held measured in units of *constant dollars.*

horizontal analysis. *Time-series analysis.*

horizontal integration. The extension of activity by an organization in the same general line of business or expansion into supplementary, complementary or compatible products. (Compare *vertical integration.)*

house account. An account with a customer who does not pay sales commissions.

human resource accounting. A term used to describe a variety of proposals that seek to report and emphasize the importance of human resources – knowledgeable, trained, and loyal employees – in a company's earning process and total assets.

hurdle rate. Required rate of return in a *discounted cash flow* analysis.

hybrid security. *Security,* such as a *convertible bond,* containing elements of both *debt* and *owners' equity.*

hypothecation. The *pledging* of property, without transfer of title or possession, to secure a loan.

I

I. *Identity matrix.*

IAA. *Interamerican Accounting Association.*

IASC. *International Accounting Standards Committee.*

ICMA. *Institute of Certified Management Accountants.* See *CMA* and *IMA.*

ideal standard costs. *Standard costs* set equal to those that a firm would incur under the best possible conditions.

Identity matrix. A square *matrix* with ones on the main diagonal and zeros elsewhere; a matrix **I** such that for any other matrix **A**, **IA** = **AI** = **A**. The matrix equivalent to the number one.

IIA. *Institute of Internal Auditors.*

IMA. *Institute of Management Accountants.*

Implicit interest. *Interest* not paid or received. See *interest, imputed*. All transactions involving the deferred payment or receipt of cash involve interest, whether explicitly stated or not. The implicit interest on a single-payment *note* is the difference between the amount collected at maturity less the amount lent at the start of the loan. The implicit *interest rate* per year can be computed from

$$\left[\frac{\text{Cash Received at Maturity}}{\text{Cash Lent}} \right]^{(1/t)} - 1.$$

where t is the term of the loan in years; t need not be an integer.

Imprest fund. *Petty cash fund.*

Improvement. An *expenditure* to extend the useful life of an *asset* or to improve its performance (rate of output, cost) over that of the original asset. Such expenditures are *capitalized* as part of the asset's cost. Sometimes called "betterment." Contrast with *maintenance* and *repair*.

Imputed cost. A cost that does not appear in accounting records, such as the *interest* that could be earned on cash spent to acquire inventories rather than, say, government bonds. Or, consider a firm that owns the buildings it occupies. This firm has an imputed cost for rent in an amount equal to what it would have to pay to use similar buildings owned by another. *Opportunity cost.*

Imputed interest. See *interest, imputed*.

Incentive compatible compensation. Said of a compensation plan for managers that induces them to act for the interests of owners while acting in their own interests. For example, consider a time of rising prices and increasing inventories when using a *LIFO cost flow assumption* implies paying lower *income taxes* than using *FIFO*. A bonus scheme for managers based on accounting *net income* would not be incentive compatible because the owners benefit more under LIFO, while managers benefit more if they report using FIFO. (See *LIFO conformity rule*.) See *goal congruence*.

Income. *Excess of revenues* and *gains* over *expenses* and *losses* for a period; *net income*. Sometimes used with an appropriate modifier to refer to the various intermediate amounts shown in a *multiple-step income statement*. Sometimes used to refer to revenues, as in "rental income." See *comprehensive income*.

Income accounts. *Revenue* and *expense accounts*.

Income before taxes. On the *income statement*, the difference between all *revenues* and *expenses* except *income tax* expense. Contrast with *net income* and *taxable income*.

Income determination. See *determine*.

Income distribution account. *Temporary account* sometimes debited when *dividends* are declared; closed to *retained earnings*.

Income from continuing operations. As defined by *APB Opinion No. 30*, all *revenues* less all *expenses* except for the following: results of operations (including *income tax* effects) that a firm has discontinued or will discontinue; *gains* or *losses*, including income tax effects, on disposal of segments of the business; gains or losses, including income tax effects, from *extraordinary items*; and the cumulative effect of *accounting changes*.

Income from discontinued operations. *Income*, net of tax effects, from parts of the business that the firm has discontinued during the period or will discontinue in the near future. Accountants report such items on separate lines of the *income statement*, after *income from continuing operations* but before *extraordinary items*.

Income (revenue) bond. See *special revenue debt*.

Income smoothing. A method of timing business *transactions* or choosing *accounting principles* so that variations in reported *income* from year to year are reduced from what they would otherwise be. Although income smoothing is an objective of some managements, it is not an official *accounting principle* or *reporting objective*.

Income statement. The statement of *revenues, expenses, gains*, and *losses* for the period ending with *net income* for the period. Accountants usually show the *earnings-per-share* amount on the income statement; the *reconciliation* of beginning and ending balances of *retained earnings* may also appear in a combined statement of income and retained earnings. See *income from continuing operations, income from discontinued operations, extraordinary items, multiple-step, single-step*.

Income summary. An *account* used in problem solving that serves as a surrogate for the *income statement*. All *revenues* are closed to the Income Summary as *credits* and all *expenses*, as *debits*. The *balance* in the account, after all other *closing entries* are made, is then closed to the retained earnings or other *owners' equity* account and represents *net income* for the period.

Income tax. An annual tax levied by the federal and other governments on the income of an entity.

Income tax allocation. See *deferred tax liability* and *tax allocation: intrastatement*.

Incremental. See *differential*. An adjective used to describe the increase in *cost, expense, investment, cash flow, revenue, profit*, and the like if the firm produces or sells one or more units or if it undertakes an activity.

Incremental cost. See *incremental*.

Incur. Said of an obligation a firm has, whether *accrued* or not. For example, a firm incurs interest expense on a loan as time passes, but accrues that interest only on payment dates or when it makes an *adjusting entry*.

Indenture. See *bond indenture*.

Independence. The mental attitude required of the *CPA* in performing the *attest* function. It implies impartiality and that the members of the auditing CPA firm own no stock in the corporation being audited.

Independent accountant. The *CPA* who performs the *attest* function for a firm.

Independent variable. See *regression analysis*.

Indeterminate-term liability. A *liability* lacking the criterion of being due at a definite time. This term is our own coinage to encompass the *minority interest*.

Indexation. An attempt by lawmakers or parties to a contract to cope with the effects of *inflation*. Amounts fixed in law or contracts are "indexed" when these amounts change as a given measure of price changes. For example, a so-called escalator clause (COLA – cost of living allowance or adjustment) in a labor contract might provide that hourly wages will be increased as the *Consumer Price Index* increases. Many economists have suggested the indexation of numbers fixed in the *income tax* laws. If, for example, the personal *exemption* is $1,000 at the start of the period, prices rise by 10 percent during the period, and the personal exemption is indexed, then the personal exemption would automatically rise to $1,100 (= $1,000 + .10 x $1,000) at the end of the period.

Indirect cost pool. Any grouping of individual costs that a firm does not identify with a *cost objective*.

Indirect costs. Costs of production not easily associated with the production of specific goods and services; *overhead costs*. Accountants may *allocate* them on some arbitrary basis to specific products or departments.

Indirect labor (material) cost. An *indirect cost* for labor (material) such as for supervisors (supplies).

Indirect method. See *statement of cash flows*.

Individual proprietorship. *Sole proprietorship*.

Industry Audit Guide. A series of publications by the *AICPA* providing specific accounting and *auditing principles* for specialized situations. Audit guides have been issued covering government contractors, state and local government units, investment companies, finance companies, brokers and dealers in securities, and many others.

Inescapable cost. A *cost* that is not *avoidable* because of an action. For example, if two operating rooms in a hospital are closed, but security is still employed, the security costs are "inescapable" with respect to the decision to close the operating rooms.

Inflation. A time of generally rising prices.

Inflation accounting. Strictly speaking, *constant dollar accounting*. Some writers use the term, incorrectly, to mean *current cost accounting*.

Information circular. Canada. A document, accompanying the notice of a shareholders' meeting, prepared in connection with the solicitation of proxies by or on behalf of the management of the corporation. It contains information concerning the persons making the solicitation, election of directors, appointment of auditors, and other particulars of matters to be acted upon at the meeting.

Information system. A system, sometimes formal and sometimes informal, for collecting, processing, and communicating data that are useful for the managerial functions of decision making, planning, and control, and for financial reporting under the *attest* requirement.

Inherent interest rate. *Implicit interest* rate.

Insolvent. Unable to pay debts when due. Said of a company even though *assets* exceed *liabilities*.

Installment. Partial payment of a debt or collection of a receivable, usually according to a contract.

Installment contracts receivable. The name used for *accounts receivable* when the *installment method* of recognizing revenue is used. Its *contra account, unrealized gross margin*, is shown on the balance sheet as a subtraction from the amount receivable.

Installment (sales) method. Recognizing *revenue* and *expense* (or *gross margin*) from a sales transaction in proportion to the fraction of the selling price collected during a period. Allowed by the *IRS* for income tax reporting, but acceptable in *GAAP* (*APB Opinion No. 10*) only when cash collections are uncertain. See *realized* (and *unrealized*) *gross margin*.

Installment sales. Sales on account where the buyer promises to pay in several separate payments, called *installments*. Sometimes are, but need not be, accounted for on the *installment method*. If installment sales are accounted for with the sales *basis of revenue recognition* for financial reporting but with the installment method for income tax returns, then a *deferred income tax liability* arises.

Institute of Certified Management Accountants. See *ICMA*.

Institute of Internal Auditors. IIA. The national association of accountants who are engaged in internal auditing and are employed by business firms. Administers a comprehensive professional examination; those who pass qualify to be designated *CIA*, certified internal auditor.

Institute of Management Accountants. IMA. Formerly, the National Association of Accountants, NAA. A society opent to those engaged in management accounting. Parent orginzation of the *ICMA*, which oversees the *CMA* prgoram. See *ICMA*.

Insurance. A contract for reimbursement of specific losses; purchased with insurance premiums. Self-insurance is not insurance but merely the willingness to assume risk of incurring losses while saving the premium.

intangible asset. A nonphysical, *noncurrent* right that gives a firm an exclusive or preferred position in the marketplace. Examples are a *copyright, patent, trademark, goodwill, organization costs, capitalized* advertising cost, computer programs, licenses for any of the preceding, government licenses (e.g., broadcasting or the right to sell liquor), *leases,* franchises, mailing lists, exploration permits, import and export permits, construction permits, and marketing quotas.

Interamerican Accounting Association. IAA. An organization, headquartered in Mexico City, devoted to facilitating interaction between accounting practitioners in Central America, North America, and South America.

intercompany elimination. See *eliminations.*

intercompany profit. If one *affiliated company* sells to another, and the goods remain in the second company's *inventory* at the end of the period, then the first company's *profit* has not been realized by a sale to an outsider. That profit is "intercompany profit" and the accounting eliminates it from net *income* in *consolidated income statements* or when the firm uses the *equity method.*

intercompany transaction. *Transaction* between *parent company* and *subsidiary* or between subsidiaries in a *consolidated entity* whose effects are eliminated in preparing *consolidated financial statements.* See *intercompany profit.*

intercorporate investment. A given *corporation* owns *shares* or *debt* issued by another.

interdepartment monitoring. One of the advantages of allocating *service department costs* to *production departments* is that those charged with the costs will have an incentive to control the costs incurred in the service department.

interest. The charge or cost for using money, usually borrowed funds. Interest on own money used is an *opportunity cost, imputed interest.* The amount of interest for a loan is the total amount paid by borrower to lender less the amount paid by lender to borrower. See *interest rate* for discussion of quoted amount. See *effective interest rate* and *nominal interest rate.*

interest, imputed. If a borrower merely promises to pay a single amount, sometime later than the present, then the present value (computed at a *fair market* interest rate, called the "imputed interest rate") of the promise is less than the *face amount* to be paid at *maturity.* Usage calls the difference between the face amount and the present value of a promise "imputed interest." See also *imputed cost.*

interest factor. One plus the *interest* rate.

interest method. See *effective interest method.*

interest rate. See *interest.* A basis used for computing the cost of borrowing funds usually expressed as a ratio per period of time between the number of currency units (e.g., dollars) charged per number of currency units borrowed for that same period of time. See *simple interest, compound interest, effective (interest) rate, nominal interest rate.*

interfund accounts. In governmental accounting, the accounts that show transactions between funds, especially interfund receivables and payables.

interim statements. Statements issued for periods less than the regular, annual *accounting period.* Most corporations are required to issue interim statements on a quarterly basis. The basic issue in preparing interim reports is whether their purpose is to report on the interim period (1) as a self-contained accounting period or (2) as an integral part of the year of which they are a part so that forecasts of annual performance can be made. For example, assume that at the end of the first quarter, a retailer has depleted its *inventory* so that *LIFO cost of goods sold* is artificially low and *net income* is artificially high, relative to their amounts if purchases for inventory had been "normal" and equal to or greater than sales. The retailer expects to purchase inventory sufficiently large so that when cost of goods sold is computed for the year, there will be no *dips into old LIFO layers* and income will not be artificially high. Under the first approach, the quarterly income will be computed from cost of goods sold using data for the dips that have actually occurred by the end of the quarter. Under the second, quarterly income will be computed from cost of goods sold assuming that purchases were equal to "normal" amounts and that there are no dips into old LIFO layers. *APB Opinion No. 28* and the *SEC* require that interim reports be constructed largely to satisfy the second purpose.

internal audit. An *audit* conducted by employees to ascertain whether *internal control* procedures are working, as opposed to an external audit conducted by a *CPA.*

internal control. See *control system.*

internal rate of return. IRR. The discount rate that equates the net *present value* of a stream of cash outflows and inflows to zero.

internal controls. Policies and procedures designed to provide management with reasonable assurances that employees behave in a way that enables the firm to meet its organizational goals.

internal reporting. Reporting for management's use in planning and control; contrast with *external reporting* for financial statement users.

Internal Revenue Service. IRS. Agency of the U.S. Treasury Department responsible for administering the Internal Revenue Code and collecting income, and certain other, taxes.

International Accounting Standards Committee. IASC. An organization that promotes the international harmonization of accounting standards.

interperiod tax allocation. See *deferred income tax liability.*

interpolation. The estimation of an unknown number intermediate between two (or more) known numbers.

Interpretations. See *FASB Interpretations.*

in the black (red). Operating at a profit (loss).

intrastatement tax allocation. See *tax allocation: intrastatement.*

inventoriable costs. *Costs* incurred that are added to the cost of manufactured products. *Product costs (assets)* as opposed to *period expenses.*

inventory. As a noun, the *balance* in an asset *account* such as raw materials, supplies, work in process, and finished goods. As a verb, to calculate the *cost* of goods on hand at a given time or to count items on hand physically.

inventory equation. *Beginning inventory* + net additions – withdrawals = ending inventory. Ordinarily, additions are net purchases and withdrawals are *cost of goods sold.* Notice that ending inventory, appearing on the balance sheet, and cost of goods sold, appearing on the income statement, are not independent of each other. The larger is one, the smaller must be the other. In valuing inventories, beginning inventory and net purchases are usually known. Some inventory methods (for example, some applications of the *retail inventory method),* measure costs of goods sold and use the equation to find the cost of ending inventory. Most methods measure cost of ending inventory and use the equation to find the cost of goods sold (withdrawals). In *current cost* (in contrast to *historical cost)* accounting *additions* (in the equation) include holding gains, whether realized or not. Thus the current cost inventory equation is: Beginning Inventory (at Current Cost) + Purchases (where Current Cost is Historical Cost) + Holding Gains (whether Realized or Not) – Ending Inventory (at Current Cost) = Cost of Goods Sold (Current Cost).

inventory holding gains. See *inventory profit.*

inventory layer. See *LIFO inventory layer.*

inventory profit. This term has several possible meanings. Consider the data in the accompanying illustration. The *historical cost* data are derived in the conventional manner; the firm uses a *FIFO cost flow assumption.* The assumed *current cost* data resemble those that the FASB suggests in *SFAS No. 89.* The term *income from continuing operations* refers to revenues less expenses based on current, rather than historical, costs. To that subtotal, add realized holding gains to arrive at realized (conventional) income. To that, add unrealized holding gains to arrive at *economic income.* The term "inventory profit" often refers (for example in some *SEC* releases) to the realized holding gain, $110 in the illustration. The amount of inventory profit will usually be material when FIFO is used and prices are rising. Others, including us, prefer to use the term "inventory profit" to refer to the total *holding gain,* $300 (= $110 + $190, both realized and unrealized), but writers use this meaning less often. In periods of rising prices and increasing inventories, the realized holding gains under a FIFO cost flow assumption will be substantially larger than under LIFO. In the illustration, for example, assume under LIFO that the historical cost of goods sold is $4,800, that historical LIFO cost of beginning inventory is $600, and that historical LIFO cost of ending inventory is $800. Then income from continuing operations, based on current costs, remains $350 (= $5,200 – $4,850), realized holding gains are $50 (= $4,850 – $4,800), realized income is $400 (= $350 + $50), the unrealized holding gain for the year is $250 [= ($1,550 – $800) – ($1,100 – $600)], and economic income is $650 (= $350 + $50 + $250). Because the only real effect of the cost flow assumption is to split the total holding gain into realized and unrealized portions, economic income is the same, independent of the cost flow assumption. The total of holding gains is $300 in the illustration. The

choice of cost flow assumption merely determines the portion reported as realized.

Inventory Profit Illustration

	(Historical) Acquisition Cost Assuming FIFO	Current Cost
Assumed Data		
Inventory, 1/1	$ 900	$1,100
Inventory, 12/31	1,150	1,550
Cost of Goods Sold for Year .	4,740	4,850
Sales for Year	$5,200	$5,200
INCOME STATEMENT FOR YEAR		
Sales	$5,200	$5,200
Cost of Goods Sold	4,740	4,850
(1) Income from Continuing Operations		$ 350
Realized Holding Gains		110[a]
(2) Realized Income = Conventional Net Income (under FIFO)	$ 460	$ 460
Unrealized Holding Gain		190[b]
(3) Economic Income		$ 650

[a]Realized holding gain during a period is current cost of goods sold less historical cost of goods sold; the realized holding gain for the year under FIFO is $110 = $4,850 – $4,750. Some refer to this as inventory profit"

[b]The total unrealized holding gain at any time is current cost of inventory on hand at that time less historical cost of that inventory. The unrealized holding gain during a period is unrealized holding gain at the end of the period less the unrealized holding gain at the beginning of the period. Unrealized holding gain prior to this year is $200 = $1,100 – $900. Unrealized holding gain during this year = ($1,550 – 1,160) – ($1,100 – $900) = $390 – $200 = $190.

inventory turnover. Number of times the average *inventory* has been sold during a period; *cost of goods sold* for a period divided by average inventory for the period. See *ratio.*

invested capital. *Contributed capital.*

investee. A company whose *stock* is owned by another.

investing activities. Lending money and collecting *principal* (but not *interest,* which is an *operating activity)* on those loans; acquiring and selling *securities* or productive *assets* expected to produce *revenue* over several *periods.*

Investment. An *expenditure* to acquire property or other *assets* in order to produce *revenue;* the asset so acquired; hence a *current* expenditure made in anticipation of future income. Said of *securities* of other companies held for the long term and appearing in a separate section of the *balance sheet;* in this context, contrast with *marketable securities.*

Investment center. A *responsibility center,* with control over *revenues, costs,* and *assets.*

Investment credit. A reduction in income tax liability sometimes granted by the federal government to firms that buy new equipment. This item is a credit, in that it is deducted from the tax bill, not from pretax income. The tax credit has been a given percentage of the purchase price of certain assets purchased. The government has changed the actual rules and rates over the years. As of 1991, there is no investment credit. See *flow-through method* and *carryforward.*

Investment decision. The decision whether to undertake an action involving production of goods or services; contrast with the *financing decision.*

Investment tax credit. *Investment credit.*

Investment turnover ratio. This term means the same thing as *total assets turnover ratio,* but we sometimes use it for a *division.*

Investments. A balance sheet heading for tangible assets held for periods longer than the operating cycle and not used in revenue production (assets not meeting the definitions of *current assets* or *property, plant, and equipment).*

Invoice. A document showing the details of a sale or purchase *transaction.*

I.O.U. An informal document acknowledging a debt, setting out the amount of the debt and signed by the debtor.

IRR. *Internal rate of return.*

IRS. *Internal Revenue Service.*

Isoprofit line. On a graph delimiting feasible production possibilities of two products that require the use of the same, limited resources, a line showing all feasible production possibility combinations with the same *profit* or, perhaps, *contribution margin.*

Issue. When a corporation exchanges its stock (or *bonds)* for cash or other *assets,* the corporation is said to issue, not sell, that stock (or bonds). Also used in the context of withdrawing supplies or materials from inventory for use in operations and drawing of a *check.*

Issued shares. Those shares of *authorized capital stock* of a *corporation* that have been distributed to the shareholders. See *issue.* Shares of *treasury stock* are legally issued but are not considered to be *outstanding* for the purpose of voting, *dividend declarations,* and *earnings-per-share* calculations.

J

JIT. See *just-in-time inventory.*

Job cost sheet. A schedule showing actual or budgeted inputs for a special order.

Job development credit. The name used for the *investment credit* in the 1971 tax law, since repealed, on this subject.

Job (-order) costing. Accumulation of *costs* for a particular identifiable batch of product, known as a job, as it moves through production.

Joint cost. Cost of simultaneously producing or otherwise acquiring two or more products, called joint products, that a firm must, by the nature of the process, produce or acquire together, such as the cost of beef and hides of cattle. Generally, accounting allocates the joint costs of production to the individual products in proportion to their respective sales value (or, sometimes and usually not preferred, physical quantities) at the *splitoff* point. Other examples include *central corporate expenses* and *overhead* of a department when it manufactures several products. See *common cost.* See *sterilized allocation.*

Joint cost allocation. See *joint cost.*

Joint product. One of two or more outputs with significant value produced by a process that a firm must produce or acquire simultaneously. See *by-product* and *joint cost.*

Journal. The place where transactions are recorded as they occur. The book of original entry.

Journal entry. A dated recording in a *journal,* showing the accounts affected, of equal *debits* and *credits,* with an explanation of the *transaction,* if necessary.

Journal of Accountancy. A monthly publication of the *AICPA.*

Journal of Accounting and Economics. Scholarly journal published three times a year by the William E. Simon Graduate School of Business Administration of the University of Rochester.

Journal of Accounting Research. Scholarly journal containing articles on theoretical and empirical aspects of accounting. Published three times a year by the Graduate School of Business of the University of Chicago.

Journal voucher. A *voucher* documenting (and sometimes authorizing) a *transaction,* leading to an entry in the *journal.*

Journalize. To make an entry in a *journal.*

Judgment(al) sampling. A method of choosing a sample in which the analyst determines subjectively the selection of items to be examined, in contrast to selecting them by statistical methods. Compare *random sampling.*

Junk bond. A low rated *bond* that lacks the merit and characteristics of an investment grade bonds. They offer high yields, typically in excess of 15 percent per year, but also possess high risk of default. Sometimes writers, less pejoratively, call these "high-yield bonds."

just-in-time inventory (production). JIT. System of managing *inventory* for manufacturing where a firm purchases or manufactures each component just before the firm uses it. Contrast with systems where firms acquire or manufacture many parts in advance of needs. JIT systems have much smaller, ideally no, carrying costs for inventory, but run higher risks of incurring *stockout* costs.

K

K. Two to the tenth power (2^{10} or 1,024), when referring to computer storage capacity. The one-letter abbreviation derives from the first letter of the prefix "kilo-" which means 1,000 in decimal notation.

KG. Kommanditgesellschaft. Germany. Similar to a general partnership (*OHG*) except that some of its members may limit their liability. One of the partners must be a *general partner* with unlimited liability.

kiting. This term means slightly different things in banking and auditing contexts. In both, however, it refers to the wrongful practice of taking advantage of the *float*, the time that elapses between the deposit of a *check* in one bank and its collection at another. In the banking context, an individual deposits in Bank A a check written on Bank B. He (or she) then writes checks against the deposit created in Bank A. Several days later, he deposits in Bank B a check written on Bank A, to cover the original check written on Bank B. Still later, he deposits in Bank A a check written on Bank B. The process of covering the deposit in Bank A with a check written on Bank B and vice versa is continued until an actual deposit of cash can be arranged. In the auditing context, kiting refers to a form of *window dressing* where the amount of the account Cash in Bank is made to appear larger than it actually is by depositing in Bank A a check written on Bank B without recording the check written on Bank B in the *check register* until after the close of the *accounting period*.

know-how. Technical or business information of the type defined under *trade secret*, but that a firm does not maintain as a secret. The rules of accounting for this *asset* are the same as for other *intangibles*.

L

labor variances. The *price* (or *rate*) and *quantity* (or *usage*) variances for *direct labor* inputs in a *standard costing system*.

laid-down cost. Canada and the United Kingdom. The sum of all direct costs incurred for procurement of goods up to the time of physical receipt, such as invoice cost plus customs and excise duties, freight and cartage.

land. An *asset shown at acquisition cost* plus the *cost* of any nondepreciable *improvements*. In accounting, implies use as a plant or office site, rather than as a *natural resource,* such as timberland or farm land.

lapping (accounts receivable). The theft, by an employee, of cash sent in by a customer to discharge the latter's *payable*. The theft from the first customer is concealed by using cash received from a second customer. The theft from the second customer is concealed by using the cash received from a third customer, and so on. The process is continued until the thief returns the funds or can make the theft permanent by creating a fictitious *expense* or receivable write-off, or until the fraud is discovered.

lapse. To expire; said of, for example, an insurance policy or discounts made available for prompt payment that are not taken.

last-in, first-out. See *LIFO*.

layer. See *LIFO inventory layer.*

lead time. The time that elapses between placing an order and receipt of the *goods or services* ordered.

learning curve. A mathematical expression of the phenomenon that incremental unit costs to produce decrease as managers and labor gain experience from practice.

lease. A contract calling for the lessee (user) to pay the lessor (owner) for the use of an asset. A cancelable lease allows the lessee to cancel at any time. A noncancelable lease requires payments from the lessee for the life of the lease and usually shares many of the economic characteristics of *debt financing*. Most long-term noncancelable leases meet the usual criteria classifying them as *liabilities* but the firm need not show some leases entered into before 1977 as liabilities. *SFAS No. 13* and the *SEC* require disclosure in notes to the financial statements of the commitments for long-term noncancelable leases. See *capital lease* and *operating lease*.

leasehold. The *asset* representing the right of the lessee to use leased property. See *lease* and *leasehold improvement*.

leasehold improvement. An *improvement* to leased property. Should be *amortized* over *service life* or the life of the lease, whichever is shorter.

least and latest rule. Pay the least amount of taxes as late as possible within the law to minimize the *present value* of tax payments for a given set of operations.

ledger. A book of accounts. See *general ledger* and *subsidiary ledger;* contrast with *journal*. Book of final entry.

legal capital. The amount of *contributed capital* that, according to state law, must remain permanently in the firm as protection for creditors.

legal entity. See *entity*.

lender. See *loan*.

lessee. See *lease*.

lessor. See *lease*.

letter stock. Privately placed *common shares;* so called because the *SEC* requires the purchaser to sign a letter of intent not to resell the shares.

leverage. "Operating leverage" refers to the tendency of *net income* to rise at a faster rate than sales when *fixed costs* are present. A doubling of sales, for example, usually implies a more than doubling of net income. "Financial leverage" (or "capital leverage") refers to the increased rate of return on *owners' equity* (see *ratio*) when an *investment* earns a return larger than the after-tax *interest rate* paid for *debt* financing. Because the interest charges on debt are usually fixed, any *incremental* income benefits owners and none benefits debtors. When writers use the term "leverage" without a qualifying adjective, the term usually refers to financial leverage, the use of *long-term* debt in securing *funds* for the *entity*.

leveraged lease. A special form of lease involving three parties a *lender,* a *lessor,* and a *lessee.* The lender, such as a bank or insurance company, lends a portion, say 80 percent, of the cash required for acquiring the *asset.* The lessor puts up the remainder, 20 percent, of the cash required. The lessor acquires the asset with the cash, using the asset as security for the loan and leases it to the lessee on a *noncancelable* basis. The lessee makes periodic lease payments to the lessor, who in turn makes payments on the loan to the lender. Typically, the lessor has no obligation for the debt to the lender other than transferring a portion of the receipts from the lessee. If the lessee should default on required lease payments, then the lender can repossess the leased asset. The lessor is usually entitled to deductions for tax purposes for *depreciation* on the asset, for *interest expense* on the loan from the lender, and for any *investment credit.* The lease is leveraged in the sense that the lessor, who enjoys most of the risks and rewards of ownership, usually borrows most of the funds needed to acquire the asset. See *leverage*.

liability. An obligation to pay a definite (or reasonably definite) amount at a definite (or reasonably definite) time in return for a past or current benefit. That is, the obligation arises from other than an *executory contract*. A probable future sacrifice of economic benefits arising from present obligations of a particular *entity* to *transfer assets* or to provide services to other entities in the future as a result of past *transactions* or events. *SFAC No. 6* says that "probable" refers to that which we can reasonably expect or believe but that is neither certain nor proved. A liability has three essential characteristics: (1) an obligation to transfer assets or services at a specified or knowable date, (2) the entity has little or no discretion to avoid the transfer, and (3) the event causing the obligation has already happened; that is, it is not executory.

lien. The right of person A to satisfy a claim against person B by holding B's property as security or by seizing B's property.

life annuity. A *contingent annuity* in which payments cease at death of a specified person(s), usually the *annuitant(s)*.

LIFO. *Last-in, first-out.* An *inventory* flow assumption where the *cost of goods sold* equals the cost of the most recently acquired units and a firm computes the *ending inventory cost* from costs of the oldest units; contrast with *FIFO*. In periods of rising prices and increasing inventories, LIFO leads to higher reported expenses and therefore lower reported income

and lower balance sheet inventories than does FIFO. See also *FISH* and *inventory profit*.

LIFO conformity rule. The *IRS* requires that companies which use a *LIFO cost flow assumption for income taxes* also use LIFO in computing *income* reported in *financial statements* and forbids disclosure of *pro forma* results from using any other cost flow assumption.

LIFO, dollar-value method. See *dollar-value LIFO method*.

LIFO inventory layer. The *ending inventory* for a period is likely to be larger than the *beginning inventory*. Under a *LIFO cost flow assumption,* this increase in physical quantities is assigned a cost computed from the prices of the earliest purchases during the year. The LIFO inventory then consists of layers, sometimes called "slices," which typically consist of relatively small amounts of physical quantities from each of the past several years. Each layer carries the prices from near the beginning of the period when it was acquired. The earliest layers will typically (in periods of rising prices) have prices much less than current prices. If inventory quantities should decline in a subsequent period, the latest layers enter cost of goods sold first.

LIFO reserve. *Unrealized holding gain* in *ending inventory:* current or *FIFO historical* cost of ending inventory less LIFO *historical cost.* See *reserve;* a better term for this concept is "excess of current cost over LIFO historical cost."

limited liability. Shareholders of corporations are not personally liable for debts of the company.

limited partner. Member of a *partnership* not personally liable for debts of the partnership; every partnership must have at least one *general partner* who is fully liable.

line of business reporting. See *segment reporting*.

line of credit. An agreement with the bank or set of banks for short-term borrowings on demand.

linear programming. A mathematical tool for finding profit maximizing (or cost minimizing) combinations of products to produce when a firm has several products that it can produce but faces linear constraints on the resources available in the production processes or on maximum and minimum production requirements.

line-of-business reporting. See *segment reporting*.

liquid. Said of a business with a substantial amount (the amount is unspecified) of *working capital,* especially *quick assets*.

liquid assets. *Cash, current marketable securities,* and, sometimes, *current receivables*.

liquidating dividend. *Dividend* declared in the winding up of a business to distribute the assets of the company to the shareholders. Usually treated by recipient as a return of *investment,* not as *revenue*.

liquidation. Payment of a debt. Sale of assets in closing down a business or a segment thereof.

liquidation value per share. The amount each *share* of stock will receive if the corporation is dissolved. For *preferred stock* with a liquidation preference, a stated amount per share.

liquidity. Refers to the availability of *cash,* or near cash resources, for meeting a firm's obligations.

LISH. An acronym, conceived by George H. Sorter, for *last in, still here.* LISH is the same cost flow assumption as *FIFO.* Many readers of accounting statements find it easier to think about inventory questions in terms of items still on hand. Think of FIFO in connection with *cost of goods sold* but of LISH in connection with *ending inventory.* See *FISH.*

list price. The published or nominally quoted price for goods.

list price method. See *trade-in transaction.*

loan. An arrangement where the owner of property, called the lender, allows someone else, called the borrower, the use of the property for a period of time that is usually specified in the agreement setting up the loan. The borrower promises to return the property to the lender and, often, to make a payment for use of the property. Generally used when the property is *cash* and the payment for its use is *interest.*

LOCOM. *Lower of cost or market.*

long-lived (term) asset. An asset whose benefits are expected to be received over several years. A *noncurrent* asset, usually includes *investments, plant assets,* and *intangibles.*

long-run. long-term. A term denoting a time or time periods in the future. How far in the future depends on context. For some securities traders, "long-term" can mean anything beyond the next hour or two. For most managers, it means anything beyond the next year or two. For government policy makers, it can mean anything beyond the next decade or two. For geologists, it can mean millions of years.

long-term (construction) contract accounting. The *percentage of completion method* of *revenue* recognition. Sometimes used to mean the *completed contract method.*

long-term debt ratio. *Noncurrent liabilities* divided by total *assets.*

long-term liability (debt). *Noncurrent liability.*

long-term solvency risk. The risk that a firm will not have sufficient *cash* to pay its *debts* sometime in the *long-run.*

loophole. Imprecise term meaning a technicality allowing a taxpayer (or *financial statements)* to circumvent a law's (or *GAAP*'s) intent without violating its letter.

loss. Excess of *cost* over net proceeds for a single transaction; negative *income* for a period. A cost expiration that produced no *revenue.* See *gain* for a discussion of related and contrasting terms.

loss contingency. See *contingency.*

lower of cost or market. LOCOM. A basis for valuation of *inventory* or *marketable equity securities.* The inventory value

is set at the lower of *acquisition cost* or *current replacement cost* (market), subject to the following constraints: First, the market value of an item used in the computation cannot exceed its *net realizable value* – an amount equal to selling price less reasonable costs to complete production and to sell the item. Second, the market value of an item used in the computation cannot be less than the net realizable value minus the normal *profit* ordinarily realized on disposition of completed items of this type. The lower-of-cost-or-market valuation is chosen as the lower of acquisition *cost* or replacement cost *(market)* subject to the upper and lower bounds on replacement cost established in the first two steps. Thus,

Market Value　=　Midvalue of (Replacement Cost, Net
　　　　　　　　　　Realizable Value, Net Realizable
　　　　　　　　　　Value less Normal Profit Margin)

Lower of Cost　=　Minimum (Acquisition Cost, Market
or Market　　　　Value).
Valuation

The accompanying exhibit illustrates the calculation of the lower-of-cost-or-market valuation for four inventory items. Notice that each of the four possible outcome occurs once in determining lower of cost or market. Item 1 uses acquisition cost; item 2 uses net realizable value; item 3 uses replacement cost; and item 4 uses net realizable value less normal profit.

	Item			
	1	**2**	**3**	**4**
Calculation of Market Value				
(a) Replacement Cost	$92	$96	$92	$96
(b) Net Realizable Value	95	95	95	95
(c) Net Realizable Value Less Normal Profit Margin [= (b) – $9]	86	86	86	86
(d) Market = Midvalue [(a), (b), (c)]	92	95	92	95
Calculation of Lower of Cost or Market				
(e) Acquisition Cost	90	97	96	90
(f) Market [= (d)]	92	95	92	95
(g) Lower of Cost or Market = Minimum [(e), (f)]	90	95	92	90

Lower of cost or market cannot be used for inventory on tax returns in a combination with a *LIFO cost flow assumption.* In the context of inventory, once the asset is written down, a new "original cost" basis is established and subsequent increases in market value are ignored in the accounts.

The firm may apply lower or cost or market to individual items of inventory or to groups (usually called *pools)* of items. The smaller the group, the more *conservative* the resulting valuation.

Note that hyphens are not used when the term is used as a noun but hyphens are used when the term is used as an adjectival phrase.

Ltd.; Limited. United Kingdom. A private limited corporation. The name of a private limited company must include the word "Limited" or its abbreviation "Ltd."

lump-sum acquisition. *Basket purchase.*

M

MD&A. *Management discussion and analysis* section of *financial statements.*

maintenance. *Expenditures* undertaken to preserve an *asset's* service potential for its originally intended life; these expenditures are treated as *period expenses* or *product costs;* contrast with *improvement.* See *repair.*

make-or-buy decision. A managerial decision about whether the firm should produce a product internally or purchase it from others. Proper make-or-buy decisions in the short run result when a firm considers only *incremental costs* in decision making.

maker (of note) (of check). One who signs a *note* to borrow. One who signs a *check;* in this context synonymous with drawer; see *draft.*

management. Executive authority that operates a business.

management accounting. See *managerial accounting.*

Management Accounting. Monthly publication of the *IMA.*

management audit. An audit conducted to ascertain whether a firm or one of its operating units properly carries out its objectives, policies, and procedures. Generally applies only to activities for which accountants can specify qualitative standards. See *audit* and *internal audit.*

management by exception. A principle of management where managers focus attention on performance only if it differs significantly from that expected.

management by objective. A management approach designed to focus on the definition and attainment of overall and individual objectives with the participation of all levels of management.

management discussion and analysis. A discussion of management's views of the company's performance required by the *SEC* since 1974 to be included in the *10-K* and in the *annual report* to shareholders. The information typically contains discussion of such items and liquidity, results of *operations, segments,* and the effects of *inflation.*

management information system. A system designed to provide all levels of management with timely and reliable information required for planning, control, and evaluation of performance.

managerial (management) accounting. Reporting designed to enhance the ability of management to do its job of decision making, planning, and control; contrast with *financial accounting.*

manufacturing cost. Cost of producing goods, usually in a factory.

manufacturing expense. An imprecise, and generally incorrect, alternative title for *manufacturing overhead.*

manufacturing overhead. General manufacturing *costs* incurred in providing a capacity to carry on productive activities not directly associated with identifiable units of product. Accounting treats *fixed* manufacturing overhead cost as a *product cost* under *full absorption costing* but as an *expense* of the period under *variable costing.*

margin. *Revenue* less specified expenses. See *contribution margin, gross margin,* and *current margin.*

margin of safety. Excess of actual, or budgeted, sales over *breakeven* sales. Usually expressed in dollars; may be expressed in units of product.

marginal cost. The *incremental cost* or *differential cost* of the last unit added to production or the first unit subtracted from production. See *cost terminology.*

marginal costing. *Direct costing.*

marginal revenue. The increment in *revenue* from sale of one additional unit of product.

marginal tax rate. The tax imposed on the next dollar of taxable income generated; contrast with *average tax rate.*

markdown. See *markup* for definition and contrast.

markdown cancellation. See *markup* for definition and contrast.

market-based transfer price. A *transfer price* based on external market data, rather than internal company data.

market price. See *fair market price.*

market rate. The rate of *interest* a company must pay to borrow *funds* currently. See *effective rate.*

marketable equity securities. *Marketable securities* representing *owners' equity* interest in other companies, rather than *loans* to them.

marketable securities. *Stocks* and *bonds* of other companies held that can be readily sold on stock exchanges or over-the-counter markets and that the company plans to sell as cash is needed. Classified as *current assets* and as part of "cash" in preparing the *statement of cash flows.* The same securities held for *long-term* purposes would be classified as *noncurrent assets.* *SFAS No. 115* requires that all marketable equity and all debt securities (except those the holder has the ability and intent to hold to maturity) appear at market value on the balance sheet. Changes in market value flow through income for *trading securities* but are debited (holding losses) or credited (holding gains) directly to owners' equity accounts for *securities available for sale.*

marketing costs. Costs incurred to sell; includes locating customers, persuading them to buy, delivering the goods or services, and collecting the sales proceeds.

markon. See *markup* for definition and contrast.

markup. When a retailer acquires items for *inventory,* the items are given a selling price. Precise usage calls the difference between the original selling price and cost "markon," although many business people use the term "markup." Because of confusion of this use of "markup" with its precise definition (see below), terminology sometimes uses "original markup." If the originally established retail price increases, the precise term for the amount of price increase is "markup," although terminology sometimes uses "additional markup." If a firm reduces selling price, terminology uses the terms "markdown" and "markup cancellation." "Markup cancellation" refers to reduction in price following "additional markups" and can, by definition, be no more than the amount of the additional markup; "cancellation of additional markup," although not used, is descriptive. "Markdown" refers to price reductions from the original retail price. A price increase after a markdown is a "markdown cancellation." If original cost is $12 and original selling price is $20, then markon (original markup) is $8; if the price is later increased to $24, the $4 increase is markup (additional markup); if the price is later lowered to $21, the $3 reduction is markup cancellation; if price is lowered further to $17, the $4 reduction comprises $1 markup cancellation and $3 markdown; if price is later increased to $22, the $5 increase comprises $3 of markdown cancellation and $2 of markup (additional markup). Accountants track markup cancellations and markdowns separately because they deduct the former (but not the latter) in computing the selling prices of goods available for sale for the denominator of the *cost percentage* used in the conventional *retail inventory method*.

markup cancellation. See *markup* for definition and contrast.

markup percentage. *Markup* divided by (acquisition cost plus *markup).*

master budget. A *budget* projecting all *financial statements* and their components.

matching convention. The concept of recognizing cost expirations *(expenses)* in the same accounting period when the related *revenues* are recognized. Combining or simultaneously recognizing the revenues and expenses that jointly result from the same *transactions* or other events.

material. As an adjective, it means relatively important. See *materiality.* Currently, no operational definition exists. As a noun, *raw material.*

materials variances. *Price* and *quantity variances* for *direct materials* in *standard costing systems.* Difference between actual cost and standard cost.

materiality. The concept that accounting should disclose separately only those events that are relatively important (no operable definition yet exists) for the business or for understanding its statements. *SFAC No. 2* suggests that accounting information is material if "the judgment of a reasonable person relying on the information would have been changed or influenced by the omission or misstatement."

matrix. A rectangular array of numbers or mathematical symbols.

matrix inverse. For a given square *matrix* **A**, the square matrix inverse is the matrix, $\mathbf{A}^{-1}$, such that $\mathbf{AA}^{-1} = \mathbf{A}^{-1}\mathbf{A} = \mathbf{I}$, the *identity matrix.* Not all square matrices have inverses. Those that do not we call "singular"; those that do are nonsingular.

maturity. The date at which an obligation, such as the *principal* of a *bond* or a *note,* becomes due.

maturity value. The amount expected to be collected when a loan reaches *maturity.* Depending upon the context, the amount may be *principal* or principal and *interest.*

MBO. Abbreviation for *management by objective.*

measuring unit. See *attribute measured* for definition and contrast.

merchandise. *Finished goods* bought by a retailer or wholesaler for resale; contrast with finished goods of a manufacturing business.

merchandise turnover. *Inventory turnover* for merchandise; see *ratio.*

merchandising business. As opposed to a manufacturing or service business, one that purchases (rather than manufactures) *finished goods* for resale.

merger. The joining of two or more businesses into a single *economic entity.* See *holding company.*

minority interest. A *balance sheet account* on *consolidated statements* showing the *equity* in a less-than-100-percent-owned *subsidiary* company allocable to those who are not part of the controlling (majority) interest. May be classified either as shareholders' equity or as a liability of *indeterminate term* on the consolidated balance sheet. On the *income statement,* the minority's interest in current period's income of the less-than-100-percent-owned subsidiary must be subtracted to arrive at consolidated *net income* for the period.

minority investment. A holding of less than 50 percent of the *voting stock* in another corporation. Accounted for with the *equity method* when sufficient shares are owned so that the investor can exercise "significant influence," and with the *lower-of-cost-or-market* otherwise. See *mutual fund.*

minutes book. A record of all actions authorized at corporate *board of director's* or shareholders' meetings.

MIS. Abbreviation for *management information system.*

mix variance. Many *standard cost* systems specify combinations of inputs, for example, labor of a certain skill and materials of a certain quality grade. Sometimes combinations of inputs used differ from those contemplated by the standard. The mix variance attempts to report the cost difference that changing the combination of inputs causes.

mixed cost. A *semifixed* or a *semivariable* cost.

modified accelerated cost recovery system. See *MACRS.*

modified cash basis. The *cash basis of accounting* with long-term assets accounted for with the *accrual basis of accounting.* Most uses of the term "cash basis of accounting" actually mean "modified cash basis."

monetary assets and liabilities. See *monetary items.*

monetary gain or loss. The *gain* or *loss* in *general purchasing power* as a result of holding *monetary assets* or liabilities during a period when the *general purchasing power of the dollar* changes. During periods of *inflation*, holders of net monetary assets lose, and holders of net monetary liabilities gain, general purchasing power. During periods of *deflation*, holders of net monetary assets gain, and holders of net monetary liabilities lose, general purchasing power. Explicitly reported in *constant dollar accounting*.

monetary items. Amounts fixed in terms of dollars by statute or contract. *Cash, accounts receivable, accounts payable,* and *debt*. The distinction between monetary and nonmonetary items is important for *constant dollar accounting* and for *foreign exchange gain* or *loss* computations. In the foreign exchange context, account amounts denominated in dollars are not monetary items, whereas amounts denominated in any other currency are monetary.

monetary-nonmonetary method. *Foreign currency translation* where all *monetary items* are translated at the *current exchange rate* and all *nonmonetary items* are translated at the *historical rate*.

money. A word seldom used with precision in accounting, at least in part because economists have not yet agreed on its definition. Economists use the term to refer to both a medium of exchange and a unit of value. See *cash* and *monetary items*.

money purchase plan. A *pension plan* where the employer contributes a specified amount of cash each year to each employee's pension fund. Benefits ultimately received by the employee are not specifically defined but depend on the rate of return on the cash invested. Sometimes called a "defined-contribution" pension plan; contrast with *defined-benefit plan*. As of the mid-1980's most corporate pension plans were defined-benefit plans because both the law and *generally accepted accounting principles* for pensions made defined-benefit plans more attractive than money purchase plans. *ERISA* makes money purchase plans relatively more attractive than they had been. We expect the relative number of money purchase plans to increase.

mortality table. Data of life expectancies or probabilities of death for persons of specified ages and sex.

mortgage. A claim given by the borrower (mortgagor) to the lender (mortgagee) against the borrower's property in return for a loan.

moving average. An *average* computed on observations over time. As a new observation becomes available, analysts drop the oldest one so that they always compute the average for the same number of observations and only the most recent ones. Some, however, use this term synonymously with *weighted average*.

moving average method. *Weighted-average method*.

multiple-step. Said of an *income statement* where various classes of *expenses* and *losses* are subtracted from *revenues* to show intermediate items such as *operating income*, income of the enterprise (operating income plus *interest* income), income to investors (income of the enterprise less *income taxes)*, net income to shareholders (income to investors less

interest charges), and income retained (income to shareholders less dividends). See *entity theory*.

municipal bond. A *bond* issued by a village, town, or city. *Interest* on such bonds is generally exempt from federal *income taxes* and from some state income taxes. Because bonds issued by state and county governments often have these characteristics, terminology often calls such bonds "municipals" as well. Sometimes called "tax exempts."

mutual fund. An investment company that issues its own stock to the public and uses the proceeds to invest in securities of other companies. A mutual fund usually owns less than five or ten percent of the stock of any one company and accounts for its investments using current *market values;* contrast with *holding company*.

mutually exclusive projects. Competing investment projects, where accepting one project eliminates the possibility of undertaking the remaining projects.

N

NAARS. *National Automated Accounting Research System.*

NASDAQ. National Association of Securities Dealers Automated Quotation System; a computerized system to provide brokers and dealers with price quotations for securities traded *over the counter* as well as for some *NYSE* securities.

National Association of Accountants. NAA. Former name for the *Institute of Management Accountants, IMA*.

National Automated Accounting Research System. NAARS. A computer-based information retrieval system containing, among other things, the complete text of most public corporate annual reports and *Forms 10-K*. The system is available to users through the *AICPA*.

natural business year. A 12-month period chosen as the reporting period so that the end of the period coincides with a low point in activity or inventories. See *ratio* for a discussion of analyses of financial statements of companies using a natural business year.

natural classification. *Income statement* reporting form in which *expenses* are classified by nature of items as acquired, that is, materials, wages, salaries, insurance, and taxes, as well as depreciation; contrast with *functional classification*.

natural resources. Timberland, oil and gas wells, ore deposits, and other products of nature that have economic value. The cost of natural resources is subject to *depletion*. Natural resources are "nonrenewable" (for example, oil, coal, gas, ore deposits) or "renewable" (timberland, sod fields); terminology often calls the former "wasting assets." See also *reserve recognition accounting* and *percentage depletion*.

negative confirmation. See *confirmation*.

negative goodwill. Refer to *goodwill*. When the purchase price of the company acquired is less than the sum of the *fair market* *value* of the *net assets* acquired, *APB Opinion No. 16* requires that the valuation of noncurrent assets (except *investments* in *marketable securities)* acquired be reduced until the purchase price equals the adjusted valuation of the fair market value of net assets acquired. If, after the adjusted valuation of noncurrent assets is reduced to zero, the purchase price is still less than the net assets acquired, then the difference is shown as a credit balance in the balance sheet as negative goodwill and is amortized to income over a period not to exceed forty years. For negative goodwill to exist, someone must be willing to sell a company for less than the fair market value of net current assets and marketable securities. Because such a bargain purchase is rare, negative goodwill is rarely found in the financial statements; when it does appear, it generally signals unrecorded obligations, such as for *pensions* or contingent liability in a law suit.

negotiable. Legally capable of being transferred by *endorsement.* Usually said of *checks* and *notes* and sometimes of *stocks* and *bearer bonds.*

negotiated transfer price. A *transfer price* set jointly by the buying and selling divisions.

net. Reduced by all relevant deductions.

net assets. *Owners' equity;* total *assets* minus total *liabilities.*

net bank position. From a firm's point of view, *cash* in a specific bank less *loans* payable to that bank.

net current assets. *Working capital = current assets − current liabilities.*

net current asset value (per share). *Working capital* divided by the number of common shares outstanding. Many security analysts think that when a common share trades in the market for an amount less than net current asset value, then the shares are undervalued and should be purchased. We find this view naive because it ignores the efficiency of capital markets generally and, specifically, unrecorded obligations such as for some *pension plans,* not currently reported as *liabilities* in the *balance sheet* under *GAAP.*

net income. The excess of all *revenues* and *gains* for a period over all *expenses* and *losses* of the period. See *comprehensive income.*

net loss. The excess of all *expenses* and *losses* for a period over all *revenues* and *gains* of the period. Negative *net income.*

net markup. In the context of *retail inventory methods, markups* less markup cancellations; a figure that usually ignores *markdowns* and markdown cancellations.

net of tax method. A nonsanctioned method for dealing with the problem of *income tax allocation;* described in *APB Opinion No. 11.* Deferred tax items are subtracted from specific *asset* amounts rather than being shown as a deferred credit or *liability.*

net of tax reporting. Reporting, such as for *income from discontinued operations, extraordinary items,* and *prior-period adjustments,* where the amounts presented in *financial statements* have been adjusted for all income tax effects. For example, if an extraordinary loss amounted to $10,000 and the

marginal tax rate were 40 percent, then the extraordinary item would be reported "net of taxes" as a $6,000 loss. Hence, all income taxes may not be reported on one line of the income statement. The taxes will be allocated to *income from continuing operations, income from discontinued operations, extraordinary items,* cumulative effects of *accounting changes,* and *prior-period adjustments.*

net operating profit. Income from *continuing operations.*

net present value. Discounted or *present value* of all cash inflows and outflows of a project or from an *investment* at a given *discount rate.*

net price method (of recording purchase or sales discounts). The *purchase* (or *sale)* is recorded at its *invoice* price less all *discounts* made available under the assumption that nearly all discounts will be taken. Discounts lapsed through failure to pay promptly are debited to an *expense* account. For purchases, management usually prefers to know about the amount of discounts lost because of inefficient operations, not the amounts taken, so that most managers prefer the net price method to the *gross price method.*

net realizable (sales) value. A method for *allocating joint costs* in proportion to *realizable values* of the joint products. For example, joint products A and B together cost $100, and A sells for $60 whereas B sells for $90. Then a firm would allocate to A ($60/$150) x $100 = .40 x $100 = $40 of cost while it would allocate to B ($90/$150) x $100 = $60 of cost.

net sales. Sales (at gross invoice amount) less *returns, allowances,* freight paid for customers, and *discounts* taken.

net working capital. *Working capital;* the "net" is redundant in accounting. Financial analysts sometimes mean *current assets* when they speak of working capital, so for them the "net" is not redundant.

net worth. A misleading term, to be avoided, that means the same as *owners' equity.*

network analysis. A method of planning and scheduling a project, usually displayed in diagrammatic form, in order to identify the interrelated sequences that must be accomplished to complete the project.

New York Stock Exchange. NYSE. A public market where various corporate *securities* are traded.

next in, first out. See *NIFO.*

NIFO. Next *in, first out.* In making decisions, many managers consider *replacement costs* (rather than *historical costs)* and refer to them as NIFO costs.

no par. Said of *stock* without a *par value.*

nominal accounts. *Temporary accounts,* such as *revenue* and *expense* accounts, as opposed to *balance sheet accounts.* All nominal accounts are *closed* at the end of each *accounting period.*

nominal amount (value). An amount stated in dollars, in contrast to an amount stated in *constant dollars.* Contrast with *real amount (value).*

nominal dollars. The measuring unit giving no consideration to differences in the *general purchasing power of the dollar* over time. The face amount of currency or coin, a *bond,* an *invoice,* a *receivable* is a nominal dollar amount. When that amount is adjusted for changes in *general purchasing power,* it is converted into a *constant dollar* amount.

nominal interest rate. A rate specified on a *debt* instrument, which usually differs from the market or *effective rate.* Also, a rate of *interest* quoted for a year. If the interest is compounded more often than annually, then the *effective interest rate* is higher than the nominal rate.

noncancelable. See *lease.*

nonconsolidated subsidiary. An *intercorporate investment* where more than 50 percent of the shares of the *subsidiary* are owned but the investment is accounted for with the *cost method* or *lower-of-cost-or-market method.*

noncontributory. Said of a *pension plan* where only the employer makes payments to a pension *fund;* contrast with *contributory.*

noncontrollable cost. A cost that a particular manager cannot *control.*

noncurrent. Due more than one year (or more than one *operating cycle)* hence.

nonexpendable fund. A governmental fund, whose *principal,* and sometimes earnings, may not be spent.

non-interest-bearing note. A *note* that bears no explicit interest. The *present value* of such a note at any time before *maturity* is less than the *face value* so long as *interest rates* are positive. *APB Opinion No. 21* requires that the present value, not face value, of long-term non-interest-bearing notes be reported as the *asset* or *liability* amount in financial statements. For this purpose, the *historical interest rate* is used. See *interest, imputed.*

nonmanufacturing costs. All *costs* incurred other than those to produce goods.

nonmonetary items. All items that are not monetary; see *monetary items.*

nonoperating. In the *income statement* context, said of *revenues* and *expenses* arising from *transactions* incidental to the company's main line(s) of business. In the *statement of cash flows* context, said of all sources or uses of cash other than cash provided by operations. See *operations.*

nonprofit corporation. An incorporated *entity,* such as a hospital, with owners who do not share in the earnings. It usually emphasizes providing services rather than maximizing income.

nonrecurring. Said of an event that is not expected to happen often for a given firm. Under *APB Opinion No. 30,* the effects of such events should be disclosed separately, but as part of *ordinary* items unless the event is also unusual. See *extraordinary* item.

normal cost. Former name for *service cost.*

normal costing. Method of charging costs to products using actual *direct materials,* actual *direct labor,* and predetermined *factory overhead* rates.

normal costing system. *Costing* based on *actual material* and *labor* costs, but using *predetermined overhead* rates per unit of some *activity* basis (such as *direct labor hours* or machine hours) to apply overhead to production. Management decides the rate to charge to production for overhead at the start of the period. At the end of the period the accounting multiplies this rate by the actual number of units of the base activity (such as actual direct labor hours worked or actual machine hours used during the period) to apply overhead to production.

normal spoilage. Costs incurred because of ordinary amounts of spoilage; accounting prorates such costs to units produced as *product costs;* contrast with *abnormal spoilage.*

normal standard cost. normal standards. The *cost* a firm expects to incur under reasonably efficient operating conditions with adequate provision for an average amount of rework, spoilage, and the like.

normal volume. The level of production over a time span, usually 1 year, that will satisfy purchasers' demands and provide for reasonable *inventory* levels.

note. An unconditional written promise by the maker (borrower) to pay a certain amount on demand or at a certain future time. See *footnotes* for another context.

note receivable discounted. A *note* assigned by the holder to another. The new holder of the note typically pays the old holder an amount less than the *face value* of the note; hence the word "discounted." But this word is used even if the payment by the new holder to the old is at or above face value. If the note is assigned with recourse, it is the *contingent liability* of the assignor until the debt is paid. See *factoring.*

NOW account. Negotiable order of withdrawal. A *savings account* on which orders to pay, much like *checks* but technically not checks, can be drawn and given to others who can redeem the order at the savings institution.

number of days sales in inventory (or receivables). Days of average inventory on hand (or average collection period for receivables). See *ratio.*

NYSE. *New York Stock Exchange.*

OASD(H)I. *Old Age, Survivors, Disability, and (Hospital) Insurance.*

objective. See *reporting objective* and *objectivity.*

objective function. In *linear programming,* the name of the profit or cost criterion the analyst wants to optimize.

objectivity. The reporting policy implying that formal recognition will not be given to an event in financial statements until the magnitude of the events can be measured with reasonable accuracy and is subject to independent verification.

obsolescence. A decline in *market value* of an *asset* caused by improved alternatives becoming available that will be more *cost effective;* the decline in market value is unrelated to physical changes in the asset itself. See *partial obsolescence.*

Occupational Safety and Health Act. *OSHA.*

off-balance-sheet financing. A description often used for an obligation meeting all the tests to be a liability, except that the obligation arises from an *executory contract* and, hence, is not a *liability.* Consider the following example.

Miller Corporation desires to acquire land costing $25 million, on which it will build a shopping center. It could borrow the $25 million from its bank, paying interest at 12 percent, and buy the land outright from the seller. If so, both an asset and a liability will appear on the balance sheet. Instead, it borrows $5 million and purchases for $5 million from the seller an *option* to buy the land from the seller at any time within the next 6 years for a price of $20 million. The option costs Miller Corporation $5 million immediately and provides for continuing "option" payments of $2.4 million per year, which is just equal to Miller Corporation's borrowing rate multiplied by the remaining purchase price of the land: $2.4 million = .12 x $20 million. Although Miller Corporation need not continue payments and can let the option lapse at any time, it also has an obligation to begin developing on the site immediately. Because Miller Corporation has invested a substantial sum in the option, will invest more, and will begin immediately developing the land, Miller Corporation is almost certain to exercise its option before it expires. The seller of the land can take the option contract to the bank and borrow $20 million, paying interest at Miller Corporation's borrowing rate, 12 percent per year. The continuing option payments from Miller Corporation will be sufficient to enable the seller to make its payments to the bank. *Generally accepted accounting principles* view Miller Corporation as having acquired an option for $5 million, rather than having acquired land costing $25 million in return for $5 million of "debt" off the balance sheet until it borrows more funds to exercise the option.

OHG. *Offene Handelsgesellschaft.* Germany. A general *partnership.* The partners have unlimited *liability.*

Old Age, Survivors, Disability, and (Hospital) Insurance. OASD(H)I. The technical name for Social Security under the Federal Insurance Contributions Act (FICA).

on (open) account. Said of a *purchase* or *sale* when payment is expected sometime after delivery and no *note* evidencing the *debt* is given or received. The purchaser has generally signed an agreement sometime in the past promising to pay for such purchases according to an agreed time schedule. When a sale (purchase) is made on open account, *Accounts Receivable (Payable)* is *debited (credited).*

on consignment. Said of goods delivered by the owner (the consignor) to another (the consignee) to be sold by the consignee; the owner is entitled to the return of the property or payment of an amount agreed upon in advance. The goods are *assets* of the consignor. Such arrangements provide the consignor with better protection than an outright *sale on account* to the consignee in case the consignee becomes bankrupt. In event of *bankruptcy,* the consignor can reclaim the goods, without going through lengthy bankruptcy proceedings from which the consignor might recover only a small percentage of the amounts owed to it.

one-line consolidation. Said of an *intercorporate investment* accounted for with the *equity method.* The effects of this method on reported *income* and *balance sheet* total *assets* and *equities* are identical to those that would appear if the investee firm were consolidated, even though the income from the investment appears on a single line of the income statement and the net investment appears on a single line in the assets section of the balance sheet.

one-write system. A system of bookkeeping which produces several records, including original documents, in one operation by the use of reproductive paper and special equipment which provides for proper alignment of the documents being processed.

open account. Any *account* with a nonzero *debit* or *credit balance.* See *on (open) account.*

operating. An adjective used to refer to *revenue* and *expense* items relating to the company's main line(s) of business. See *operations.*

operating accounts. *Revenue, expense,* and *production cost accounts;* contrast with *balance sheet accounts.*

operating activities. See *operations.* For purposes of the *statement of cash flows,* all *transactions* and *events* that are neither *financing activities* nor *investing activities.*

operating budget. A formal *budget* for the *operating cycle* or for a year.

operating cash flow. Financial statement analysts use this term to mean *cash flow – capital expenditures – dividends.*

operating cycle. *Earnings cycle.*

operating expenses. *Expenses* incurred in the course of *ordinary* activities of an *entity.* Frequently, a classification including only *selling, general,* and *administrative expenses,* thereby excluding *cost of goods sold, interest,* and *income tax* expenses. See *operations.*

operating lease. A *lease* accounted for by the *lessee* without showing an *asset* for the lease rights (*leasehold*) or a *liability* for the lease payment obligations. Rental payments of the lessee are merely shown as *expenses* of the period. The asset remains on the lessor's *books* where rental collections appear as *revenues;* contrast with *capital lease.*

operating leverage. Usually said of a firm with a large proportion of *fixed costs* in its *total costs.* Consider a book publisher or a railroad: the *incremental costs* of producing another book or transporting another freight car are much less than *average cost,* so the *gross margin* upon sale of the unit is relatively large. Contrast, for example, a grocery store, where the *contribution margin* is usually less than 5 percent of the selling price. For firms with equal profitability, however defined, we say the one with the larger percentage increase in income from a given percentage increase in unit sales has the larger operating leverage. See *leverage* for contrast of this term with "financial leverage." See *cost terminology* for definition of terms involving the word "cost."

operating margin (based on current costs). *Revenues* from *sales* minus *current cost* of goods sold. A measure of operating efficiency that is independent of the *cost flow assumption* for *inventory.* Sometimes called "current (gross) margin." See *inventory profit* for illustrative computations.

operating ratio. See *ratio.*

operational control. See *control system.*

operations. A word not precisely defined in *accounting.* Generally, operating activities (producing and selling *goods* or *services)* are distinguished from financing activities (raising funds) and *investing activities.* Acquiring goods on account and then paying for them in one month, though generally classified as an operating activity, has the characteristics of a financing activity. Or consider the transaction of selling plant assets for a price in excess of book value. On the *income statement,* the gain is part of income from operations (continuing operations or discontinued operations, depending on the circumstances) but on the *statement of cash flows,* all of the funds received on disposition are reported below the "cash from operations" section, as a nonoperating source of cash, disposition of noncurrent assets. In income tax accounting an "operating loss" results whenever deductions are greater than taxable revenues.

opinion. The *auditor's report* containing an attestation or lack thereof. Also, *APB Opinion.*

opinion paragraph. Section of *auditor's report,* generally following the *scope paragraph,* giving the auditor's conclusion that the *financial statements* are (rarely, are not) in accordance with *GAAP* and present fairly the *financial position,* changes in financial position, and the results of *operations.*

opportunity cost. The *present value* of the *income* (or *costs)* that a firm could earn (or save) from using an *asset* in its best alternative use to the one under consideration.

opportunity cost of capital. *Cost of capital.*

option. The legal right to buy something during a specified period at a specified price, called the *exercise* price. Employee stock options should not be confused with *put* and *call* options traded in various public markets.

ordinary annuity. An *annuity in arrears.*

ordinary income. For income tax purposes, reportable *income* not qualifying as *capital gains.*

organization costs. The *costs* incurred in planning and establishing an *entity;* example of an *intangible* asset. Often, since the amounts are not *material,* the costs are treated as *expenses* in the period incurred even though the *expenditures* clearly provide future benefits and meet the test to be *assets.*

original cost. *Acquisition cost.* In public utility accounting, the acquisition cost of the *entity* first devoting the *asset* to public use. See *aboriginal cost.*

original entry. Entry in a *journal.*

OSHA. *Occupational Safety and Health Act.* The federal law that governs working conditions in commerce and industry.

outlay. The amount of an *expenditure.*

outlier. Said of an observation (or data point) which appears to differ significantly in some regard from other observations (or data points) of supposedly the same phenomenon. Often used in describing the results of a *regression analysis* when an observation is not "near" the fitted regression equation.

out-of-pocket. Said of an *expenditure* usually paid for with cash. An *incremental* cost.

out-of-stock cost. The estimated decrease in future *profit* as a result of losing customers because a firm has insufficient quantities of *inventory* currently on hand to meet customers' demands.

output. Physical quantity or monetary measurement of *goods* and *services* produced.

outside director. A member of a corporate board of directors who is not a company officer and does not participate in the corporation's day-to-day management.

outstanding. Unpaid or uncollected. When said of *stock,* the shares issued less *treasury stock.* When said of *checks,* it means a check issued that did not clear the *drawer's* bank prior to the *bank statement* date.

over-and-short. Title for an *expense account* used to account for small differences between book balances of cash and actual cash and vouchers or receipts in *petty cash* or *change funds.*

overapplied (overabsorbed) overhead. An excess of costs applied, or *charged,* to product for a period over actual *overhead costs* during the period. A *credit balance* in an overhead account after overhead is assigned to product.

overdraft. A *check* written on a checking account that contains funds less than the amount of the check.

overhead costs. Any *cost* not directly associated with the production or sale of identifiable goods and services. Sometimes called "burden" or "indirect costs" and, in Britain, "oncosts." Frequently limited to manufacturing overhead. See *central corporate expenses* and *manufacturing overhead.*

overhead rate. Standard, or other predetermined rate, at which a firm applies *overhead costs* to products or to services.

over-the-counter. Said of a *security* traded in a negotiated transaction, rather than in an auctioned one on an organized stock exchange, such as the *New York Stock Exchange.*

owners' equity. *Proprietorship; assets* minus *liabilities; paid-in capital* plus *retained earnings* of a corporation; partners' capital accounts in a *partnership;* owner's capital account in a *sole proprietorship.*

P

P & L. Profit and loss statement; *income statement.*

paid-in capital. Sum of balances in *capital stock* and *capital contributed in excess of par (or stated) value* accounts. Same as *contributed capital* (minus *donated capital*). Some use the term to mean only *capital contributed in excess of par (or stated value).*

paid-in surplus. See *surplus.*

paper profit. A *gain* not yet realized through a *transaction.* An *unrealized holding gain.*

par. See *at par* and *face amount.*

par value. *Face amount* of a *security.*

par value method. The method of accounting for *treasury stock* that *debits* a common stock account with the *par value* of the shares required and allocates the remaining debits between the *additional paid-in capital* and *retained earnings* accounts; contrast with *cost method.*

parent company. Company owning more than 50 percent of the voting shares of another company, called the *subsidiary.*

partial obsolescence. As technology improves, the economic value of existing *assets* declines. In many cases, however, it will not pay a firm to replace the existing asset with a new one even though the new type, rather than the old, would be acquired if a new acquisition were to be made currently. In these cases, the accountant should theoretically recognize a loss from partial obsolescence from the firm's owning an old, out-of-date asset, but *GAAP* does not permit recognition of partial obsolescence. The old asset will be carried at *cost* less *accumulated depreciation* until it is retired from service so long as the *undiscounted* future *cash flows* from the asset exceed its book value. See *obsolescence.*

partially funded. Said of a *pension plan* where not all earned benefits have been funded. See *funded* for funding requirements.

partially vested. Said of a *pension plan* where not all employee benefits are *vested.* See *graded vesting.*

participating dividend. *Dividend* paid to preferred shareholders in addition to the minimum preferred dividends when the *preferred stock* contract allows such sharing in earnings. Usually applied after dividends on *common stock* have reached a certain level.

participating preferred stock. *Preferred stock* with rights to *participating dividends.*

partner's drawing. A payment to a partner to be charged against his or her share of income or capital. The name of a *temporary account* to record such payments.

partnership. Contractual arrangement between individuals to share resources and operations in a jointly run business. See *general* and *limited partner* and *Uniform Partnership Act.*

patent. A right granted for up to 17 years by the federal government to exclude others from manufacturing, using or selling a claimed design, product or plant (e.g., a new breed of rose) or from using a claimed process or method of manufacture. An *asset* if acquired by purchase. If developed internally, the development costs are *expensed* when incurred under current *GAAP.*

payable. Unpaid but not necessarily due or past due.

pay as you go. Said of an *income tax* scheme where periodic payments of income taxes are made during the period when the income to be taxed is being earned; in contrast to a scheme where no payments are due until the end of, or after, the period whose income is being taxed. (Called PAYE – pay as you earn – in Britain.) Sometimes used to describe an *unfunded pension plan,* where payments to pension plan beneficiaries are made from general corporate funds, not from cash previously contributed to a pension fund. Not acceptable as a method of accounting for pension plans under *SFAS No. 87* nor as a method of *funding* under *ERISA.*

payback period. Amount of time that must elapse before the cash inflows from a project equal the cash outflows.

payback reciprocal. One divided by the *payback period.* This number approximates the *internal rate of return* on a project when the project life exceeds twice the payback period and the cash inflows are identical in every period after the initial period.

PAYE. See *pay as you go.*

payee. The person or entity to whom a cash payment is made or who will receive the stated amount of money on a *check.* See *draft.*

payout ratio. *Common stock dividends* declared for a year divided by net *income* to common stock for the year. A term used by financial analysts; contrast with *dividend yield.*

payroll taxes. Taxes levied because salaries or wages are paid; for example, *FICA* and unemployment compensation insurance taxes. Typically, the employer pays a portion and withholds part of the employee's wage fund.

P/E ratio. *Price-earnings ratio.*

Pension Benefit Guarantee Corporation. PBGC. A federal corporation established under *ERISA* to guarantee basic pension benefits in covered pension plans by administering terminated pension plans and placing *liens* on corporate assets for certain unfunded pension liabilities.

pension fund. *Fund,* the assets of which are to be paid to retired ex-employees, usually as a *life annuity.* Usually held by an independent trustee and thus is not an *asset* of the employer.

pension plan. Details or provisions of employer's contract with employees for paying retirement *annuities* or other benefits. See *funded, vested, service cost, prior service cost, money purchase plan,* and *defined-benefit plan.*

per books. An expression used to refer to the *book value* of an item at a specific time.

percent. Any number, expressed as a decimal, multiplied by 100.

percentage depletion (allowance). Deductible *expense* allowed in some cases by the federal *income tax* regulations; computed as a percentage of gross income from a *natural resource* independent of the unamortized cost of the *asset*. Because the amount of the total deductions for tax purposes is usually greater than the cost of the asset being *depleted*, many people think the deduction is an unfair tax advantage or *loophole*.

percentage-of-completion method. Recognizing *revenues* and *expenses* on a job, order, or contract (a) in proportion to the *costs* incurred for the period divided by total costs expected to be incurred for the job or order ("cost to cost") or (b) in proportion to engineers' or architects' estimates of the incremental degree of completion of the job, order, or contract during the period. Contrast with *completed contract method.*

percentage statement. A statement containing, in addition to (or instead of) dollar amounts, ratios of dollar amounts to some base. In a percentage *income statement,* the base is usually either *net sales* or total *revenues* and in a percentage *balance sheet,* the base is usually total *assets.*

period. *Accounting period.*

period cost. An inferior term for *period expense.*

period expense (charge). *Expenditure,* usually based upon the passage of time, charged to operations of the accounting period rather than *capitalized* as an asset; contrast with *product cost.*

periodic inventory. A method of recording *inventory* that uses data on beginning inventory, additions to inventories, and ending inventory to find the cost of withdrawals from inventory. Contrast with *perpetual inventory.*

periodic procedures. The process of making *adjusting entries, closing entries,* and preparing the *financial statements,* usually by use of *trial balances* and *work sheets.*

permanent account. An account which appears on the *balance sheet;* contrast with *temporary account.*

permanent difference. Difference between reported income and taxable income that will never be reversed and, hence, requires no entry in the *deferred income tax liability* account. An example is the difference between taxable and reportable income from interest earned on state and municipal *bonds;* contrast with *timing difference* and see *deferred income tax liability.*

permanent file. The file of working papers prepared by a public accountant containing information required for reference in successive professional engagements for a particular organization, as distinguished from working papers applicable only to a particular engagement.

perpetual annuity. *Perpetuity.*

perpetual inventory. Records on quantities and amounts of *inventory* that are changed or made current with each physical addition to or withdrawal from the stock of goods; an inventory so recorded. The records will show the physical quantities and, frequently, the dollar valuations that should be on hand at any time. Because *cost of goods sold* is explicitly computed, the *inventory equation* can be used to compute an amount for what *ending inventory* should be. The computed amount of ending

inventory can be compared to the actual amount of ending inventory as a *control* device. Contrast with *periodic inventory.*

perpetuity. An *annuity* whose payments continue forever. The *present value* of a perpetuity in *arrears* is p/r where p is the periodic payment and r is the *interest rate* per period. If $100 is promised each year, in arrears, forever and the interest rate is 8 percent per year, then the value of the perpetuity is $1,250 = $100/.08.

personal account. *Drawing account.*

PERT. Program evaluation and review technique. A method of *network analysis* in which three time estimates are made for each activity – the optimistic time, the most likely time, and the pessimistic time – and which gives an expected completion date for the project within a probability range.

petty cash fund. Currency and coins maintained for expenditures that are made with cash on hand.

physical units method. A method of allocating a *joint cost* to the *joint products* based on a physical measure of the joint products. For example, allocating the cost of a cow to sirloin steak and to hamburger, based on the weight of the meat. This method usually provides nonsensical (see *sterilized allocation*) results unless the physical units of the joint products tend to have the same value.

physical verification. *Verification,* by an *auditor,* performed by actually inspecting items in *inventory, plant assets,* and the like; may be based on statistical sampling procedures; in contrast to mere checking of written records.

planning and control process. General name for the techniques of management comprising the setting of organizational goals and *strategic plans, capital budgeting, operations* budgeting, comparison of plans with actual results, performance evaluation and corrective action, and revisions of goals, plans, and budgets.

plant. *Plant assets.*

plant assets. *Assets* used in the revenue production process. Plant assets include buildings, machinery, equipment, land, and natural resources. The phrase "property, plant, and equipment" while often used as a balance sheet heading, is therefore a redundancy. In this context, "plant" used alone means buildings.

plant asset turnover. Number of dollars of *sales* generated per dollar of *plant assets.* Equal to sales divided by average *plant assets.*

plantwide allocation method. First, use one *cost pool* for the entire plant. Then, allocate all costs from that pool to product using a single overhead *allocation* rate, or one set of rates, to all of the products of the plant, independent of the number of departments in the plant.

PLC. Public Limited Company. United Kingdom. A publicly held *corporation.* Contrast with *Ltd.*

pledging. The borrower assigns *assets* as security or *collateral* for repayment of a loan.

pledging of receivables. The process of using expected collections on *accounts receivable* as *collateral* for a loan. The borrower remains responsible for collecting the receivable but promises to use the proceeds for repaying the debt.

plow back. To retain *assets* generated by earnings for continued investment in the business.

plug. For any *account*, beginning balance + additions – deductions = ending balance; if any three of the four items are known, the fourth can be found by plugging. In making a *journal entry*, often all *debits* are known, as are all but one of the *credits* (or vice versa). Because *double-entry* bookkeeping requires equal debits and credits, the unknown quantity can be computed by subtracting the sum of the known credits from the sum of all the debits (or vice versa). This process is also known as plugging. Accountants often call the unknown the "plug." For example, if a *discount* on *bonds payable* is being *amortized* with the *straight-line method*, then *interest expense* is a plug: interest expense = interest payable + *discount amortization*. See *trade-in transaction* for an example. The term sometimes has a bad connotation for accountants because plugging occurs in a slightly different context: In preparing a *preclosing trial balance* (or *balance sheet*), often the sum of the debits does not equal the sum of the credits. Rather than find the error, some accountants are tempted to force equality by changing one of the amounts, with a plugged debit or credit to an account such as Other Expenses. There is really nothing wrong with this procedure if the amount of the error is very small compared to asset totals because it is not cost effective to spend tens or hundreds of dollars in bookkeeper's or accountant's time to find an error of a few dollars. Still, most accounting teachers and auditors gravely frown on the process.

pooling-of-interests method. Accounting for a *business combination* by merely adding together the *book value* of the *assets* and *equities* of the combined firms. Contrast with *purchase method*. Generally leads to a higher reported *net income* for the combined firms than would be reported had the business combination been accounted for as a purchase because the *market values* of the merged assets are generally larger than their book values. *APB Opinion No. 16* states the conditions that, when met, require the pooling-of-interests treatment.

population. The entire field of numbers or items which is to be the subject of sampling or other analysis.

positive confirmation. See *confirmation*.

post. To record entries in an *account* in a *ledger*; usually the entries are transferred from a *journal*.

post-closing trial balance. *Trial balance* taken after all *temporary accounts* have been closed.

post-statement events. Events with *material* impact that occur between the end of the *accounting period* and the formal publication of the *financial statements*. Such events must be disclosed in notes for the auditor to give a *clean opinion*, even though the events are subsequent to the period being reported on.

potentially dilutive. A *security* that may be converted into, or exchanged for, common stock and thereby reduce reported *earnings per share*: options, warrants, convertible bonds, and convertible preferred stock.

PPB. *Program budgeting*; the second "P" means "plan".

practical capacity. Maximum level at which the plant or department can operate efficiently.

precision. The degree of accuracy with which the estimate derived from sampling process is stated, usually expressed as a range of values around the estimate. A sample estimate may be expressed in the following terms: "Based on the sample, we are 95% sure [confidence level] that the true population value is within the range of X to Y [precision]". See *confidence level*.

preclosing trial balance. *Trial balance* taken at the end of the period before *closing entries*. In this sense, an *adjusted trial balance*. Sometimes taken before *adjusting entries* and then is synonymous with *unadjusted trial balance*.

predetermined (factory) overhead rate. Rate used in applying *overhead* to products or departments developed at the start of a period by dividing estimated overhead cost by the estimated number of units of the overhead allocation base (or *denominator volume)* activity. See *normal costing*.

preemptive right. The privilege of a *shareholder* to maintain a proportionate share of ownership by purchasing a proportionate share of any new stock issues. Most state corporation laws allow corporations to pay shareholders to waive their preemptive rights or state that preemptive rights exist only if the *corporation charter* explicitly grants them. In practice, then, preemptive rights are the exception, rather than the rule.

preference as to assets. The rights of *preferred shareholders* to receive certain payments in case of dissolution before common shareholders receive payments.

preferred shares. *Capital stock* with a claim to *income* or *assets* after *bondholders* but before *common shares. Dividends* on preferred shares are *income distributions*, not *expenses*. See *cumulative preferred stock*.

premium. The excess of issue (or market) price over *par value*. For a different context, see *insurance*.

premium on capital stock. Alternative but inferior title for *capital contributed in excess of (par) or stated value*.

prepaid expense. An *expenditure* that leads to a *deferred charge* or *prepayment*; strictly speaking, a contradiction in terms because an *expense* is a gone asset and this title refers to past *expenditures*, such as for rent or insurance premiums, that still have future benefits and thus are *assets*.

prepaid income. An inferior alternative title for *advances from customers*. Do not call an item *revenue* or *income* until earned, when the firm delivers goods or renders services.

prepayments. *Deferred charges. Assets* representing *expenditures* for future benefits. Rent and insurance premiums paid in advance are usually classified as *current* prepayments.

present value. Value today (or at some specific date) of an amount or amounts to be paid or received later (or at other, different dates), discounted at some *interest* or *discount rate*.

price. The quantity of one *good* or *service*, usually *cash*, asked in return for a unit of another good or service. See *fair market price.*

price-earnings ratio. At a given time, the market value of a company's *common stock*, per share, divided by the *earnings per* common *share* for the past year. The denominator is usually based on *income from continuing operations* or, if the analyst thinks the current figure for that amount is not representative – such as when the number is negative – on some estimate of the number. See *ratio.*

price index. A series of numbers, one for each period, that purports to represent some *average* of prices for a series of periods, relative to a base period.

price level. The number from a *price index* series for a given period or date.

price level-adjusted statements. *Financial statements* expressed in terms of dollars of uniform purchasing power. *Nonmonetary* items are restated to reflect changes in general *price levels* since the time specific *assets* were acquired and *liabilities* were incurred. A *gain* or *loss* is recognized on *monetary items* as they are held over time periods when the general *price level changes.* Conventional financial statements show *historical costs* and ignore differences in purchasing power in different periods.

price variance. In accounting for *standard costs,* and amount equal to (actual cost per unit – standard cost per unit) times actual quantity.

primary earnings per share. Net *income* to *common shareholders* plus *interest* (*net of tax* effects) or *dividends* paid on *common stock equivalents* divided by (weighted average of common share outstanding plus the net increase in the number of common shares that would become *outstanding* if all common stock equivalents were exchanged for common shares with cash proceeds, if any, used to retire common shares).

prime cost. Sum of *direct materials* plus *direct labor* costs assigned to product.

prime rate. The rate for loans charged by commercial banks to their creditworthy customers. Some customers pay even less than the prime rate and others, more. The *Federal Reserve Bulletin* is considered the authoritative source of information about historical prime rates.

principal. An amount in which *interest* is charged or earned. The *face amount* of a *loan.* Also, the absent owner (principal) who hires the manager (agent) in a "principal-agent" relationship.

principle. See *generally accepted accounting principles.*

prior-period adjustment. A *debit* or *credit* made directly to *retained earnings* (that does not affect *income* for the period) to adjust earnings as calculated for prior periods. Such adjustments are now extremely rare. Theory might suggest that corrections of errors in accounting estimates (such as the *depreciable life* or *salvage value* of an asset) should be treated as adjustments to retained earnings. But *GAAP* require that corrections of such estimates flow through current, and perhaps future, *income statements.* See *accounting changes* and *accounting errors.*

prior service cost. *Present value* at a given time of a *pension plan's* retroactive *benefits.* "Unrecognized prior service cost" refers to that portion of prior service cost not yet *debited* to *expense.* See *actuarial accrued liability* and *funded;* contrast with *normal cost.*

pro forma statements. Hypothetical statements. Financial statements as they would appear if some event, such as a *merger* or increased production and sales had occurred or were to occur. Pro forma is often spelled as one word.

proceeds. The *funds* received from disposition of assets or from the issue of securities.

process costing. A method of *cost accounting* based on average costs (total cost divided by the *equivalent units* of work done in a period). Typically used for assembly lines or for products that are produced in a series of steps that are more continuous than discrete.

product. *Goods* or *services* produced.

product cost. Any *manufacturing cost* that can be inventoried. See *flow of costs* for example and contrast with *period expenses.*

production cost. *Manufacturing cost.*

production cost account. A *temporary account* for accumulating *manufacturing costs* during a period.

production department. A department producing salable *goods* or *services;* contrast with *service department.*

production method (depreciation). The depreciable asset (e.g., a truck) is given a *depreciable life* measured, not in elapsed time, but in units of output (e.g., miles) or perhaps in units of time of expected use. Then the *depreciation* charge for a period is a portion of depreciable cost equal to a fraction computed by dividing the actual output produced during the period by the expected total output to be produced over the life of the asset. Sometimes called the "units-of-production (or output) method."

production method (revenue recognition). *Percentage-of-completion method* for recognizing *revenue.*

production volume variance. Standard fixed *overhead* rate per unit of normal *capacity* (or base activity) times (units of base activity budgeted or planned for a period minus actual units of base activity worked or assigned to product during the period). Often called a "volume variance."

productive capacity. In computing *current cost* of *long-term assets,* we are interested in the cost of reproducing the productive capacity (for example, the ability to manufacture one million units a year), not the cost of reproducing the actual physical assets currently used (see *reproduction cost).* Replacement cost of productive capacity will be the same as reproduction cost of assets only in the unusual case when there has been no technological improvement in production processes and the relative prices of goods and services used in production have remained approximately the same as when the currently used ones were acquired.

profit. Excess of *revenues* over *expenses* for a *transaction;* sometimes used synonymously with *net income* for the period.

profit and loss sharing ratio. The fraction of *net income* or loss allocable to a partner in a *partnership*. Need not be the same fraction as the partner's share of capital.

profit and loss statement. *Income statement.*

profit center. A *responsibility center* for which a firm accumulates both *revenue* and *expenses;* contrast with *cost center.*

profit margin. *Sales* minus all *expenses.*

profit margin percentage. *Profit margin* divided by *net sales.*

profit maximization. The doctrine that a given set of operations should be accounted for so as to make reported *net income* as large as possible; contrast with *conservatism.* This concept in accounting is slightly different from the profit-maximizing concept in economics where the doctrine states that operations should be managed to maximize the present value of the firm's wealth, generally by equating *marginal costs* and *marginal revenues.*

profit sharing plan. A *defined contribution plan,* where the employer contributes amounts based on *net income.*

profit variance analysis. Analysis of the causes of the difference between *budgeted profit* in the *master budget* and the profits earned.

profit-volume analysis (equation). Analysis of effects on *profits* caused by changes in volume or *contribution margin* per unit or *fixed costs.* See *breakeven chart.*

profit-volume graph. See *breakeven chart.*

profit-volume ratio. *Net income* divided by net sales in dollars.

profitability accounting. *Responsibility accounting.*

program budgeting. Specification and analysis of inputs, outputs, costs, and alternatives that link plans to *budgets.*

programmed costs. A *fixed cost* not essential for carrying out operations. A firm can control research and development and advertising designed to generate new business, but once it commits to incur them, they become fixed costs. Sometimes called managed costs or *discretionary costs;* contrast with *capacity costs.*

progressive tax. Tax for which the rate increases as the taxed base, such as income, increases; contrast with *regressive tax.*

project financing arrangement. As defined by *SFAS No. 47,* the financing of an investment project in which the lender looks principally to the *cash flows* and *earnings* of the project as the source of funds for repayment and to the *assets* of the project as *collateral* for the loan. The general *credit* of the project entity is usually not a significant factor, either because the entity is a *corporation* without other assets or because the financing is without direct *recourse* to the entity's owners.

projected benefit obligation. The *actuarial present value* at a given date of all pension benefits attributed by a *defined-benefit pension* formula to employee service rendered before that date. The obligation is measured using assumptions as to future compensation levels if the formula incorporates future compensation, as happens, for example, when the eventual pension benefit is based on wages of the last several years of employees' work lives. Contrast to "accumulated benefit obligation," where the obligation is measured using employee compensation levels at the time of the measurement date of the obligation.

projected financial statement. *Pro forma* financial statement.

projection. See *financial projection* for definition and contrast.

promissory note. An unconditional written promise to pay a specified sum of money on demand or at a specified date.

proof of journal. The process of checking arithmetic accuracy of *journal entries* by testing for the equality of all *debits* with all *credits* since the last previous proof.

property dividend. A *dividend in kind.*

property, plant and equipment. See *plant assets.*

proportionate consolidation. Canada. A presentation of the *financial statements* of any investor-investment relationship, whereby the investor's pro rata share of each *asset, liability, income* item, and *expense* item appears in the *financial statements* of the investor under the various *balance sheet and income statement* headings.

proprietary accounts. See *budgetary accounts* for definition and contrast in context of governmental accounting.

proprietorship. *Assets* minus *liabilities* of an *entity;* equals *contributed capital* plus *retained earnings.*

proprietorship theory. The view of the corporation that emphasizes the form of the *accounting equation* that says *assets – liabilities = owners' equity;* contrast with *entity theory.* The major implication of a choice between these theories deals with the treatment of *subsidiaries.* For example, the view that *minority interest* is an *indeterminate term liability* is based on the proprietorship theory. The proprietorship theory implies using a *single-step income statement.*

prorate. To *allocate* in proportion to some base; for example, allocate *service department* costs in proportion to hours of service used by the benefitted department. Or, to allocate *manufacturing variances* to product sold and to product added to *ending inventory.*

prorating variances. See *prorate.*

prospectus. Formal written document describing *securities* to be issued. See *proxy.*

protest fee. Fee charged by banks or other financial agencies when items (such as *checks)* presented for collection cannot be collected.

provision. Often the exact amount of an *expense* is uncertain, but must, nevertheless, be recognized currently. The entry for the estimated expense, such as for *income taxes* or expected costs under *warranty,* is:

Expense (Estimated)...............	X	
Liability (Estimated)		X

In American usage, the term "provision" is often used in the expense account title of the above entry. Thus, Provision for Income Taxes is used to mean the estimate of income tax expense. (In British usage, the term "provision" is used in the title for the estimated liability of the above entry, so that Provision for Income Taxes is a balance sheet account.)

proxy. Written authorization given by one person to another so that the second person can act for the first, such as to vote shares of stock. Of particular significance to accountants because the *SEC* presumes that financial information is distributed by management along with its proxy solicitations.

public accountant. Generally, this term is synonymous with *certified public accountant.* In some jurisdictions, individuals have been licensed as public accountants without being CPAs.

public accounting. That portion of accounting primarily involving the *attest* function, culminating in the *auditor's report.*

PuPU. An acronym for *purchasing power unit* conceived by John C. Burton, former Chief Accountant of the *SEC.* Those who think *constant dollar accounting* not particularly useful poke fun at it by calling it "PuPU accounting."

purchase allowance. A reduction in sales *invoice price* usually granted because the *goods* received by the purchaser were not exactly as ordered. The goods are not returned to the seller, but are purchased at a price lower than originally agreed upon.

purchase discount. A reduction in purchase *invoice price* granted for prompt payment. See *sales discount* and *terms of sale.*

purchase investigation. An investigation of the financial affairs of a company for the purpose of disclosing matters that may influence the terms or conclusion of a potential acquisition.

purchase method. Accounting for a *business combination* by adding the acquired company's assets at the price paid for them to the acquiring company's assets. Contrast with *pooling-of-interests method.* The acquired assets are put on the books at current values, rather than original costs; the subsequent *amortization expenses* are usually larger (and reported income, smaller) than for the same business combination accounted for as a pooling of interests. The purchase method is required unless all the criteria in *APB Opinion No. 16* to be a pooling are met.

purchase order. Document authorizing a seller to deliver goods with payment to be made later.

purchasing power gain or loss. *Monetary gain or loss.*

push-down accounting. Assume that Company A purchases substantially all of the *common shares* of Company B but that Company B must still issue its own *financial statements.* The question arises, shall the *basis* for Company B's *assets* and *equities* be changed on its own books to the same updated amounts at which they appear on Company A's *consolidated* statements? When Company B shows the new asset and equity bases reflecting Company A's purchase, Company B is using "push-down accounting," because the new bases are "pushed down" from Company A (where they are required in *GAAP* to Company B (where the new bases would not appear in *historical cost accounting).* Since 1983, the *SEC* has required push-down accounting under some circumstances.

put. An option to sell *shares* of a publicly-traded corporation at a fixed price during a fixed time span. Contrast with *call.*

Q

qualified report (opinion). *Auditor's report* containing a statement that the auditor was unable to complete a satisfactory examination of all things considered relevant or that the auditor has doubts about the financial impact of some *material* item reported in the financial statements. See *except for* and *subject to.*

quantitative performance measure. A measure of output based on an objectively observable quantity, like units produced or *direct costs* incurred, rather than on an unobservable quantity or one observable only non-objectively, like quality of service provided.

quantity discount. A reduction in purchase price as quantity purchased increases; amount of the discount is constrained by law (Robinson-Patman Act). Not to be confused with *purchase discount.*

quantity variance. *Efficiency variance.* In *standard cost* systems, the standard price per unit times (actual quantity used minus standard quantity that should be used).

quasi-reorganization. A *reorganization* where no new company is formed or no court has intervened, as would happen in *bankruptcy.* The primary purpose is to absorb a *deficit* and get a "fresh start."

quick assets. *Assets* readily convertible into *cash;* includes cash, *current marketable securities* and *current receivables.*

quick ratio. Sum of (*cash, current marketable securities,* and *receivables)* divided by *current liabilities.* The analyst may exclude some nonliquid receivables from the numerator. Often called the "acid test ratio." See *ratio.*

R

R^2. The proportion of the statistical variance of a *dependent variable* explained by the equation fit to *independent variable(s)* in a *regression analysis.*

R & D. See *research and development.*

Railroad Accounting Principles Board. RAPB. A board brought into existence by the Staggers Rail Act of 1980 to advise the Interstate Commerce Commission on matters of accounting affecting railroads.

random number sampling. A method of choosing a sample in which the analyst selects items from the *population* by using a random number table or generator.

random sampling. A method of choosing a sample in which all items in the population have an equal chance of being selected. Compare *judgment(al) sampling*.

RAPB. *Railroad Accounting Principles Board.*

rate of return on assets. *Return on assets.*

rate of return on common stock equity. See *ratio*.

rate of return on shareholders' (owners') equity. See *ratio*.

rate of return (on total capital). See *ratio* and *rate of return on assets*.

rate variance. *Price variance*, usually for *direct labor costs*.

ratio. The number resulting when one number is divided by another. Analysts generally use ratios to assess aspects of profitability, solvency, and liquidity. The commonly used financial ratios fall in three categories: (1) those that summarize some aspect of *operations* for a period, usually a year, (2) those that summarize some aspect of *financial position* at a given moment – the moment for which a balance sheet has been prepared, and (3) those that relate some aspect of operations to some aspect of financial position.
    The accompanying exhibit lists the most common financial ratios and shows separately both the numerator and denominator used to calculate each ratio.
    For all ratios that require an average balance during the period, the analyst often derives the average as one half the sum of the beginning and ending balances. Sophisticated analysts recognize, however, that particularly when companies use a fiscal year different from the calendar year, this averaging of beginning and ending balances may be misleading. Consider, for example, the *rate of return on assets* of Sears, Roebuck & Company whose fiscal year ends on January 31. Sears chooses a January 31 closing date at least in part because inventories are at a low level and are therefore easy to count – it has sold the Christmas merchandise and the Easter merchandise has not yet all arrived. Furthermore, by January 31, Sears has collected for most Christmas sales, so receivable amounts are not unusually large. Thus at January 31, the amount of total assets is lower than at many other times during the year. Consequently, the denominator of the rate of return on assets, total assets, for Sears is more likely to represent the smallest amount of total assets on hand during the year than the average amount. The return on assets rate for Sears and other companies who choose a fiscal year-end to coincide with low points in the inventory cycle is likely to be larger than if a more accurate estimate of the average amounts of total assets were used.

raw material. Goods purchased for use in manufacturing a product.

reacquired stock. *Treasury stock.*

real accounts. *Balance sheet accounts;* as opposed to *nominal accounts.* See *permanent accounts*.

real amount (value). An amount stated in *constant dollars*. For example, if an investment costing $100 is sold for $130 after a period of 10 percent general *inflation*, the *nominal amount* of *gain* is $30 (= $130 – $100) but the real amount of gain is C$20 (= $130 – 1.10 x $100), where "C$" denotes constant dollars of purchasing power on the date of sale.

real estate. *Land* and its *improvements*, such as landscaping and roads, but not buildings.

realizable value. *Market value* or, sometimes, *net realizable value*.

realization convention. The accounting practice of delaying the recognition of *gains* and *losses* from changes in the market price of *assets* until the assets are sold. However, unrealized losses on *inventory* and *marketable securities* classified as *current assets* are recognized prior to sale when the *lower-of-cost-or-market* valuation basis is used.

realize. To convert into *funds*. When applied to a *gain* or *loss*, implies that an *arm's-length transaction* has taken place. Contrast with *recognize;* a loss (as for example on *marketable equity securities*) may be recognized in the financial statements even though it has not yet been realized in a transaction.

realized gain (or loss) on marketable equity securities. An income statement account title for the difference between the proceeds of disposition and the *original cost* of *marketable equity securities*.

realized holding gain. See *inventory profit* for definition and an example.

rearrangement costs. Costs of re-installing assets perhaps in a different location. May be *capitalized* as part of the assets cost, just as is original installation cost.

recapitalization. *Reorganization.*

recapture. Various provisions of the *income tax* rules require refund by the taxpayer (recapture by the government) of various tax advantages under certain conditions. For example, the tax savings provided by the *investment credit* or by *accelerated depreciation* must be repaid if the item providing the tax savings is retired prematurely.

receipt. Acquisition of *cash*.

receivable. Any *collectible* whether or not it is currently due.

receivable turnover. See *ratio*.

reciprocal holdings. Company A owns stock of Company B and Company B owns stock of Company A.

recognize. To enter a transaction in the accounts. Not synonymous with *realize*.

reconciliation. A calculation that shows how one balance or figure is derived systematically from another, such as a *reconciliation of retained earnings* or a *bank reconciliation schedule*. See *articulate*.

Summary of Financial Statement Ratios

Ratio	Numerator	Denominator
Profitability Ratios		
Rate of Return on Assets . . .	Net Income + Interest Expense (net of tax effects)[a]	Average Total Assets During the Period[b]
Profit Margin Ratio (before interest effects)	Net Income + Interest Expense (net of tax effects)[a]	Revenues
Various Expense Ratios	Various Expenses	Revenues
Total Assets Turnover Ratio . .	Revenues	Average Total Assets During the Period
Accounts Receivable Turnover Ratio	Net Sales on Account	Average Accounts Receivable During the Period
Inventory Turnover Ratio	Cost of Goods Sold	Average Inventory During the Period
Plant Asset Turnover Ratio . .	Revenues	Average Plant Assets During the Period
Rate of Return on Common Shareholders' Equity	Net Income - Preferred Stock Dividends	Average Common Shareholders' Equity During the Period
Profit Margin Ratio (after interest expense and preferred dividends)	Net Income - Preferred Stock Dividends	Revenues
Leverage Ratio	Average Total Assets During the period	Average Common Shareholders' Equity During the Period
Earnings per Share of Stock[c] .	Net Income - Preferred Stock Dividends	Weighted-Average Number of Common Shares Outstanding During the Period
Short-Term Liquidity Ratios		
Current Ratio	Current Assets	Current Liabilities
Quick or Acid Test Ratio	Highly Liquid Assets (ordinarily, cash, marketable securities, and receivables)[d]	Current Liabilities

[a]If a consolidated subsidiary is not owned entirely by the parent corporation, the minority interest share of earnings must allso be added back to net income.

[b]Financial economists deduct the average of non-interest-bearing liabilities from the denominator. This deduction compensates for the implicit interest charges (such as for accounts payable) already subtracted in measuring net income.

[c]This calculation can be more complicated when there are convertible securities, options, or warrants outstanding.

[d]Receivables could conceivably be excluded for some firms and inventories included for others. Such refinements are seldom employed in practice.

Summary of Financial Statement Ratios

Ratio	Numerator	Denominator
Cash Flow from Operations to Current Liabilities Ratio	Cash Provided by Operations	Average Current Liabilities During the Period
Working Capital Turnover Ratio	Revenues	Average Working Capital During the Pefiod
Long-Term Liquidity Ratios		
Long-Term Debt Ratio	Total Long-Term Debt	Total Long-Term Debt Plus Shareholders'Equity
Debt-Equity Ratio	Total Liabilities	Total Equities (liabilities plus shareholders' equity)
Cash Flow from Operations to Total Liabilities Ratio	Cash Provided by Operations	Average Total Liabilities During the Period
Times Interest Charges Earned	Net Income Before Interest and Income Taxes	Interest Expense

record date. *Dividends* are paid on payment date to those who own the stock on the record date.

recourse. A borrower borrows from a lender and gives the lender a contract promising to repay. "Recourse" refers to the rights of the lender if the borrower does not repay as promised. A recourse loan gives the lender the right to take any asset of the borrower not exempted from such taking by the contract. See also *note receivable discounted.*

recovery of unrealized loss on marketable securities. An *income statement account title* for the *gain* during the current period on the *current asset* portfolio of *marketable equity securities.* This gain will be *recognized* only to the extent that net losses have been recognized in preceding periods in amounts no smaller than the current gain. (The Allowance for Declines in Marketable Equity Securities account can never have a *debit balance.)*

redemption. Retirement by the issuer, usually by a purchase or *call,* of *stocks* or *bonds.*

redemption premium. *Call premium.*

redemption value. The price to be paid by a corporation to retire *bonds* or *preferred stock* if called before *maturity.*

refinancing. An adjustment in the *capital structure* of a *corporation,* involving changes in the nature and amounts of the various classes of *debt* and, in some cases, *capital* as well as other components of *shareholders' equity; asset* carrying values in the accounts remain unchanged.

refunding bond issue. Said of a *bond* issue whose proceeds are used to retire bonds already *outstanding.*

register. Collection of consecutive entries, or other information, in chronological order, such as a check register or an insurance register, which lists all insurance policies owned. If entries are recorded, it may serve as a *journal.*

registered bond. *Principal* of such a *bond* and *interest,* if registered as to interest, is paid to the owner listed on the books of the issuer. As opposed to a bearer bond where the possessor of the bond is entitled to interest and principal.

registrar. An *agent,* usually a bank or trust company, appointed by a corporation to keep track of the names of shareholders and distributions of earnings.

registration statement. Statement required by the Securities Act of 1933 of most companies wishing to have their securities traded in public markets. The statement discloses financial data and other items of interest to potential investors.

regression analysis. A method of *cost estimation* based on statistical techniques for fitting a line (or its equivalent in higher mathematical dimensions) to an observed series of data points, usually by minimizing the sum of squared deviations of the observed data from the fitted line. Common usage calls the cost the analysis explains the "dependent variable"; it calls the variable(s) we use to estimate cost behavior "independent variable(s)." If we use more than one independent variable, the term for the analysis is "multiple regression analysis." See R^2, *standard error, t-value.*

regressive tax. Tax for which the rate decreases as the taxed base, such as income, increases. Contrast with *progressive tax.*

Regulation S-X. The *SEC*'s regulation specifying the form and content of financial reports to the SEC.

rehabilitation. The improving of a used *asset* via an extensive repair. Ordinary *repairs* and *maintenance* restore or maintain expected *service potential* of an asset and are treated as *expenses.* A rehabilitation improves the asset beyond its current service potential, enhancing the service potential to significantly higher level than before the rehabilitation. Once rehabilitated, the asset may be better, but need not be, than it was when new. *Expenditures* for rehabilitation, like those for *betterments* and *improvements,* are *capitalized.*

reinvestment rate. In a *capital budgeting* context, the rate at which cash inflows from a project occurring before the project's completion are invested. Once such a rate is assumed, there will never be multiple *internal rates of return.* See *Descartes' rule of signs.*

relative performance evaluation. Setting performance targets and, sometimes, compensation in relation to performance of others, perhaps in different firms or divisions, facing a similar environment.

relevant cost. *Incremental cost. Opportunity cost.* Cost used by analyst in making a decision.

relevant range. Activity levels over which costs are linear or for which *flexible budget* estimates and *breakeven charts* will remain valid.

relative sales value method. *Net realizable (sales) value method.*

remittance advice. Information on a *check stub,* or on a document attached to a check by the *drawer,* which tells the *payee* why a payment is being made.

rent. A charge for use of land, buildings, or other assets.

reorganization. A major change in the *capital structure* of a corporation that leads to changes in the rights, interests, and implied ownership of the various security owners. Usually results from a *merger* or agreement by senior security holders to take action to forestall *bankruptcy.*

repair. An *expenditure* to restore an *asset's* service potential after damage or after prolonged use. In the second sense, after prolonged use, the difference between repairs and maintenance is one of degree and not of kind. Treated as an *expense* of the period when incurred. Because repairs and maintenance are treated similarly in this regard, the distinction is not important. A repair helps to maintain capacity intact at levels planned when the *asset* was acquired; contrast with *improvement.*

replacement cost. For an asset, the current fair market price to purchase another, similar asset (with the same future benefit or service potential). *Current cost.* See *reproduction cost* and *productive capacity.* See also *distributable income* and *inventory profit.*

replacement cost method of depreciation. The original cost *depreciation* charge is augmented by an amount based upon a portion of the difference between the *current replacement cost* of the asset and its *original cost.*

replacement system of depreciation. See *retirement method of depreciation* for definition and contrast.

report. *Financial statement; auditor's report.*

report form. This form of *balance sheet* typically shows *assets* minus *liabilities* as one total. Then, below that appears

the components of *owners' equity* summing to the same total. Often, the top section shows *current* assets less current liabilities before *noncurrent assets* less noncurrent liabilities. Contrast with *account form.*

reporting objectives (policies). The general purposes for which *financial statements* are prepared. The *FASB* has discussed these in *SFAC No. 1.*

representative item sampling. Sampling where the sample selected is believed to be typical of the entire population from which it is drawn. Compare *specific item sampling.*

reproduction cost. The *cost* necessary to acquire an *asset* similar in all physical respects to another asset for which a *current value* is wanted. See *replacement cost* and *productive capacity* for further contrast.

required rate of return. *Cost of capital.*

requisition. A formal written order or request, such as for withdrawal of supplies from the storeroom.

resale value. *Exit value. Net realizable value.*

research and development. Firms engage in research in hopes of discovering new knowledge that will create a new product, process, or service or improving a present product, process, or service. Development translates research findings or other knowledge into a new or improved product, process, or service. *SFAS No. 2* requires that firms expense costs of such activities as incurred on the grounds that the future benefits are too uncertain to warrant *capitalization* as an asset. This treatment seems questionable to us because we wonder why firms would continue to undertake R&D if there were no expectation of future benefit; if future benefits exist, then its *costs* should be assets.

reserve. When properly used in accounting, the term refers to an account that appropriates *retained earnings* and restricts dividend declarations. Appropriating retained earnings is itself a poor and vanishing practice, so the word should seldom be used in accounting. In addition, used in the past to indicate an asset *contra account* (for example, "reserve for depreciation") or an *estimated liability* (for example, "reserve for warranty costs"). In any case, reserve accounts have *credit* balances and are not pools of *funds* as the unwary reader might infer. If a company has set aside a pool of *cash* (or *marketable securities)* to serve some specific purpose such as paying for a new factory, then it will call that cash a *fund.* No other word in accounting is so misunderstood and misused by laymen and "experts" who should know better. A leading unabridged dictionary defines "reserve" as "Cash, or assets readily convertible into cash, held aside, as by a corporation, bank, state or national government, etc. to meet expected or unexpected demands." This definition is absolutely wrong in accounting. Reserves are not funds. For example, a contingency fund of $10,000 is created by depositing cash in a fund and this entry is made:

Dr. Contingency Fund...............	10,000	
Cr. Cash...................		10,000

The following entry may accompany this entry, if retained earnings are to be appropriated:

Dr. Retained Earnings.	10,000	
Cr. Reserve for Contingencies. . .		10,000

The transaction leading to the first entry is an event of economic significance. The second entry has little economic impact for most firms. The problem with the word "reserve" arises because the second entry can be made without the first – a company can create a reserve, that is appropriate retained earnings, without creating a fund. The problem is at least in part caused by the fact that in common usage, "reserve" means a pool of assets, as in the phrase "oil reserves." The *Internal Revenue Service* does not help in dispelling confusion about the term *reserves*. The federal *income tax* return for corporations uses the title "Reserve for Bad Debts" to mean "Allowance for Uncollectible Accounts" and speaks of the "Reserve Method" in referring to the *allowance method* for estimating *revenue* or *income* reductions from estimated *uncollectibles*.

reserve recognition accounting. In exploration for natural resources, there is the problem of what to do with the expenditures for exploration. Suppose that $10 million is spent to drill 10 holes ($1 million each) and that nine of them are dry whereas one is a gusher containing oil with a *net realizable value* of $40 million. Dry hole, or *successful efforts,* accounting would expense $9 million and *capitalize* $1 million to be *depleted* as the oil was lifted from the ground. *SFAS No. 19,* now suspended, required successful efforts accounting. Full costing would expense nothing, but capitalize the $10 million of drilling costs to be depleted as the oil is lifted from the single productive well. Reserve recognition accounting would capitalize $40 million to be depleted as the oil is lifted, with a $30 million *credit* to *income* or *contributed capital.* The *balance sheet* shows the *net realizable value* of proven oil and gas reserves. The *income statement* has three sorts of items: (1) current income resulting from production or "lifting profit," which is the *revenue* from sales of oil and gas less the expense based on the current valuation amount at which these items had been carried on the balance sheet, (2) profit or loss from exploration efforts where the current value of new discoveries is revenue and all the exploration cost is expense, and (3) gain or loss on changes in current value during the year, which accountants other contexts call a *holding gain or loss.*

reset bond. A bond, typically a *junk bond,* which specifies that periodically the issuer will reset the coupon rate so that the bond sells at *par* in the market. Investment bankers created this type of instrument to make the purchasers of such bonds more sure of getting a fair rate of return, given the riskiness of the issuer. If the issuer gets into financial trouble, then its bonds will trade for less than par in the market. The issuer of a reset bond promises to raise the interest rate and preserve, in principle, the value of the bond. Ironically, the reset feature has often had just the opposite effect. The default risk of many issuers of reset bonds has deteriorated so much that the bonds have dropped to less than 50 percent of par. In order to raise the value to par, the issuer would have to raise the interest rate to more than 25 percent per year. That rate is so large that issuers have declared bankruptcy, rather than attempt to make the large new interest payments.

residual income. In an external reporting context, this term refers to *net income* to *common shares* (= net income less *preferred stock dividends).* In *managerial accounting,* this term refers to the excess of income for a *division* or *segment* of a company over the product of the *cost of capital* for the company multiplied by the average amount of capital invested in the division during the period over which the income was earned.

residual security. A *potentially dilutive security. Options, warrants, convertible bonds,* and *convertible preferred stock.*

residual value. At any time, the estimated or actual, *net realizable value* (that is, proceeds less removal costs) of an *asset,* usually a depreciable *plant asset.* In the context of depreciation accounting, this term is equivalent to *salvage value* and is preferable to *scrap value* because the asset need not be scrapped. Sometimes used to mean net *book value.* In the context of a *noncancelable* lease, the estimated value of the leased asset at the end of the lease period. See *lease.*

responsibility accounting. Accounting for a business by considering various units as separate entities, or *profit centers,* giving management of each unit responsibility for the unit's *revenues* and *expenses.* See *transfer price.*

responsibility center. Part or *segment* of an organization that top management holds accountable for a specified set of activities. Also called "accountability center." See *cost center, investment center, profit center, revenue center.*

restricted assets. Governmental resources restricted by legal or contractual requirements for specific purpose.

restricted retained earnings. That part of *retained earnings* not legally available for *dividends.* See *retained earnings, appropriated.* Bond indentures and other loan contracts can curtail the legal ability of the corporation to declare dividends without formally requiring a retained earnings appropriation, but disclosure is required.

retail inventory method. Ascertaining cost amounts of *ending inventory* as follows (assuming *FIFO): cost of ending inventory = (selling price of *goods available for sale* – sales) x *cost percentage.* Cost of goods sold is then computed from the inventory equation; costs of beginning inventory, purchases and ending inventory are all known. (When *LIFO* is used, the method is similar to the *dollar-value LIFO method).* See *markup.*

retail terminology. See *markup.*

retained earnings. Net *income* over the life of a corporation less all *dividends* (including capitalization through *stock dividends); owners' equity* less *contributed capital.*

retained earnings, appropriated. An *account* set up by crediting it and debiting *retained earnings.* Used to indicate that a portion of retained earnings is not available for dividends. The practice of appropriating retained earnings is misleading unless all capital is earmarked with its use, which is not practicable. Use of formal retained earnings appropriations is declining.

retained earnings statement. *Generally accepted accounting principles* require that whenever *comparative balance sheets* and an *income statement* are presented, there must also be presented a *reconciliation* of the beginning and ending balances in the *retained earnings account.* This reconciliation can appear in a separate statement, in a combined statement of income and retained earnings, or in the balance sheet.

retirement method of depreciation. No entry is recorded for *depreciation expense* until an *asset* is retired from service. Then, an entry is made *debiting* depreciation expense and *crediting* the asset account for the cost of the asset retired. If the retired asset has a *salvage value*, the amount of the debit to depreciation expense is reduced by the amount of salvage value with a corresponding debit to cash, receivables, or salvaged materials. The "replacement system of depreciation" is similar, except that the debit to depreciation expense equals the cost of the new asset less the salvage value, if any, of the old asset. These methods were used by some public utilities. For example, if ten telephone poles are acquired in Year 1 for $60 each and are replaced in Year 10 for $100 each when the salvage value of the old poles is $5 each, then the accounting would be as follows:

Retirement Method.

Plant Assets......................	600	
Cash........................		600
To acquire assets in Year 1.		

Depreciation Expense..............	550	
Salvage Receivable................	50	
Plant Assets......................		600
To record retirement and depreciation in Year 10.		

Plant Assets......................	1,000	
Cash........................		1,000
To record acquisition of new assets in Year 10.		

Replacement Method.

Plant Assets......................	600	
Cash........................		600
To acquire assets in Year 1.		

Depreciation Expense..............	950	
Salvage Receivable................	50	
Cash........................		1,000
To record depreciation on old asset in amount quantified by net cost of replacement asset in Year 10.		

The retirement method is like *FIFO*, in that it records the cost of the first assets as depreciation and puts the cost of the second assets on the balance sheet. The replacement method is like *LIFO* in that it records the cost of the second assets as depreciation expense and leaves the cost of the first assets on the balance sheet.

retirement plan. *Pension plan.*

retroactive benefits. *Pension plan* benefits granted in initiating or amending a *defined-benefit* pension plan that are attributed by the benefit formula to employee services rendered in periods prior to the initiation or amendment. See *prior service costs.*

return. A schedule of information required by governmental bodies, such as the tax return required by the *Internal Revenue Service.* Also the physical return of merchandise. See also *return on investment.*

return of investment. return on capital. *Income* (before distributions to suppliers of capital) for a period. As a rate, this amount divided by average total assets. *Interest,* net of tax effects, should be added back to *net income* for the numerator. See *ratio.*

return on assets. *Net income* plus after-tax *interest charges* plus *minority interest* in income divided by average total *assets.* Perhaps the single most useful ratio for assessing management's overall operating performance. Most financial economists would subtract average non-interest bearing *liabilities* from the denominator. Economists realize that when liabilities do not provide for explicit interest charges, the creditor adjusts the terms of contract, such as setting a higher selling price or lower discount, to those who do not pay cash immediately. (To take an extreme example, consider how much higher salary a worker who receives salary once per year, rather than once per month, would demand.) This ratio requires in the numerator the income amount before the firm accrues any charges to suppliers of funds. We cannot measure the interest charges implicit in the non-interest bearing liabilities because items such as cost of goods sold and salary expense are somewhat larger because of these charges. Subtracting their amount from the denominator adjusts for their implicit cost. Such subtraction assumes that assets financed with non-interest bearing liabilities have the same rate of return as all the other assets.

revenue. The increase in *owners' equity* caused by a service rendered or the sale of goods. *Sales* of products, merchandise, and services, and earnings from *interest, dividends, rents,* and the like. The amount of revenue is the expected *net present value* of the net assets to be received. Do not confuse with *receipt* of *funds,* which may occur before, when, or after revenue is recognized. Contrast with *gain* and *income.* See also *holding gain.* Some writers use the term *gross income* synonymously with *revenue;* avoid such usage.

revenue center. A *responsibility center* within a firm that has control only over revenues generated; contrast with *cost center.* See *profit center.*

revenue expenditure. A phrase sometimes used to mean an *expense,* in contrast to a capital *expenditure* to acquire an *asset* or to discharge a *liability.* Avoid using this phrase; use *period expense* instead.

revenue received in advance. An inferior term for *advances from customers.*

reversal (reversing) entry. An *entry* in which all *debits* and *credits* are the credits and debits, respectively, of another entry, and in the same amounts. It is usually made on the first day of an *accounting period* to reverse a previous *adjusting entry,* usually an *accrual.* The purpose of such entries is to make the bookkeeper's tasks easier. Suppose that salaries are paid every other Friday, with paychecks compensating employees for the 2 weeks just ended. Total salaries accrue at the rate of $5,000 per 5-day work week. The bookkeeper is accustomed to making the following entry every other Friday:

(1) Salary Expense	10,000	
Cash........................		10,000
To record salary expense and salary payments.		

If paychecks are delivered to employees on Friday, November 25, 1988, then the *adjusting entry* made on November 30 (or, perhaps, later) to record accrued salaries for November 28, 29, and 30 would be as follows:

(2) Salary Expense	3,000	
Salaries Payable		3,000
To charge November operations with		
all salaries earned in November.		

The Salary Expense account would be closed as part of the November 30 closing entries. On the next pay day, December 9, the salary entry would have to be as follows:

(3) Salary Expense	7,000	
Salaries Payable	3,000	
Cash.		10,000
To record salary payments split between		
expense for December (7 days) and		
liability carried over from November.		

To make entry (3), the bookkeeper must look back into the records to see how much of the debit is to Salaries Payable accrued from the previous year so that total debits are properly split between third quarter expense and the liability carried over from the second quarter. Notice that this entry forces the bookkeeper both (a) to refer to balances in old accounts and (b) to make an entry different from the one customarily made, entry (1). The reversing entry, made just after the books have been closed for the second quarter, makes the salary entry for December 9, 1988, the same as that made on all other Friday pay days. The reversing entry merely *reverses* the adjusting entry (2):

(4) Salaries Payable	3,000	
Salary Expense.		3,000
To reverse the adjusting entry.		

This entry results in a zero balance in the Salaries Payable account and a credit balance in the Salary Expense account. If entry (4) is made just after the books are closed for November, then the entry on December 9 will be the customary entry (1). Entries (4) and (1) together have exactly the same effect as entry (3).

The procedure for using reversal entries is as follows: The required adjustment to record an accrual (*payable* or *receivable*) is made at the end of an *accounting period;* the closing entry is made as usual; as of the first day of the following period, an entry is made reversing the adjusting entry; when a payment is made (or received), the entry is recorded as though no adjusting entry had been recorded. Whether or not reversal entries are used affects the record-keeping procedures, but not the financial statements.

Also used to describe the entry reversing an incorrect entry before recording the correct entry.

reverse stock split. A stock split in which the number of shares *outstanding* is decreased. See *stock split.*

revolving fund. A fund whose amounts are continually expended and then replenished; for example, a *petty cash fund.*

revolving loan. A *loan* that is expected to be renewed at *maturity.*

right. The privilege to subscribe to new *stock* issues or to purchase stock. Usually, rights are contained in securities called warrants and its owner may sell the *warrant.* See also *preemptive right.*

risk. A measure of the variability of the *return on investment.* For a given expected amount of return, most people prefer less risk to more risk. Therefore, in rational markets, investments with more risk usually promise, or investors are expected to yield, a higher rate of return than investments with lower risk. Most people use "risk" and "uncertainty" as synonyms. In technical language, however, these terms have different meanings. We use "risk" when we know the probabilities attached to the various outcomes are known, such as the probabilities of heads or tails in the flip of a fair coin. "Uncertainty" refers to an event where the probabilities of the outcomes, such as winning or losing a lawsuit, can only be estimated.

risk adjusted discount rate. In a *capital budgeting* context, a decision analyst compares projects by comparing their net *present values* for a given *interest* rate, usually the cost of capital. If the analyst considers a given project's outcome to be much more or much less risky than the normal undertakings of the company, then the analyst will use a larger interest rate in discounting (if the project is more risky) or smaller (if less risky), and the rate used is said to be "risk-adjusted."

risk premium. Extra compensation paid to an employee or extra *interest* paid to a lender, over amounts usually considered normal, in return for their undertaking to engage in activities more risky than normal.

ROA. *Return on assets.*

ROI. *Return on investment,* but usually used to refer to a single project and expressed as a ratio: *income* divided by average *cost* of *assets* devoted to the project.

royalty. Compensation for the use of property, usually a patent, copyrighted material, or natural resources. The amount is often expressed as a percentage of receipts from using the property or as an amount per unit produced.

RRA. See *Reserve recognition accounting.*

RRR. Required rate of return.

rule of 69. An amount of money invested at r percent per period will double in $69/r + .35$ periods. This approximation is accurate to one tenth of a period for interest rates between 1/4 and 100 percent per period. For example, at 10 percent per period, the rule says that a given sum will double in $69/10 + .35 = 7.25$ periods. At 10 percent per period, a given sum actually doubles in 7.27+ periods.

rule of 72. An amount of money invested at r percent per period will double in $72/r$ periods. A reasonable approximation for interest rates between 4 and 10 percent, but not nearly as accurate as the *rule of 69* for interest rates outside that range. For example, at 10 percent per period, the rule says that a given sum will double in $72/10 = 7.2$ periods.

rule of 78. The rule followed by many finance companies for allocating earnings on *loans* among the months of a year on the sum-of-the-months'-digits basis when the borrower makes equal monthly payments to the lender. The sum of the digits from 1 through 12 is 78, so 12/78 of the year's earnings are allocated to the first month, 11/78 to the second month, and so on. This approximation allocates more of the early payments to interest and less to principal than does the correct, compound interest method. Hence, lenders still use this method even though present day computers can make the compound interest computation as easily as the they can carry out the approximation. See *sum-of-the-years'-digits depreciation.*

ruling (and balancing) an account. The process of summarizing a series of entries in an *account* by computing a new *balance* and drawing double lines to indicate the information above the double lines has been summarized in the new balance. The process is illustrated below. The steps are as follows: (1) Compute the sum of all *debit* entries including opening debit balance, if any – $1,464.16. (2) Compute the sum of all credit entries including opening credit balance, if any – $413.57. (3) If the amount in (1) is larger than the amount in (2), then write the excess as a credit with a check mark – $1,464.16 – $413.57 = $1,050.59. (4) Add both debit and credit columns, which should both now sum to the same amount, and show that identical total at the foot of both columns. (5) Draw double lines under those numbers and write the excess of debits over credits as the new debit balance with a check mark. (6) If the amount in (2) is larger than the amount in (1), then write the excess as a debit with a check mark. (7) Do steps (4) and (5) except that the excess becomes the new credit balance. (8) If the amount in (1) is equal to the amount in (2), then the balance is zero and only the totals with the double lines beneath them need be shown. This process is illustrated in the accompanying figure.

S

SA; Société anonyme. France. A *corporation.*

SAB. Staff Accounting Bulletin of the *SEC.*

safe-harbor lease. A form of *tax-transfer lease.*

safety stock. Extra items of *inventory* kept on hand to protect against running out.

salary. Compensation earned by managers, administrators, and professionals, not based on an hourly rate. Contrast with *wage.*

sale. A *revenue* transaction where *goods* or *services* are delivered to a customer in return for cash or a contractual obligation to pay.

sale and leaseback. Describes a *financing* transaction where improved property is sold but is taken back for use on a long-term *lease.* Such transactions often have advantageous income tax effects but usually have no effect on *financial statement income.*

sales activity variance. *Sales volume variance.*

sales allowance. A reduction in sales *invoice* price usually given because the *goods* received by the buyer are not exactly what was ordered. The amounts of such adjustments are often accumulated by the seller in a temporary *revenue contra account* having this, or a similar, title. See *sales discount.*

sales basis of revenue recognition. The firm recognizes *revenue,* not as it produces goods nor as it receives orders, but only when it has completed the sale by delivering the goods or services and has received cash or a claim to cash. Most firms recognize revenue on this basis. Compare with the *percentage-of-completion method* and the *installment method.* Identical with the *completed contract method* but this latter term ordinarily applies only to *long-term* construction projects.

sales contra, estimated uncollectibles. A title for the *contra- revenue account* to recognize estimated reductions in income caused by accounts receivable that will not be collected. See *bad debt expense, allowance for uncollectibles,* and *allowance method.*

sales discount. Reduction in sales *invoice* price usually offered for prompt payment. See *terms of sale* and *2/10, n/30.*

sales return. The physical return of merchandise; the amounts of such returns are often accumulated by the seller in a temporary *revenue contra account.*

An Open Account, Ruled and Balanced
(Steps indicated in parentheses correspond to steps described in "ruling an account")

	Date 1990	Explanation	Ref.	Debit (1)		Date 1990	Explanation	Ref.	Credit (2)		
	Jan. 1	Balance	✓	100	00						
	Jan. 13		VR	121	37	Sept. 15		J		42	
	Mar. 20		VR	56	42	Nov. 12		J	413	15	
	June 5		J	1,138	09	Dec. 31	Balance	✓	1,050	59	(3)
	Aug. 18		J	1	21						
	Nov. 20		VR	38	43						
	Dec. 7		VR	8	64						
(4)			VR	1,464	16				1,464	16	(4)
(5)	Jan. 1	Balance	✓	1,050	59						

sales-type (capital) lease. See *capital lease.* When a manufacturer (or other firm) that ordinarily sells goods enters a capital lease as *lessor,* the lease is called a "sales-type lease." When a financial firm, such as a bank or insurance company or leasing company, acquires the asset from the manufacturer and then enters a capital lease as lessor, the lease is called a "direct-financing-type lease." The manufacturer recognizes its ordinary profit on executing the sales-type capital lease, but the financial firm does not recognize profit on executing a capital lease of the direct-financing type.

sales value method. *Relative sales value method.* See *net realizable value method.*

sales volume variance. *Budgeted contribution margin* per unit times (planned sales volume minus actual sales volume).

salvage value. Actual or estimated selling price, net of removal or disposal costs, of a used *plant asset* to be sold or otherwise retired. See *residual value.*

SAR. *Summary annual report.*

SARL. Société à responsabilité limitée. France. A *corporation* with limited liability and a life of no more than 99 years. Must have at least two and no more than 50 *shareholders.*

SAS. *Statement on Auditing Standards* of the *AICPA.*

scale effect. See *discounted cash flow.*

scatter diagram. A graphic representation of the relationship between two or more variables within a population.

schedule. A supporting set of calculations, with explanations, that show how figures in a *financial statement* or tax return are derived.

scientific method. *Effective interest method* of amortizing *bond discount* or *premium.*

scrap value. *Salvage value* assuming item is to be junked. A *net realizable value. Residual value.*

SEC. Securities and Exchange Commission. An agency authorized by the U.S. Congress to regulate, among other things, the financial reporting practices of most public corporations. The SEC has indicated that it will usually allow the *FASB* to set accounting principles but it often requires more disclosure than required by the FASB. The SEC states its accounting requirements in its *Accounting Series Releases (ASR), Financial Reporting Releases (FRR)*, Accounting and Auditing Enforcement Releases, *Staff Accounting Bulletins* (these are, strictly speaking, interpretations by the accounting staff, not rules of the Commissioners themselves) and *Regulation S-X.* See also *registration statement, 10-K,* and *20-F.*

secret reserve. *Hidden reserve.*

Securities and Exchange Commission. *SEC.*

security. Document that indicates ownership, such as a *share* of *stock,* or indebtedness, such as a *bond,* or potential ownership, such as an *option* or *warrant.*

security available for sale. According to *SFAS No. 115* (1993), a *debt* or *equity security* which is not a *trading security* or a debt security which is not a *security held to maturity.*

security held to maturity. According to *SFAS No. 115* (1993), a *debt security* the holder has both the ability and intent to hold to *maturity.*

segment (of a business). As defined by *APB Opinion No. 30,* "a component of an *entity* whose activities represent a separate major line of business or class of customer.... [It may be] a *subsidiary,* a division, or a department,... provided that its *assets,* results of *operations,* and activities can be clearly distinguished, physically and operationally for financial reporting purposes, from the other assets, results of operations, and activities of the entity." In *SFAS No. 14* a segment is defined as "A component of an enterprise engaged in promoting a product or service or a group of related products and services primarily to unaffiliated customers... for a profit."

segment reporting. Reporting of *sales, income* and *assets* by *segments of a business,* usually classified by nature of products sold but sometimes by geographical area where goods are produced or sold or by type of customers. Sometimes called "line of business reporting." *Central corporate expenses* are not allocated to the segments.

self balancing. A set of records with equal *debits* and *credits* such as the *ledger* (but not individual accounts), the *balance sheet,* and a *fund* in nonprofit accounting.

self-check(ing) digit. A digit forming part of an account or code number, normally the last digit of the number, which is mathematically derived from the other numbers of the code and is used to detect errors in transcribing the code number.

self insurance. See *insurance.*

self-sustaining foreign operation. A foreign operation which is financially and operationally independent of the reporting enterprise such that the exposure to exchange rate changes is limited to the reporting enterprise's net investment in the foreign exchange.

selling and administrative expenses. *Expenses* not specifically identifiable with, nor assigned to, production.

semifixed costs. *Costs* that increase with activity as a step function.

semivariable costs. *Costs* that increase strictly linearly with activity but that are positive at zero activity level. Royalty fees of 2 percent of sales are variable; royalty fees of $1,000 per year plus 2 percent of sales are semivariable.

senior securities. *Bonds* as opposed to *preferred stock; preferred stock* as opposed to *common stock.* The senior security has a claim against *earnings* or *assets* that must be met before the claim of less senior securities.

sensitivity analysis. Most decision making requires the use of assumptions. Sensitivity analysis is the study of how the outcome of a decision-making process changes as one or more of the assumptions change.

sequential access. Access to computer storage where information can be located only by a sequential search of the storage file. Compare *direct access*.

serial bonds. An *issue* of *bonds* that mature in part at one date, another part on another date, and so on; the various maturity dates usually are equally spaced; contrast with *term bonds*.

service bureau. A commercial data center providing service to various customers.

service basis of depreciation. *Production method.*

service cost. (current) service cost. *Pension plan expenses incurred* during an *accounting period* for employment services performed during that period; contrast with *prior service cost* and see *funded*.

service department. A department, such as the personnel or computer department, that provides services to other departments, rather than direct work on a salable product; contrast with *production department*. A firm must allocate costs of service departments whose services benefit manufacturing operations to *product costs* under *full absorption costing*.

service life. Period of expected usefulness of an asset; may not be the same as *depreciable life* for income tax purposes.

service potential. The future benefits embodied in an item that cause the item to be classified as an *asset*. Without service potential, an item has no future benefits, and accounting will not classify the item as an asset. *SFAC No. 6* suggests that the primary characteristic of service potential is the ability to generate future net cash inflows.

services. Useful work done by a person, a machine, or an organization. See *goods and services*.

setup. The time or costs required to prepare production equipment for doing a job.

SFAC. *Statement of Financial Accounting Concepts* of the *FASB*.

SFAS. *Statement of Financial Accounting Standards* of the *FASB*.

shadow price. One output of a *linear programming* analysis is the potential value of having available more of the scarce resources that constrain the production process; for example, the value of having more time available on a machine tool critical to the production of two products. Common terminology refers to this value as "shadow price" or the "dual value" of the scarce resource.

share. A unit of *stock* representing ownership in a corporation.

shareholders' equity. *Proprietorship* or *owners' equity* of a corporation. Because *stock* means inventory in Australian, British, and Canadian usage, the term "shareholders' equity" is usually used by Australian, British, and Canadian writers, who do not use the term "stockholders' equity."

short-run. short-term. The opposite of *long-run* or *long-term*. This pair of terms is equally imprecise.

short-term. Current; ordinarily, due within one year.

short-term liquidity risk. The risk that an *entity* will not have enough *cash* in the *short run* to pay its *debts*.

shrinkage. An excess of *inventory* shown on the *books* over actual physical quantities on hand. Can result from theft or shoplifting as well as from evaporation or general wear and tear. Some accountants, in an attempt to downplay their own errors, use the term to mean mistakes in record keeping that later must be embarrassingly corrected, resulting in material changes in reported income. There is no need to use the term "shrinkage" for the correction of mistakes because adequate terminology exists for describing mistakes.

shutdown cost. Those fixed cost which continue to be incurred after production has ceased. The costs of closing down a particular production facility.

sight draft. A demand for payment drawn by a person to whom money is owed. The *draft* is presented to the borrower's (the debtor's) bank in expectation that the borrower will authorize its bank to disburse the funds. Such drafts are often used when a seller sells goods to a new customer in a different city. The seller is not sure whether the buyer will pay the bill. The seller sends the *bill* of lading, or other evidence of ownership of the goods, along with a sight draft to the buyer's bank. Before the goods can be released to the buyer, the buyer must instruct its bank to honor the sight draft by withdrawing funds from the buyers' account. Once the sight draft is honored, the bill of lading or other document evidencing ownership is handed over to the buyer and the goods become the property of the buyer.

simple interest. *Interest* calculated on *principal* where interest earned during periods before maturity of the loan is neither added to the principal nor paid to the lender. *Interest = principal x interest rate x time,* where the rate is a rate per period (typically a year) and time is expressed in units of that period. For example, if the *rate* is annual and the time is two months, then in the formula, use 2/12 for *time.* Seldom used in economic calculations except for periods less than one year and then only for computational convenience; contrast with *compound interest.*

single-entry accounting. Accounting that is neither *self-balancing* nor *articulated;* that is, it does not rely on equal *debits* and *credits. No journal entries* are made. *Plugging* is required to derive *owners' equity* for the *balance sheet.*

single proprietorship. *Sole proprietorship.*

single-step. Said of an *income statement* where *ordinary revenue* and *gain* items are shown first and totaled. Then all ordinary *expenses* and *losses* are totaled. Their difference, plus the effect of *income from discontinued operations* and *extraordinary items,* is shown as *net income;* contrast with *multiple-step* and see *proprietorship theory.*

sinking fund. *Assets* and their earnings earmarked for the retirement of bonds or other long-term obligations. Earnings of sinking fund investments are taxable income of the company.

sinking fund method of depreciation. The periodic charge is an amount so that when the charges are considered to be an *annuity,* the value of the annuity at the end of depreciable life is equal to the *acquisition cost* of the asset. In theory, the charge for a period ought also to include interest on the accumulated depreciation at the start of the period as well. A *fund* of cash is not necessarily, or even usually, accumulated. This method is rarely used.

skeleton account. *T-account.*

slide. The name of the error made by a bookkeeper in recording the digits of a number correctly with the decimal point misplaced; for example, recording $123.40 as $1,234.00 or as $12.34. If the only errors in a *trial balance* result from one or more slides, then the difference between the sum of the *debits* and the sum of the *credits* will be divisible by nine. Not all differences between sums of debits and sums of credits in trial balances divisible by nine result from slides. See *transposition error.*

SMAC. The Society of Management Accountants of Canada. The national association of accountants whose provincial associations engage in industrial and governmental accounting. The association undertakes research and administers an educational program and comprehensive examinations; those who pass qualify to be designated RIAs.

SNC. Société en nom collectif. France. A *partnership.*

soak-up method. The *equity method.*

Social Security taxes. Taxes levied by the federal government on both employers and employees to provide *funds* to pay retired persons (or their survivors) who are entitled to receive such payments, either because they paid Social Security taxes themselves or because the Congress has declared them eligible. Unlike a *pension plan,* the Social Security system does not collect funds and invest them for many years. The tax collections in a given year are used primarily to pay benefits for that year. At any given time the system has a multi-trillion dollar unfunded obligation to current workers for their eventual retirement benefits. See *Old Age, Survivors, Disability,* and *(Hospital) Insurance.*

software. The programming aids, such as compilers, sort and report programs, and generators, which extend the capabilities of and simplify the use of the computer, as well as certain operating systems and other control programs. Compare *hardware.*

sole proprietorship. All *owners' equity* belongs to one person.

solvent. Able to meet debts when due.

SOP. *Statement of Position* (of *AcSEC* of the *AICPA*).

sound value. A phrase used mainly in appraisals of *fixed assets* to mean *fair market value* or *replacement cost* in present condition.

source of funds. Any *transaction* that increases *cash* and *marketable securities* held as *current assets.*

sources and uses statement. *Statement of cash flows.*

SOYD. *Sum-of-the years'-digits depreciation.*

SP. Société en participation. France. A silent *partnership,* where the managing partner acts for the partnership as an individual in transacting with others who need not know that the person represents a partnership.

special assessment. A compulsory levy made by a governmental unit on property to pay the costs of a specific improvement or service presumed not to benefit the general public but only the owners of the property so assessed. Accounted for in a special assessment fund.

special journal. A *journal,* such as a sales journal or cash disbursements journal, to record *transactions* of a similar nature that occur frequently.

special revenue debt. Debt of a governmental unit backed only by revenues from specific sources such as tolls from a bridge.

specific identification method. Method for valuing *ending inventory* and *cost of goods sold* by identifying actual units sold and in inventory and summing the actual costs of those individual units. Usually used for items with large unit value, such as precious jewelry, automobiles, and fur coats.

specific item sampling. Sampling where particular items are selected because of their nature, value, or method of recording. Compare *representative item sampling.*

specific price changes. Changes in the market prices of specific *goods and services;* contrast with *general price level changes.*

specific price index. A measure of the price of a specific good or service, or a small group of similar goods or services, at one time relative to the price during a base period; contrast with *general price index.* See *dollar-value LIFO method.*

spending variance. In *standard cost systems,* the *rate* or *price variance* for *overhead costs.*

split. *Stock split.* Sometimes called "splitup."

splitoff point. The point where all costs are no longer *joint costs* but an analyst can identify costs associated with individual products or perhaps with a smaller number of *joint products.*

spoilage. See *abnormal spoilage* and *normal spoilage.*

spread sheet. For many years, this term referred specifically to a *work sheet* organized like a *matrix* that provides a two-way classification of accounting data. The rows and columns both have labels which are *account* titles. An entry in a row represents a *debit* whereas an entry in a column represents a *credit.* Thus, the number "100" in the "cash" row and the "accounts receivable" column records an entry debiting cash and crediting accounts receivable for $100. A given row total indicates all debit entries to the account represented by that row, and a given column total indicates the sum of all credit entries to the account represented by the column.

Since personal computer software has become familiar, this term refers to any file created by programs such as Lotus 1-2-3® and Microsoft Excel®. Such files have rows and columns but they need not represent debits and credits. Moreover, they can have more than two dimensions.

squeeze. A term sometimes used for *plug.*

SSARS. See *Statement on Standards for Accounting and Review Services.*

stabilized accounting. *Constant dollar accounting.*

stable monetary unit assumption. In spite of *inflation* that appears to be a way of life, the assumption that underlies *historical cost/nominal dollar accounting* – namely that current dollars and dollars of previous years can be meaningfully added together. No specific recognition is given to changing values of the dollar in the usual *financial statements*. See *constant dollar accounting.*

Staff Accounting Bulletin. An interpretation issued by the Staff of the Chief Accountant of the *SEC* "suggesting" how the various *Accounting Series Releases* should be applied in practice. The suggestions are effectively part of *GAAP.*

standard cost. Anticipated *cost* of producing a unit of output; a predetermined cost to be assigned to products produced. Standard cost implies a norm – what costs should be. Budgeted cost implies a forecast – something likely, but not necessarily a "should," as implied by a norm. Firms use standard costs as the benchmark for gauging good and bad performance. While a firm may similarly use a budget, it need not. A budget may simply be a planning document, subject to changes whenever plans change, whereas standard costs usually change annually or when technology significantly changes or costs of labor and materials significantly change.

standard costing. *Costing* based on *standard costs.*

standard costing system. *Product costing* using *standard costs* rather than actual costs. May be based on either *full absorption* or *variable costing* principles.

standard error (of regression coefficients). A measure of the uncertainty about the magnitude of the estimated parameters of an equation fit with a *regression analysis.*

standard manufacturing overhead. *Overhead costs* expected to be incurred per unit of time and per unit produced.

standard price (rate). Unit price established for materials or labor used in *standard cost systems.*

standard quantity allowed. The quantity of direct material or direct labor (inputs) that production should have used if it produced the units of output in accordance with preset *standards.*

standby costs. A type of *capacity cost*, such as property taxes, incurred even if a firm shuts down operations completely. Contrast with *enabling costs.*

stated capital. Amount of capital contributed by shareholders. Sometimes used to mean *legal capital.*

stated value. A term sometimes used for the *face amount of capital stock*, when no *par value* is indicated. Where there is stated value per share, it may be set by the directors (in which case, capital *contributed in excess of stated value* may come into being).

statement of affairs. A *balance sheet* showing immediate *liquidation* amounts, rather than *historical costs*, usually prepared when *insolvency* or *bankruptcy* is imminent. The *going-concern assumption* is not used.

statement of cash flows. The *FASB* requires that all for-profit companies present a schedule of *cash receipts* and *payments*, classified by *investing, financing,* and *operating activities.* Companies may report operating activities with either the direct method (where only receipts and payments of cash appear) or the indirect method (which starts with *net income* and shows adjustments for *revenues* not currently producing cash and for *expenses* not currently using cash). "Cash" includes cash equivalents such as Treasury bills, commercial paper, and *marketable securities* held as *current assets.* Sometimes called the "funds statement." Before 1987, the FASB required the presentation of a similar statement called the *statement of changes in financial position*, which tended to emphasize *working capital*, not cash. See *dual transactions assumption.*

statement of changes in financial position. As defined by *APB Opinion No. 19*, a statement that explains the changes in *working capital* (or cash) balances during a period and shows the changes in the working capital (or cash) accounts themselves. This statement has been replaced with the *statement of cash flows.*

statement of charge and discharge. A financial statement, showing *net assets* or *income*, drawn up by an executor or administrator, to account for receipts and dispositions of cash or other assets in an estate or trust.

Statement of Financial Accounting Concepts. SFAC. One of a series of *FASB* publications in its *conceptual framework* for *financial accounting* and reporting. Such statements set forth objectives and fundamentals to be the basis for specific financial accounting and reporting standards.

Statement of Financial Accounting Standards. SFAS. See *FASB.*

statement of financial position. *Balance sheet.*

Statement of Position. SOP. A recommendation on an emerging accounting problem issued by the *AcSEC* of the *AICPA.* The AICPA's Code of Professional Ethics specifically states that *CPAs* need not treat *SOPs* as they do rules from the *FASB*, but a CPA would be wary of departing from the recommendations of a *SOP.*

statement of retained earnings (income). A statement that reconciles the beginning-of-period and end-of-period balances in the *retained earnings* account. It shows the effects of *earnings, dividend declarations,* and *prior-period adjustments.*

statement of significant accounting policies (principles). *APB Opinion No. 22* requires that every *annual report* summarize the significant *accounting principles* used in compiling the annual report. This summary may be a separate exhibit or the first *note* to the financial statements.

Statement on Auditing Standards. SAS. No. 1 of this series (1973) codifies all statements on auditing standards previously promulgated by the *AICPA.* Later numbers deal with specific auditing standards and procedures.

Statement on Standards for Accounting and Review Services. SSARS. Pronouncements issued by the *AICPA* on *unaudited financial statements* and unaudited financial information of nonpublic entities.

static budget. *Fixed budget.*

status quo. Events or costs incurrences that will happen or a firm expects to happen in the absence of taking some contemplated action.

statutory tax rate. The tax rate specified in the *income tax law* for each type of income (for example, *ordinary income, capital gain or loss*).

step allocation method. *Step-down method.*

step cost. *Semifixed cost.*

step-down method. The method for *allocating service department* costs that starts by allocating one service department's costs to *production departments* and to all other service departments. Then the firm allocates a second service department's costs, including costs allocated from the first, to production departments and to all other service departments except the first one. In this fashion, a firm may allocate the costs of all service departments, including previous allocations, to production departments and to those service departments whose costs it has not yet allocated.

stepped cost. *Semifixed cost.*

sterilized allocation. Optimal decisions result from considering *incremental costs,* only. *Allocations* of *joint* or *common costs* are never required for optimal decisions. An allocation of these costs that causes the optimal decision choice not to differ from the one that occurs when joint or common costs are unallocated is "sterilized" with respect to that decision. The term was first used in this context by Arthur L. Thomas. Because *absorption costing* requires that all manufacturing costs be allocated to product and because some allocations can lead to bad decisions, Thomas (and we) advocate that the allocation scheme chosen lead to sterilized allocations that do not alter the otherwise optimal decision. There is, however, no single allocation scheme that is always sterilized with respect to all decisions. Thus, Thomas (and we) advocate that decisions be made on the basis of incremental costs before any allocations.

stewardship. The function of management to be accountable for an *entity's* resources, for their efficient use, and for protecting them, as well as is practicable, from adverse impact. Some theorists believe that a primary goal of *accounting* is to aid users of *financial statements* in their assessment of management's performance in stewardship.

stock. *Inventory. Capital stock.* A measure of the amount of something on hand at a specific time; in this sense, contrast with *flow.*

stock appreciation rights. The employer promises to pay to the employee an amount of *cash* on a certain future date. The amount of cash is the difference between the *market value* of a certain number of *shares* of *stock* in the employer's company on a given future date and some base price set on the date the rights are granted. This form of compensation is sometimes used because both changes in tax laws in recent years have made *stock options* relatively less attractive. *GAAP* computes compensation based on the difference between market value of the shares and the base price set at the time of the grant. *Expense* is recognized as the holder of the rights performs the services required for the rights to be exercised.

stock dividend. A so-called *dividend* where additional *shares* of *capital stock* are distributed, without cash payments, to existing shareholders. It results in a *debit* to *retained earnings* in the amount of the market value of the shares issued and a *credit* to *capital stock* accounts. It is ordinarily used to indicate that earnings retained have been permanently reinvested in the business; contrast with a *stock split,* which requires no entry in the capital stock accounts other than a notation that the *par* or *stated value* per share has been changed.

stock option. The right to purchase a specified number of shares of *stock* for a specified price at specified times, usually granted to employees; contrast with *warrant.*

stockout. A firm needs a unit of *inventory* in production or to sell to a customer but it is unavailable.

stock-out costs. *Contribution margin* or other measure of *profits* not earned because a seller has run out of *inventory* and cannot fill a customer's order. A firm may incur an extra cost because of delay in filling an order.

stock right. See *right.*

stock split. Increase in the number of common shares outstanding resulting from the issuance of additional shares to existing shareholders without additional capital contributions by them. Does not increase the total *par* (or *stated*) *value* of *common stock* outstanding because par (or stated) value per share is reduced in inverse proportion. A three-for-one stock split reduces par (or stated) value per share to one third of its former amount. Stock splits are usually limited to distributions that increase the number of shares outstanding by 20 percent or more; compare with *stock dividend.*

stock subscriptions. See *subscription* and *subscribed stock.*

stock warrant. See *warrant.*

stockholders' equity. See *shareholders' equity.*

stores. *Raw materials,* parts, and supplies.

straight-debt value. An estimate of what the *market value* of a *convertible bond* would be if the bond did not contain a conversion privilege.

straight line depreciation. If the *depreciable life* is n periods, then the periodic *depreciation* charge is $1/n$ of the *depreciable cost.* Results in equal periodic charges and accountants sometimes call it "straight time depreciation."

strategic plan. A statement of the method for achieving an organization's goals.

stratified sampling. A method of choosing a *sample* in which the investigator divides the entire *population* first into relatively homogeneous subgroups (strata) and then selects *random samples* from these subgroups.

street security. A stock certificate in immediately transferable form, most commonly because it is registered in the name of the broker and endorsed in blank.

Subchapter S Corporation. A firm legally organized as a *corporation* but taxed as if it were a *partnership*. Tax terminology calls the corporations paying their own income taxes "C Corporations."

subject to. Qualifications in an *auditor's report* usually caused by a *material* uncertainty in the valuation of an item, such as future promised payments from a foreign government or outcome of pending litigation.

subordinated. Said of *debt* whose claim on income or assets is junior to, or comes after, claims of other debt.

subscribed stock. A *shareholders' equity* account showing the capital that will be contributed as soon as the subscription price is collected. A subscription is a legal contract so that an entry is made *debiting* an *owners' equity contra account* and *crediting* subscribed stock as soon as the stock is subscribed.

subscription. Agreement to buy a *security,* or to purchase periodicals, such as magazines.

subsequent events. *Post-statement events.*

subsidiary. Said of a company more than 50 percent of whose voting stock is owned by another.

subsidiary (ledger) accounts. The *accounts* in a *subsidiary ledger.*

subsidiary ledger. The *ledger* that contains the detailed accounts whose total is shown in a *controlling account* of the *general ledger.*

successful efforts accounting. In petroleum accounting, the *capitalization* of the drilling costs of only those wells that contain gas or oil. See *reserve recognition accounting* for an example.

sum-of-the-years'-digits depreciation. SYD. SOYD. An *accelerated depreciation* method for an asset with *depreciable life* of *n* years where the charge in period *i* ($i = 1,...,n$) is the fraction $(n + 1 - i)/[n(n + 1)/2]$ of the *depreciable cost.* If an asset has a depreciable cost of $15,000 and a 5 year depreciable life, for example, the depreciation charges would be $5,000 (= 5/15 x $15,000) in the first year, $4,000 in the second, $3,000 in the third, $2,000 in the fourth, and $1,000 in the fifth. The name derives from the fact that the denominator in the fraction is the sum of the digits from 1 through *n*.

summary annual report. Condensed financial statements distributed in lieu of the usual *annual report.* Since 1987, the *SEC* has allowed firms to include such statements in the annual report to shareholders so long as the full, detailed statements appear in SEC filings and in *proxy* materials sent to shareholders.

summary of significant accounting principles. *APB Opinion No. 22* requires that every *annual report* summarize the significant *accounting principles* used in compiling the annual report. A firm may present this summary as a separate exhibit or as the first *note* to the financial statements.

sunk cost. *Costs* incurred in the past that current and future decisions cannot affect and, hence, are irrelevant for decision making aside from *income tax* effects; contrast with *incremental costs* and *imputed costs.* For example, the *acquisition* cost of machinery is irrelevant to a decision of whether or not to scrap the machinery. The current *exit value* of the machine is the *opportunity cost* of continuing to own it, and the cost of, say, electricity to run the machine is an incremental cost of its operation. Sunk costs become relevant for decision making when the analysis requires taking *income taxes (gain* or *loss* on disposal of asset) into account because the cash payment for income taxes depends on the tax basis of the asset. Avoid the term in careful writing because it is ambiguous. Consider, for example, a machine costing $100,000 with current *salvage* value of $20,000. Some (including us) would say that $100,000 is "sunk"; others would say that only $80,000 is "sunk."

supplementary statements (schedules). Statements (schedules) in addition to the four basic *financial statements* (including the *retained earnings* reconciliation as a basic statement).

surplus. A word once used but now considered poor terminology; prefaced by "earned" to mean *retained earnings* and prefaced by "capital" to mean *capital contributed in excess of par (or stated) value.*

surplus reserves. Of all the words in accounting, *reserve* is the most objectionable and *surplus* is the second most objectionable. This phrase, then, has nothing to recommend it. It means *appropriated retained earnings.*

suspense account. A *temporary account* used to record part of a transaction prior to final analysis of that transaction. For example, if a business regularly classifies all sales into a dozen or more different categories but wants to deposit the proceeds of cash sales every day, it may credit a sales suspense account pending detailed classification of all sales into sales, type 1; sales, type 2; and so on.

sustainable income. The part of *distributable income* (computed from *current cost* data) that the firm can be expected to earn in the next accounting period if operations are continued at the same levels as during the current period. *Income from discontinued operations,* for example, may be distributable but not sustainable.

S-X. See *Regulation S-X.*

SYD. *Sum-of-the-years'-digits depreciation. SOYD.*

T

T-account. Account form shaped like the letter T with the title above the horizontal line. *Debits* are shown to the left of the vertical line, *credits* to the right.

t-statistic. For an estimated *regression* coefficient, the estimated coefficient divided by the *standard error* of the estimate.

take-home pay. The amount of a paycheck; earned wages or *salary* reduced by deductions for *income taxes, Social Security taxes,* contributions to fringe benefit plans, union dues, and so on. Take home pay might be as little as half of earned compensation.

take-or-pay contract. As defined by *SFAS No. 47,* an agreement between a purchaser and a seller that provides for the purchaser to pay specified amounts periodically in return for products or services. The purchaser must make specified minimum payments even if it does not take delivery of the contracted products or services.

taking a bath. To incur a large loss. See *big bath.*

tangible. Having physical form. Accounting has never satisfactorily defined the distinction between tangible and intangible assets. Typically, intangibles are defined by giving an exhaustive list and everything not on the list is defined as tangible. See *intangible asset* for such a list.

target cost. *Standard cost.*

tax. A nonpenal, but compulsory, charge levied by a government on income, consumption, wealth, or other basis, for the benefit of all those governed. The term does not include fines or specific charges for benefits accruing only to those paying the charges, such as licenses, permits, special assessments, admission fees, and tolls.

tax allocation: interperiod. See *deferred income tax liability.*

tax allocation: intrastatement. The showing of income tax effects on *extraordinary items, income from discontinued operations,* and *prior-period adjustments* along with these items, separately from income taxes on other income. See *net-of-tax reporting.*

tax avoidance. See *tax shelter* and *loophole.*

tax basis of assets and liabilities. A concept important for applying *SFAS No. 109* on *deferred income taxes.* Two *assets* will generally have different *book values* if the firm paid different amounts for them or *amortizes* them on a different schedule, or both. Similarly a single asset will generally have a different book value than it will have for tax purposes if the firm recorded different *acquisition* amounts for the asset for book and tax purposes or amortizes it differently for book and for tax purposes, or both. The difference between financial book value and income tax basis becomes important in computing deferred income tax amounts. The adjusted cost in the financial records is the "book basis" and the adjusted amount in the tax records is the "tax basis." Differences between book and tax basis can arise for *liabilities* as well as for assets.

tax credit. A subtraction from taxes otherwise payable, contrast with *tax deduction.*

tax deduction. A subtraction from *revenues* and *gains* to arrive at taxable income. Tax deductions are technically different from tax *exemptions,* but the effect of both is to reduce gross income in computing taxable income. Both are different from *tax credits,* which are subtracted from the computed tax itself in computing taxes payable. If the tax rate is the fraction *t* of pretax income, then a *tax credit* of $1 is worth $1/*t* of *tax deductions.*

tax evasion. The fraudulent understatement of taxable revenues or overstatement of deductions and expenses or both; contrast with *tax shelter* and *loophole.*

tax exempts. See *municipal bonds.*

tax shelter. The legal avoidance of, or reduction in, *income taxes* resulting from a careful reading of the complex income tax regulations and the subsequent rearrangement of financial affairs to take advantage of the regulations. Often the term is used pejoratively, but the courts have long held that an individual or corporation has no obligation to pay taxes any larger than the legal minimum. If the public concludes that a given tax shelter is "unfair," then the laws and regulations can be, and have been, changed. Sometimes used to refer to the investment that permits tax avoidance. See *loophole.*

tax shield. The amount of an *expense* that reduces taxable income but does not require *working capital,* such as *depreciation.* Sometimes this term is expanded to include expenses that reduce taxable income and use working capital. A depreciation deduction (or *R&D expense* in the expanded sense) of $10,000 provides a tax shield of $4,600 when the marginal tax rate is 46 percent.

taxable income. *Income* computed according to *IRS* regulations and subject to *income taxes.* Contrast with income, net income, income before taxes (in the *income statement),* and *comprehensive income* (a *financial reporting* concept). Use the term "pretax income" to refer to income before taxes on the income statement in financial reports.

tax-transfer lease. The Congress has in the past provided business with an incentive to invest in qualifying *plant and equipment* by granting an *investment credit,* which, though it occurs as a reduction in *income taxes* otherwise payable, is effectively a reduction in the purchase price of the assets. Similarly, Congress continues to grant an incentive to acquire such assets by allowing *Accelerated Cost Recovery (ACRS,* form of unusually *accelerated depreciation).* Accelerated depreciation for tax purposes allows a reduction of taxes paid in early years of an assets's life, which provides the firm with an increased *net present value* of *cash flows.* Both of these incentives are administered by the *IRS* through the income tax laws, rather than being granted as an outright cash payment by some other government agency. A business with no taxable income in many cases had difficulty reaping the benefits of the investment credit or of accelerated depreciation because the Congress had not provided for tax refunds to those who acquire qualifying assets but who have no taxable income. In principle, a company without taxable income could lease from another firm with taxable income an asset that would otherwise have been purchased by the first company. The second firm acquires the asset, gets the tax reduction benefits from the acquisition, and becomes a lessor, leasing the asset (presumably at a lower price reflecting its own costs lowered by the tax reductions) to the unprofitable company. Such leases were discouraged by the tax laws prior to 1981. That is, although firms could enter into such leases, the tax benefits could not be legally transferred. Under certain restrictive conditions, the tax law allows a profitable firm to earn tax credits and take deductions while leasing to the firm without tax liability in such leases. Sometimes called "safe-harbor leases."

Technical Bulletin. The *FASB* has authorized its staff to issue bulletins to provide guidance on financial accounting and reporting problems. Although the FASB does not formally approve the contents of the bulletins, their contents are presumed to be part of *GAAP.*

technology. The sum of a firm's technical *trade secrets* and *know-how*, as distinct from its *patents*.

temporary account. *Account* that does not appear on the *balance sheet*. *Revenue* and *expense* accounts, their *adjuncts* and *contras, production cost accounts, dividend distribution accounts,* and purchases-related accounts (which are closed to the various inventories). Sometimes called a "nominal account."

temporary difference. *SFAS No. 109* (1992) definition includes these words: "A difference between the tax basis of an asset or liability and its reported amount in the financial statements that will result in taxable or deductible amounts in future years ...." Temporary differences include *timing differences* and differences between *taxable income* and pretax income caused by different cost bases for assets. For example, a plant asset might have a cost of $10,000 for financial reporting, but a basis of $7,000 for income tax purposes. This temporary difference might arise because the firm has used an accelerated depreciation method for tax but straight-line for book, or the firm may have purchased the asset from someone else in a purchase transaction where the fair value of the asset exceeds its tax basis. Both situations create a temporary difference.

temporary investments. Investments in *marketable securities* that the owner intends to sell within a short time, usually one year, and hence classified as *current assets.*

10-K. The name of the annual report required by the *SEC* of nearly all publicly held corporations.

term bonds. A *bond issue* whose component bonds all mature at the same time; contrast with *serial bonds.*

term loan. A loan with a *maturity* date, as opposed to a demand loan which is due whenever the lender requests payment. In practice, bankers and auditors use this phrase only for loans for a year or more.

term structure. A phrase with different meanings in *accounting* and *financial economics.* In accounting, it refers to the pattern of times that must elapse before *assets* turn into, or produce, *cash* and the pattern of times that must elapse before *liabilities* require cash. In financial economics, the phrase refers to the pattern of interest rates as a function of the time that elapses for loans to come due. For example, if six-month loans cost 6 percent per year while ten-year loans cost 9 percent per year, this is called a "normal" term structure. If the six-month loan costs 9 percent per year and the ten-year loan costs 6 percent per year, the term structure is said to be "inverted."

terms of sale. The conditions governing payment for a sale. For example, the terms 2/10, n(et)/30 mean that if payment is made within 10 days of the invoice date, a *discount* of 2 percent from *invoice* price can be taken; the invoice amount must be paid, in any event, within 30 days or it becomes overdue.

thin capitalization. A state of having a high *debt-equity ratio.* Under income tax legislation, the term has a special meaning.

throughput contract. As defined by *SFAS No. 47,* an agreement between a shipper (processor) and the owner of a transportation facility (such as an oil or natural gas pipeline or a ship) or a manufacturing facility that provides for the shipper (processor) to pay specified amounts periodically in return for the transportation (processing) of a product. The shipper (processor) is obligated to make cash payments even if it does not ship (process) the contracted quantities.

tickler file. A collection of *vouchers* or other memoranda arranged chronologically to remind the person in charge of certain duties to make payments (or to do other tasks) as scheduled.

time-adjusted rate of return. *Internal rate of return.*

time cost. *Period cost.*

time deposit. Cash in bank earning interest; contrast with *demand deposit.*

time-series analysis. See *cross-section analysis* for definition and contrast.

times-interest (charges) earned. Ratio of pretax *income* plus *interest* charges to interest charges. See *ratio.*

timing difference. The major type of *temporary difference.* A difference between taxable income and pretax income reported to shareholders that will be reversed in a subsequent period and requires an entry in the *deferred income tax* account. For example, the use of *accelerated depreciation* for tax returns and *straight line depreciation* for financial reporting. Contrast with *permanent difference.*

Toronto Stock Exchange (TSE). A public market where various corporate securities are traded.

total assets turnover. *Sales* divided by average total *assets.*

traceable cost. A *cost* that a firm can identify with or assign to a specific product; contrast with a *joint cost.*

trade acceptance. A *draft* drawn by a seller which is presented for signature (acceptance) to the buyer at the time goods are purchased and which then becomes the equivalent of a *note receivable* of the seller and the *note payable* of the buyer.

trade credit. One business allows another to buy from it in return for a promise to pay later. As contrasted with consumer credit, where a business extends the privilege of paying later to a retail customer.

trade discount. A *discount* from *list price* offered to all customers of a given type; contrast with a *discount* offered for prompt payment and *quantity discount.*

trade payables (receivables). *Payables (receivables)* arising in the ordinary course of business transactions. Most accounts payable (receivable) are of this kind.

trade secret. Technical or business information such as formulas, recipes, computer programs, and marketing data not generally known by competitors and maintained by the firm as a secret. A famous example is the secret formula for Coca-Cola (a registered *trademark* of the company). Compare with *know-how.* Theoretically capable of having an infinite life, this intangible asset is capitalized only if purchased and then amortized over a period not to exceed 40 years. If the firm develops it internally, then it shows no asset.

trade-in. Acquiring a new *asset* in exchange for a used one and perhaps additional cash. See *boot* and *trade-in transaction.*

trade-in transaction. The accounting for a trade-in depends whether the asset received is "similar" to (and used in the same line of business as) the asset traded in and whether the accounting is for *financial statements* or for *income tax* returns. Assume that an old asset cost $5,000, has $3,000 of *accumulated depreciation* (after recording depreciation to the date of the trade-in), and hence has a *book value* of $2,000. The old asset appears to have a market value of $1,500, according to price quotations in used asset markets. The old asset is traded in on a new asset with a list price of $10,000. The old asset and $5,500 cash (*boot)* are given for the new asset. The generic entry for the trade-in transaction is:

New Asset	A		
Accumulated Depreciation (Old Asset) .	3,000		
Adjustment on Exchange of Asset. . . .	B	or	B
Old Asset.			5,000
Cash.			5,500

(1) The *list price* method of accounting for trade-ins rests on the assumption that the list price of the new asset closely approximates its market value. The new asset is recorded at its list price (A = $10,000 in the example); B is a *plug* (= $2,500 credit in the example). If B requires a *debit* plug, the Adjustment on Exchange of Asset is a *loss;* if a *credit* plug is required (as in the example), the adjustment is a *gain.*

(2) Another theoretically sound method of accounting for trade-ins rests on the assumption that the price quotation from used-asset markets gives a more reliable measure of the market value of the old asset than is the list price a reliable measure of the market value of the new asset. This method uses the *fair market value* of the old asset, $1,500 in the example, to determine B (= $2,000 book value – $1,500 assumed proceeds on disposition = $500 debit or loss). The exchange results in a loss if the book value of the old asset exceeds its market value and in a gain if the market value exceeds the book value. The new asset is recorded on the books by plugging for A (= $7,000 in the example).

(3) For income tax reporting, no gain or loss may be recognized on the trade in. Thus the new asset is recorded on the books by assuming B is zero and plugging for A (= $7,500 in the example). In practice, firms that wish to recognize the loss currently will sell the old asset directly, rather than trading it in, and acquire the new asset entirely for cash.

(4) *Generally accepted accounting principles (APB Opinion No. 29)* require a variant of these methods. The basic method is (1) or (2), depending on whether the list price of the new asset (1) or the quotation of the old asset's market value (2) is the more reliable indication of market value. If, when applying the basic method, a debit entry, or loss, is required for the Adjustment on Exchange of Asset, then the trade-in is recorded as described in (1) or (2) and the full amount of the loss is recognized currently. If, however, a credit entry, or gain, is required for the Adjustment on Exchange of Asset, then the amount of gain recognized currently depends on whether or not the old asset and the new asset are "similar." If the assets are not similar, then the entire gain is recognized currently. If the assets are similar and cash is not received by the party trading in, then no gain is recognized and the treatment is like that in (3); that is B = 0, plug for A. If the assets are similar and cash is received by the party trading in – a rare case – then a portion of the gain recognized currently. The portion of the

gain recognized currently is the fraction *cash received/fair market value of total consideration received.* (When the list price method, (1), is used, the market value of the old asset is assumed to be the list price of the new asset plus the amount of cash received by the party trading in.)

The results of applying *GAAP* to the example can be summarized as follows:

More Reliable Information As to Fair Market Value	Old Asset Compared with New Asset	
	Similar	Not Similar
New Asset	A = $7,500	A = $10,000
List Price	B = 0	B = 2,500 gain
Old Asset	A = $7,000	A = $ 7,000
Market Price	B = 500 loss	B = 500 loss

trademark. A distinctive word or symbol affixed to a product, its package or dispenser, which uniquely identifies the firm's products and services. See *trademark right.*

trademark right. The right to exclude competitors in sales or advertising from using words or symbols that may be confusingly similar to the firm's *trademarks.* Trademark rights last as long as the firm continues to use the trademarks in question. In the United States, trademark rights arise from use and not from government registration. They therefore have a legal life independent of the life of a registration. Registrations last 20 years and are renewable as long as the trademark is being used. Thus, as an asset, purchased trademark rights might, like land, not be subject to amortization if management believes that the life of the trademark is indefinite. In practice, accountants amortize a trademark right over some estimate of its life, not to exceed 40 years. Under *SFAS No. 2,* internally developed trademark rights must be *expensed.*

trading on the equity. Said of a firm engaging in *debt financing;* frequently said of a firm doing so to a degree considered abnormal for a firm of its kind. *Leverage.*

trading securities. *Marketable securities* a firm holds that it expects to sell within a relatively short time. Contrast with *available for sale, securities* and *held-to-maturity securities.* A classification important in *SFAS No. 115,* which requires the owner to carry marketable equity securities on the balance sheet at market value, not at cost. Under *SFAS No. 115,* the balance sheet reports trading securities at market value on the balance sheet date and the income statement reports *holding gains and losses* on trading securities. When it sells the securities the firm reports realized gain or loss as the difference between the selling price and the market value at the last balance sheet date.

transaction. A *transfer* (of more than promises – see *executory contract)* between the accounting *entity* and another party or parties.

transfer. *SFAC No. 6* distinguishes "reciprocal" and "nonreciprocal" transfers. In a reciprocal transfer, or "exchange," the entity both receives and sacrifices. In a nonreciprocal transfer the entity sacrifices but does not receive (examples include gifts, distributions to owners) or receives but does not sacrifice (investment by owner in entity). *SFAC No. 6* suggests that the term "internal transfer" is self-contradictory and that the term "internal event" be used instead.

transfer agent. Usually a bank or trust company designated by a corporation to make legal transfers of *stock (bonds)* and, perhaps, to pay *dividends (coupons).*

transfer price. A substitute for a *market,* or *arm's length, price* used in *profit,* or *responsibility center, accounting* when one segment of the business "sells" to another segment. Incentives of profit center managers will not coincide with the best interests of the entire business unless a firm sets transfer prices properly.

transfer pricing problem. The problem of setting *transfer prices* so that both buyer and seller have *goal congruence* with respect to the parent organization's goals.

translation gain (or loss). *Foreign exchange gain (or loss).*

transportation-in. *Freight-in.*

transposition error. An error in record keeping resulting from reversing the order of digits in a number, such as recording "32" for "23." If the only errors in a *trial balance* result from one or more transposition errors, then the difference between the sum of the *debits* and the sum of the *credits* will be divisible by nine. Not all differences between sums of debits and sums of credits in trial balances divisible by nine result from transposition errors. See *slide.*

treasurer. The financial officer of a business responsible for managing cash and raising funds.

treasury bond. A bond issued by a corporation and then reacquired; such bonds are treated as retired when reacquired and an *extraordinary gain or loss* on reacquisition is recognized. Also, a *bond* issued by the U.S. Treasury Department.

treasury shares. *Capital stock* issued and then reacquired by the corporation. Such reacquisitions result in a reduction of *shareholders' equity* and usually appear on the balance sheet as *contra* to shareholders' equity. Accounting recognizes neither *gain* nor *loss* on transactions involving treasury stock. The accounting debits (if positive) or credits (if negative) any difference between the amounts paid and received for treasury stock transactions to *additional paid-in capital.* See *cost method* and *par value method.*

treasury stock. *Treasury shares.*

trial balance. A two-column listing of *account balances.* The left-hand column shows all accounts with *debit* balances and their total. The right-hand column shows all accounts with *credit* balances and their total. The two totals should be equal. Accountants compute trial balances as a partial check of the arithmetic accuracy of the entries previously made. See *adjusted, preclosing, post-closing, unadjusted trial balance, plug, slide,* and *transposition error.*

troubled debt restructuring. As defined in *SFAS No. 15,* a concession (changing of the terms of a *debt)* granted by a *creditor* for economic or legal reasons related to the *debtor's* financial difficulty that the creditor would not otherwise consider.

TSE. *Toronto Stock Exchange.*

turnover. The number of times that *assets,* such as *inventory* or *accounts receivable,* are replaced on average during the period. Accounts receivable turnover, for example, is total sales on account for a period divided by average accounts receivable balance for the period. See *ratio.*

turnover of plant and equipment. See *ratio.*

t-value. In *regression analysis,* the ratio of an estimated regression coefficient divided by its *standard error.*

20-F. Form required by the *SEC* for foreign companies issuing or trading their securities in the U.S. This form reconciles the foreign accounting results using foreign *GAAP* to amounts resulting from using U.S. GAAP.

two T-account method. A method for computing either (1) *foreign exchange gains and losses* or (2) *monetary gains or losses* for *constant dollar accounting statements.* The left hand *T-account* shows actual net balances of *monetary items* and the right hand T-account shows implied *(common) dollar* amounts.

2/10, n(et)/30. See *terms of sale.*

U

unadjusted trial balance. *Trial balance* before *adjusting* and *closing entries* are made at the end of the period.

unappropriated retained earnings. *Retained earnings* not appropriated and therefore against which *dividends* can be charged in the absence of retained earnings restrictions. See *restricted retained earnings.*

unavoidable cost. A *cost* that is not an *avoidable cost.*

uncertainty. See *risk* for definition and contrast.

uncollectible account. An *account receivable* that will not be paid by the *debtor.* If the preferable *allowance method* is used, the entry on judging a specific account to be uncollectible is to *debit* the allowance for uncollectible accounts and to *credit* the specific account receivable. See *bad debt expense* and *sales contra, estimated uncollectibles.*

unconsolidated subsidiary. A *subsidiary* not consolidated and, hence, accounted for on the *equity method.*

uncontrollable cost. The opposite of *controllable cost.*

underapplied (underabsorbed) overhead. An excess of actual *overhead costs* for a period over costs applied, or charged, to products produced during the period. A *debit balance* remaining in an overhead account after the accounting assigns overhead to product.

underlying document. The record, memorandum, *voucher,* or other signal that is the authority for making an *entry* into a *journal.*

underwriter. One who agrees to purchase an entire *security issue* for a specified price, usually for resale to others.

undistributed earnings. *Retained earnings;* typically, this term refers to that amount retained for a given year.

unearned income (revenue). *Advances from customers;* strictly speaking, a contradiction in terms.

unemployment tax. See *FUTA.*

unencumbered appropriation. In governmental accounting, portion of an *appropriation* not yet spent or *encumbered.*

unexpired cost. An *asset.*

unfavorable variance. In *standard cost* accounting, an excess of expected revenue over actual revenue or an excess of actual cost over standard cost.

unfunded. Not *funded.* An obligation or *liability,* usually for *pension costs,* exists but no *funds* have been set aside to discharge the obligation or liability.

Uniform Partnership Act. A model law, enacted by many states, to govern the relations between partners where the *partnership* agreement fails to specify the agreed-upon treatment.

unissued capital stock. *Stock* authorized but not yet issued.

units-of-production method. The *production method of depreciation.*

unlimited liability. The legal obligation of *general partners* or the sole proprietor for all debts of the *partnership* or *sole proprietorship.*

unqualified opinion. See *auditor's report.*

unrealized appreciation. An *unrealized holding gain;* frequently used in the context of *marketable securities.*

unrealized gross margin (profit). A *contra* account to *installment accounts receivable* used with the *installment method* of revenue recognition. Shows the amount of profit that will eventually be realized when the receivable is collected. Some accountants show this account as a *liability.*

unrealized holding gain. See *inventory profit* for definition and an example.

unrealized loss on marketable securities. An *income statement* account title for the amount of *loss* during the current period on the portfolio of *marketable securities* held as *trading securities. SFAS No. 115* requires that losses caused by declines in price below market be *recognized* in the income statement, even though they have not been *realized.*

unrecovered cost. *Book value* of an *asset.*

usage variance. *Efficiency variance.*

use of funds. Any transaction that reduces funds (however funds is defined).

useful life. *Service life.*

V

valuation account. A *contra account* or *adjunct account.* When *marketable securities* are reported at *lower of cost or market,* any declines in market value below cost will be credited to a valuation account. In this way, the acquisition cost and the amount of price declines below cost can both be shown. *SFAC No. 6* says a valuation account is "a separate item that reduces and increases the carrying amount" of an asset (or liability). The accounts are part of the related assets (or liabilities) and are neither assets (nor liabilities) in their own right.

value. Monetary worth; the term is usually so subjective that you should not use it without a modifying adjective unless most people would agree on the amount. Do not confuse with cost. See *fair market value, entry value, exit value.*

value added. *Cost* of a product or *work in process,* minus the cost of the material purchased for the product or work in process.

value variance. *Price variance.*

variable annuity. An *annuity* whose periodic payments depend on some uncertain outcome, such as stock market prices.

variable budget. *Flexible budget.*

variable costing. This method of allocating costs assigns only *variable manufacturing costs* to products and treats *fixed manufacturing costs* as *period expenses.* Contrast with *full absorption costing.*

variable costs. *Costs* that change as activity levels change. Strictly speaking, variable costs are zero when the activity level is zero. See *semivariable costs.* In accounting this term most often means the sum of *direct costs* and variable *overhead.*

variable overhead variance. Difference between actual and *standard variable overhead costs.*

variables sampling. The use of a sampling technique whereby a particular quantitative characteristic of an entire population is inferred from a sample, e.g. money value. See also *estimation sampling.* Compare *attribute(s) sampling.*

variance. Difference between actual and *standard costs* or between *budgeted* and actual *expenditures* or, sometimes, *expenses.* The word has completely different meanings in accounting and statistics, where it means a measure of dispersion of a distribution.

variance analysis. *Variance investigation.* This term's meaning differs in statistics.

variance investigation. *Standard cost systems* produce *variance* numbers of various sorts. These numbers are seldom exactly equal to zero. Management must decide when a variance differs sufficiently from zero to study its cause. This terms refers to deciding when to study the cause and the study itself.

variation analysis. Analysis of the causes of changes in items of interest in financial statements such as net *income* or *gross margin.*

VAT. *Value added tax.*

vendor. A seller. Sometimes spelled, "vender."

verifiable. A qualitative *objective* of financial reporting specifying that items in *financial statements* can be checked by tracing back to *underlying documents* – supporting *invoices,* canceled *checks,* and other physical pieces of evidence.

verification. The auditor's act of reviewing or checking items in *financial statements* by tracing back to *underlying documents* – supporting *invoices,* canceled *checks,* and other business documents – or sending out *confirmations* to be returned. Compare with *physical verification.*

vertical analysis. Analysis of the financial statements of a single firm or across several firms for a particular time, as opposed to *horizontal* or time-series analysis where items are compared over time for a single firm or across firms.

vertical integration. The extension of activity by an organization into business directly related to the production or distribution of the organization's end products. Although products may be sold to others at various stages, a substantial portion of the output at each stage is devoted to the production of the end products. Compare *horizontal integration.*

vested. Said of an employee's *pension plan* benefits that are not contingent on the employee's continuing to work for the employer.

visual curve fitting method. Sometimes, when a firm needs only rough approximations to the amounts of *fixed* and *variable costs,* management need not perform a formal *regression analysis,* but merely plot the data and draw in a line by hand that seems to fit the data, using the parameters of that line for the rough approximations.

volume variance. *Production volume variance.* Less often, used to mean *sales volume variance.*

voucher. A document that signals recognition of a *liability* and authorizes the disbursement of cash. Sometimes used to refer to the written evidence documenting an *accounting entry,* as in the term *journal voucher.*

voucher system. A method for controlling *cash* that requires each *check* to be authorized with an approved *voucher.* No *disbursements* of currency or coins are made except from *petty cash funds.*

vouching. The function performed by an *auditor* to ascertain that underlying data or documents support a *journal entry.*

W

wage. Compensation of employees based on time worked or output of product for manual labor. But see *take-home pay.*

warrant. A certificate entitling the owner to buy a specified number of shares at a specified time(s) for a specified price. Differs from a *stock option* only in that options are granted to employees and warrants are issued to the public. See *right.*

warranty. A promise by a seller to correct deficiencies in products sold. When warranties are given, proper accounting practice recognizes an estimate of warranty *expense* and an *estimated liability* at the time of sale. See *guarantee* for contrast in proper usage.

wash sale. The sale and purchase of the same or similar *asset* within a short time period. For *income tax* purposes, *losses* on a sale of stock may not be recognized if equivalent stock is purchased within 30 days before or 30 days after the date of sale.

waste. Residue of material from manufacturing operations with no sale value. Frequently, it has negative value because a firm must incur additional costs for disposal.

wasting asset. A *natural resource* having a limited *useful life* and, hence, subject to *amortization,* called *depletion.* Examples are timberland, oil and gas wells, and ore deposits.

watered stock. Shares issued for *assets* with *fair market value* less than *par* or *stated value.* The assets are put onto the books at the overstated values. In the law, for shares to be considered watered, the *board of directors* must have acted in bad faith or fraudulently in issuing the shares under these circumstances. The term originated from a former practice of cattlemen who fed cattle ("stock") large quantities of salt to make them thirsty. The cattle then drank a lot of water before being taken to market. This was done to make the cattle appear heavier and more valuable than otherwise.

weighted average. An average computed by counting each occurrence of each value, not merely a single occurrence of each value. For example, if a firm purchases one unit for $1 and two units for $2 each, then the simple average of the purchase prices is $1.50 but the weighted average price per unit is $5/3 = $1.67. Contrast with *moving average.*

weighted-average inventory method. Valuing either *withdrawals* or *ending inventory* at the *weighted-average* purchase price of all units on hand at the time of withdrawal or of computing ending inventory. The *inventory equation* is used to calculate the other quantity. If a firm uses the *perpetual inventory* method, accountants often call it the *"moving average method."*

where-got, where-gone statement. A term used by W. M. Cole for a statement much like the *statement of cash flows.*

wind up. To bring to an end, such as the life of a corporation. The board winds up the life of a corporation by following the winding-up provisions of applicable statutes, by surrendering the charter, or by following bankruptcy proceedings. See also *liquidation.*

window dressing. The attempt to make financial statements show *operating* results, or *financial position,* more favorable than would be otherwise shown.

with recourse. See *note receivable discounted.*

withdrawals. *Assets* distributed to an owner. *Partner's drawings.* See *inventory equation* for another context.

withholding. Deductions from *salaries* or *wages,* usually for *income taxes,* to be remitted by the employer, in the employee's name, to the taxing authority.

without recourse. See *note receivable discounted.*

work in process (inventory account). Partially completed product; appears on the balance sheet as *inventory.*

work sheet (program). A computer program that is designed to combine explanations and calculations. This type of program is useful in preparing *financial statements, schedules,* and *worksheets.* It is a tabular schedule for convenient summary of *adjusting* and *closing entries.* The work sheet usually begins with an *unadjusted trial balance.* Adjusting entries are shown in the next two columns, one for *debts* and one for *credits.* The horizontal sum of each line is then carried to the right into either the *income statement or balance sheet* column, as appropriate. The *plug* to equate the income statement column totals is the income, if a debit plug is required, or loss, if a credit plug is required, for the period. That income will be closed to retained earnings on the balance sheet. The income statement credit columns are the revenues for the period, and the debit columns are the expenses (and revenue *contras)* to be shown on the income statement. Work sheet is also used to refer to *schedules* for ascertaining other items appearing on the *financial statements* that require adjustment or compilation.

working capital. *Current assets* minus *current liabilities.*

working papers. The schedules and analyses prepared by the *auditor* in carrying out investigations prior to issuing an *opinion* on *financial statements.*

worth. *Value.* See *net worth.*

worth-debt ratio. Reciprocal of the *debt-equity ratio.* See *ratio.*

write down. *Write off,* except that not all the assets' cost is charged to expense or *loss.* Generally used for nonrecurring items.

write off. *Charge* an *asset* to *expense* or *loss;* that is, *debit* expense (or loss) and *credit* asset.

write-off method. A method for treating *uncollectible accounts* that charges *bad debt expense* and credits accounts receivable of specific customers as uncollectible amounts are identified. May not be used when uncollectible amounts are significant and can be estimated. See *bad debt expense, sales contra, estimated uncollectibles,* and the *allowance method* for contrast.

write up. To increase the recorded *cost* of an *asset* with no corresponding *disbursement* of *funds;* that is, *debit* asset and *credit revenue,* or perhaps, *owners' equity.* Seldom done because currently accepted accounting principles are based on actual transactions. When a portfolio of *marketable equity securities* increases in market value subsequent to a previously recognized decrease, the *book value* of the portfolio is written up – the debit is to the *contra account.*

Y

yield. *Internal rate of return* of a stream of cash flows. Cash yield is cash flow divided by book value. See also *dividend yield.*

yield to maturity. At a given time, the *internal rate of return* of a series of cash flows. Usually said of a *bond.* Sometimes called the "effective rate."

yield variance. Measures the input-output relation holding the standard mix of inputs constant. It is the part of the *efficiency variance* not called the *mix variance.* It is (standard price multiplied by actual amount of input used in the standard mix) – (standard price multiplied by standard quantity allowed for the actual output).

Z

zero-base(d) budgeting. ZBB. In preparing an ordinary *budget* for the next period, a manager starts with the budget for the current period and makes adjustments as seem necessary because of changed conditions for the next period. Because most managers like to increase the scope of the activities managed and since most prices increase most of the time, amounts in budgets prepared in the ordinary, incremental way seem to increase period after period. The authority approving the budget assumes operations will be carried out in the same way as in the past and that next period's expenditures will have to be at least as large as the current period's. Thus, this authority tends to study only the increments to the current period's budget. In ZBB, the authority questions the process for carrying out a program and the entire budget for next period. The authority studies every dollar in the budget, not just the dollars incremental to the previous period's amounts. The advocates of ZBB claim that in this way: (1) management will more likely delete programs or divisions of marginal benefit to the business or governmental unit, rather than continuing with costs at least as large as the present ones and (2) management may discover and implement alternative, more cost-effective ways of carrying out programs. ZBB implies questioning the existence of programs and the fundamental nature of the way firms carry them out, not merely the amounts used to fund them. Experts appear to be evenly divided as to whether the middle word should be "base" or "based."

General Electric 1993 Annual Report

Authors' Introduction

GE's Annual Reports are consistently among the best we see. This is an annotated excerpt from GE's 1993 Annual Report, in which we comment on various aspects of the financial statements in numbered footnotes keyed to the report.

We leave the page numbers of the original report intact. References, both in the report and in our comments, use these numbers. The first 25 pages and pages 32 through 43 of the annual report, which we have not reproduced, give general information about the company, illustrations, and highlights of the year's operations. We have inserted circled numbers — known as callouts — in the annual report to refer to our comments. Comments begin at the bottom of this page, and generally appear on a page facing (or near) the relevant callout. The Glossary explains all accounting terms we use in our comments.

We think there is no better way to learn financial accounting than to try to understand all that appears in GE's statements. To begin, notice the GE corporate symbol — a trademark of General Electric Company — as it appears above. GE calls it "the meatball." This symbol is, perhaps, the single most valuable asset of the Company, but in accordance with generally accepted accounting principles (GAAP), this asset does not appear anywhere in the financial statements.

Authors' Comments on General Electric Annual Report

① This is the first of our numbered comments. These paragraphs, which appear on page 44 of the annual report, indicate that management takes responsibility for the preparation of the financial statements.

② The paragraphs here comprise the auditors' report, which also appears on page 44 of the annual report. This particular auditor's report is both nonqualified ("clean") and in standard format. The first two paragraphs describe the work done. The third paragraph gives the opinion. The fourth paragraph describes changes in accounting principles to alert the reader to an inconsistency across time. See GE's income statement near the callout for our comment 8 for more information about the changes in accounting methods.

③ This is the income statement.

④ GE presents income statements for three economic entities. GAAP require the first set of columns ("General Electric Company and consolidated affiliates"). GE provides the other two sets of columns ("GE" and "GECS") because the financial services operations — GECS — so differ from the company's other operations, that management feels this disaggregated information will aid investors. See GE's discussion in its Note 1 on page 45.

Management's Discussion of Financial Responsibility ①

The financial data in this report, including the audited financial statements, have been prepared by management using the best available information and applying judgment. Accounting principles used in preparing the financial statements are those that are generally accepted in the United States.

Management believes that a sound, dynamic system of internal financial controls that balances benefits and costs provides the best safeguard for Company assets. Professional financial managers are responsible for implementing and overseeing the financial control system, reporting on management's stewardship of the assets entrusted to it by share owners and maintaining accurate records.

GE is dedicated to the highest standards of integrity, ethics and social responsibility. This dedication is reflected in written policy statements covering, among other subjects, environmental protection, potentially conflicting outside interests of employees, compliance with antitrust laws, proper business practices, and adherence to the highest standards of conduct and practices in transactions with the U.S. government. Management continually emphasizes to all employees that even the appearance of impropriety can erode public confidence in the Company.

Ongoing education and communication programs and review activities such as those conducted by the Company's Policy Compliance Review Board are designed to create a strong compliance culture — one that encourages employees to raise their policy questions and concerns and prohibits retribution for doing so.

KPMG Peat Marwick provide an objective, independent review of management's discharge of its obligations relating to the fairness of reporting operating results and financial condition. Their report for 1993 appears below.

The Audit Committee of the Board (consisting solely of Directors from outside GE) maintains an ongoing appraisal — on behalf of share owners — of the activities and independence of the Company's independent auditors, the activities of its internal audit staff, financial reporting process, internal financial controls and compliance with key Company policies.

John F. Welch, Jr.
Chairman of the Board and
Chief Executive Officer
February 11, 1994

Dennis D. Dammerman
Senior Vice President
Finance

Independent Auditors' Report ②

To Share Owners and Board of Directors of
General Electric Company

We have audited the accompanying statement of financial position of General Electric Company and consolidated affiliates as of December 31, 1993 and 1992, and the related statements of earnings and cash flows for each of the years in the three-year period ended December 31, 1993. These consolidated financial statements are the responsibility of the Company's management. Our responsibility is to express an opinion on these consolidated financial statements based on our audits.

We conducted our audits in accordance with generally accepted auditing standards. Those standards require that we plan and perform the audit to obtain reasonable assurance about whether the financial statements are free of material misstatement. An audit includes examining, on a test basis, evidence supporting the amounts and disclosures in the financial statements. An audit also includes assessing the accounting principles used and significant estimates made by management, as well as evaluating the overall financial statement presentation. We believe that

our audits provide a reasonable basis for our opinion.

In our opinion, the aforementioned financial statements appearing on pages 26-31 and 45-64 present fairly, in all material respects, the financial position of General Electric Company and consolidated affiliates at December 31, 1993 and 1992, and the results of their operations and their cash flows for each of the years in the three-year period ended December 31, 1993, in conformity with generally accepted accounting principles.

As discussed in notes 1 and 22 to the consolidated financial statements, the Company in 1993 adopted required changes in its methods of accounting for investments in certain securities and for postemployment benefits. As discussed in note 6, the Company in 1991 adopted a required change in its method of accounting for postretirement benefits other than pensions.

KPMG Peat Marwick
Stamford, Connecticut
February 11, 1994

44

Statement of Earnings ③

④

		General Electric Company and consolidated affiliates		
For the years ended December 31 (In millions)		1993	1992	1991
Revenues				
Sales of goods		$29,509	$29,575	$29,434
Sales of services		8,268	8,331	8,062
Other income (note 3)		735	799	792
Earnings of GECS before accounting change		—	—	—
GECS revenues from operations (note 4)		22,050	18,368	16,341
Total revenues		60,562	57,073	54,629
Costs and expenses (note 5)				
Cost of goods sold		22,606	22,107	21,498
Cost of services sold		6,308	6,273	6,373
Interest and other financial charges (note 7)		6,989	6,860	7,401
Insurance losses and policyholder and annuity benefits		3,172	1,957	1,623
Provision for losses on financing receivables (note 8)		987	1,056	1,102
Other costs and expenses		13,774	12,494	10,834
Minority interest in net earnings of consolidated affiliates	⑤	151	53	72
Total costs and expenses		53,987	50,800	48,903
Earnings from continuing operations before income taxes and accounting changes		6,575	6,273	5,726
Provision for income taxes (note 9)	⑥	(2,151)	(1,968)	(1,742)
Earnings from continuing operations before accounting changes		4,424	4,305	3,984
Earnings from discontinued operations, net of income taxes of $44, $248 and $259, respectively (note 2)	⑦	75	420	451
Gain on transfer of discontinued operations, net of income taxes of $752		678	—	—
Earnings from discontinued operations		753	420	451
Earnings before accounting changes		5,177	4,725	4,435
Cumulative effects of accounting changes (notes 6 and 22)	⑧	(862)	—	(1,799)
Net earnings		$ 4,315	$ 4,725	$ 2,636
Net earnings per share (in dollars)				
Continuing operations before accounting changes		$ 5.18	$ 5.02	$ 4.58
Discontinued operations before accounting changes		0.88	0.49	0.52
Earnings before accounting changes		6.06	5.51	5.10
Cumulative effects of accounting changes		(1.01)	—	(2.07)
Net earnings per share	⑨	$ 5.05	$ 5.51	$ 3.03
Dividends declared per share (in dollars)		$ 2.61	$ 2.32	$ 2.08

The notes to consolidated financial statements on pages 45-64 are an integral part of this statement.

	GE			GECS		
	1993	1992	1991	**1993**	1992	1991
	$29,533	$29,595	$29,446	**$ —**	$ —	$ —
	8,289	8,348	8,075	**—**	—	—
	730	812	798	**—**	—	—
	1,807	1,499	1,275	**—**	—	—
	—	—	—	**22,137**	18,440	16,399
	40,359	40,254	39,594	**22,137**	18,440	16,399
	22,630	22,127	21,510	**—**	—	—
	6,329	6,290	6,386	**—**	—	—
	525	768	893	**6,473**	6,122	6,536
	—	—	—	**3,172**	1,957	1,623
	—	—	—	**987**	1,056	1,102
	5,124	5,319	5,422	**8,723**	7,230	5,448
	17	13	39	**134**	40	33
	34,625	34,517	34,250	**19,489**	16,405	14,742
	5,734	5,737	5,344	**2,648**	2,035	1,657
	(1,310)	(1,432)	(1,360)	**(841)**	(536)	(382)
	4,424	4,305	3,984	**1,807**	1,499	1,275
	75	420	451	**—**	—	—
	678	—	—	**—**	—	—
	753	420	451	**—**	—	—
	5,177	4,725	4,435	**1,807**	1,499	1,275
	(862)	—	(1,799)	**—**	—	(19)
	$ 4,315	$ 4,725	$ 2,636	**$ 1,807**	$ 1,499	$ 1,256

In the supplemental consolidating data on this page, "GE" means the basis of consolidation as described in note 1 to the consolidated financial statements; "GECS" means General Electric Capital Services, Inc. and all of its affiliates and associated companies. Transactions between GE and GECS have been eliminated from the "General Electric Company and consolidated affiliates" columns on page 26.

(5) GE does not own all the outstanding shares of all its consolidated subsidiaries. Some of the shares belong to outsiders, called the *minority interest*. The minority interest's share of the earnings of the subsidiary companies does not belong to GE's shareholders. Hence, the accounting to derive income to GE's shareholders subtracts the minority interest's share in earnings from the earnings of the consolidated group of companies. GE includes the minority share in the "costs and expenses" it subtracts from revenues to compute income. Note, however, that this reduction in income uses no cash, so the Statement of Cash Flows contains an adjustment for this charge against income. The item is too small, however, to appear separately in the Statement of Cash Flows, so GE places it in "All other operating activities."

(6) Provision usually means "estimated expense" in this country; see the Glossary at *provision* for the contrast in this word's meanings in the U.S. and the U.K.

(7) GE disposed of its entire Aerospace business during 1993. See GE's Note 2. APB *Opinion No. 30* requires companies that discontinue an entire line of business (as opposed to disposing of a portion of a continuing line) to segregate the results for the discontinued line for all the years reported. Thus, the amounts reported as "Earnings from discontinued operations, net of income taxes" are the after-tax earnings of the Aerospace business in 1991, 1992 and through the sale date in 1993. The gain on the sale of the unit's net assets in 1993 appears on the next line. If GE had retained some operations in aerospace, but restructured, sold or abandoned part of the business, it would have classified the gains or losses with other income from continuing operations. See also the balance sheet near the callout for comment 11; the Statement of Cash Flows near the callout for comment 20; and our comment 35.

(8) GE's Notes 6 and 22 explain the large decreases in 1991 and 1993 income from adopting new mandatory accounting rules. In 1991 the company adopted *SFAS No. 106*, which required it to record a liability for postretirement employee benefits like health care and insurance. Prior to 1991, GE recorded only the benefits paid out during a period, and did not accrue any liability for the future benefits employees earned by working that period. The cumulative after-tax effect on income of accruing the liability for all past service is $1,799 million. In 1993, the company adopted *SFAS No. 112*, which required it to record a similar liability for severance benefits. The cumulative after-tax effect on income of this change is $862 million.

(9) This is primary earnings per share, as required by APB *Opinion No. 15*. GE does not disclose fully-diluted earnings per share because the difference between fully diluted and primary earnings per share is less than 3 percent.

(10) This statement contains two balance sheets, one at the end of 1993 and the second a year earlier, for each of the three economic entities (GE, GECS and consolidated).

(11) As we described in our comment 7, GE segregates the discontinued Aerospace operations from continuing lines of business for all years reported. Since GE sold the assets in April 1993, no assets for the discontinued unit remain on GE's 1993 year-end balance sheet.

⑫ GE uses the completed contract method of recognizing revenue from long term construction contracts; see GE's Note 1 near the callout for comment 28. As GE incurs costs on these contracts it makes journal entries such as:

Work in Process Inventory for Long Term Contracts.	X	
Various Assets and Liabilities		X
To record cost of construction activity.		

Some of GE's long-term construction contracts provide that the customer shall make progress payments to GE as GE performs the work. GE does not recognize revenue until it completes all work on the contract, so when GE receives cash it makes a journal entry such as:

Cash	Y	
Advances from Customers on Long-Term Contracts		Y
To record cash received and to set up the corresponding liability.		

When GE prepares the balance sheet, it nets the amounts in the inventory accounts, X (debit balance), against the amounts in the liability accounts, Y (credit balance). If cash collections exceed the amounts in the inventory account, as here, then GE records the difference, Y – X, as a liability. GE shows this liability under the title "Progress collections." On contracts where the amounts in the inventory account exceed the cash collections, the difference X – Y appears as an asset under a title such as "Costs incurred on long-term contracts in excess of billings." *ARB No. 45* requires this netting of costs incurred against cash collections, with excesses shown separately. On many of its contracts, the only cash GE collects before completion of construction is for engineering costs incurred in preparation to undertake construction. GE expenses these engineering costs, rather than accumulating them in Work in Process inventory accounts. Thus, there is no asset account to net against the liability, so GE uses the title "Progress collections" rather than the more typical "Billings on uncompleted contracts in excess of related costs." The "price adjustments accrued" represent amounts that GE expects to pay in the future for which it will not receive reimbursement from the buyer under the contract.

⑬ This account represents the equity of the minority shareholders in the consolidated affiliates. Refer to our comment 5 for a description of "minority interest" on the income statement. From the point of view of GE's shareholders, this equity belonging to the minority is a liability. From the point of view of the consolidated entity, the minority shareholders' interest is part of total owners' equity. Thus, whether one believes that minority interest is a liability or an item of owners' equity depends upon whether one views the financial statements as being prepared for the shareholders of GE (the proprietorship theory) or for all potential readers (the entity theory). Note that GE avoids the issue by classifying "minority interest" neither with liabilities nor with owners' equity.

⑭ GE uses the cost method of accounting for treasury stock and shows the cost of its own shares acquired on the market as contra to all of owners' equity. Refer to our comment 74.

⑮ In the middle set of columns, GE uses the equity method to account for its subsidiary, General Electric Capital Services (GECS). Because GE has owned 100 percent of GECS since the subsidiary was organized, GE's investment (asset) account for GECS is the mirror image of GECS's owners' equity accounts. See GECS's balance sheet near the callout for our comment 16. Consider the following example transactions.

(1) GE makes an investment in GECS by sending it cash:
GE debits the investment account and credits cash;
GECS debits cash and credits a contributed capital account.

(2) GECS earns income:
GECS debits various net asset accounts and (after closing entries) credits retained earnings;
GE, using the equity method, debits the investment account and credits income.

(3) GECS declares and pays a dividend:
GECS debits retained earnings and credits cash;
GE, using the equity method, debits cash and credits the investment account.

Statement of Financial Position ⑩

	General Electric Company and consolidated affiliates	
At December 31 (In millions)	1993	1992
Assets		
Cash and equivalents	$ 3,218	$ 3,129
GECS trading securities (note 10)	30,165	24,154
Investment securities (note 11)	26,811	11,256
Securities purchased under agreements to resell	43,463	26,788
Current receivables (note 12)	8,195	7,150
Inventories (note 13)	3,824	4,574
GECS financing receivables (investment in time sales, loans and financing leases) — net (note 14)	63,948	59,388
Other GECS receivables	15,616	8,025
Property, plant and equipment (including equipment leased to others) — net (note 15)	21,228	20,387
Investment in GECS	—	—
Intangible assets (note 16)	10,364	9,510
All other assets (note 17)	24,674	16,625
Net assets of discontinued operations ⑪	—	1,890
Total assets	$251,506	$192,876
Liabilities and equity		
Short-term borrowings (note 18)	$ 62,135	$ 56,389
Accounts payable, principally trade accounts	11,956	8,245
Securities sold under agreements to repurchase	56,669	36,014
Securities sold but not yet purchased, at market (note 19)	15,332	11,413
Progress collections and price adjustments accrued ⑫	2,608	2,150
Dividends payable	615	539
All other GE current costs and expenses accrued (note 20)	6,414	5,725
Long-term borrowings (note 18)	28,270	25,376
Insurance reserves and annuity benefits (note 21)	22,909	7,948
All other liabilities (note 22)	12,009	9,734
Deferred income taxes (note 23)	5,109	4,540
Total liabilities	224,026	168,073
Minority interest in equity of consolidated affiliates (note 24) ⑬	1,656	1,344
Common stock (926,564,000 shares issued)	584	584
Other capital	1,398	755
Retained earnings	28,613	26,527
Less common stock held in treasury ⑭	(4,771)	(4,407)
Total share owners' equity (notes 25 and 26)	25,824	23,459
Total liabilities and equity	$251,506	$192,876

The notes to consolidated financial statements on pages 45-64 are an integral part of this statement.

	GE		GECS	
	1993	1992	1993	1992
	$ 1,536	$ 1,189	$ 1,682	$ 1,940
	—	—	30,165	24,154
	19	32	26,792	11,224
	—	—	43,463	26,788
	8,561	7,462	—	—
	3,824	4,574	—	—
	—	—	63,948	59,388
	—	—	15,799	8,476
	9,542	9,932	11,686	10,455
(15)	10,809	8,884	—	—
	6,466	6,607	3,898	2,903
	10,377	7,505	14,297	9,196
	—	1,890	—	—
	$51,134	$48,075	$211,730	$154,524
	$ 2,391	$ 3,448	$ 60,003	$ 53,183
	2,331	2,217	9,885	6,624
	—	—	56,669	36,014
	—	—	15,332	11,413
	2,608	2,150	—	—
	615	539	—	—
	6,414	5,725	—	—
	2,413	3,420	25,885	21,957
	—	—	22,909	7,948
	8,482	7,096	3,529	2,638
	(299)	(329)	5,408	4,869
	24,955	24,266	199,620	144,646
	355	350	1,301	994
	584	584	1	1
	1,398	755	2,596	1,868
	28,613	26,527	8,212	7,015
	(4,771)	(4,407)	—	—
(16)	25,824	23,459	10,809	8,884
	$51,134	$48,075	$211,730	$154,524

In the supplemental consolidating data on this page, "GE" means the basis of consolidation as described in note 1 to the consolidated financial statements; "GECS" means General Electric Capital Services, Inc. and all of its affiliates and associated companies. Transactions between GE and GECS have been eliminated from the "General Electric Company and consolidated affiliates" columns on page 28.

(16) *SFAS No. 94* requires firms to consolidate majority-owned and controlled subsidiaries. In compliance with this standard, GE consolidates GECS in its first set of columns, where all GECS's assets and liabilities appear on the consolidated balance sheet. In consolidation, GE adds $10,809 (= $211,730 – $199,620 – $1,301) million of net assets to its December 31, 1993 balance sheet and eliminates the account "Investments in GECS." Notice that GECS's owners' equity equals GE's equity-method investment in GECS, as we explained in comment 15.

    GE's consolidated retained earnings in the first set of columns, however, are the same as retained earnings in the second set of columns where GE accounts for GECS using the equity method. This equality results from the fact that, under the equity method, the parent records the income of unconsolidated subsidiaries.

    Consolidating GECS affects the appearance of the financial statements. Below, we show two key financial ratios calculated from year-end account balances. See the Glossary for definitions of the ratios.

RATIOS: GENERAL ELECTRIC AND GE CAPITAL SERVICES, 1993
(For Authors' comment 16. Dollar amounts are in millions)

Using the Equity Method for GECS
(from the middle set of columns)

Rate of Return on Assets:

$$\frac{\$4,315 + \$17^a + (.65 \times \$525)^b}{\$51,134}$$

$$= \frac{\$4,673}{\$51,134} = 9.1\%$$

Debt-Equity Ratio:

$$\frac{\$24,955}{\$51,134} = 49\%$$

Consolidating GECS
(from the first set of columns)

Rate of Return on Assets:

$$\frac{\$4,315 + \$151^a + (.65 \times \$6,989)^b}{\$251,506}$$

$$= \frac{\$9,009}{\$251,506} = 3.6\%$$

Debt-Equity Ratio:

$$= \frac{\$224,026}{\$251,506} = 89\%$$

a. Minority interest in net income, from the income statement.
b. Interest expense, multiplied by .65 (= 1.00 – .35 federal tax rate) to place it on an after-tax basis.

---

(17) This statement starts with net income as shown in the income statement on pages 28 and 29. The next line segregates the earnings from the discontinued Aerospace unit, for which GE reports cash flows separately (see our comment 7). The following eleven lines adjust net income from continuing operations for non-cash components of revenues and expenses, to derive cash flow from operations. This presentation, known as the "indirect method," derives operating cash flow indirectly by making adjustments to income. The acceptable alternative format, the "direct method," would show operating cash collections, less operating cash expenditures, and would require no adjustments.

(18) The next four lines show subtractions for revenues and other credits to income that did not produce cash or working capital, and additions for expenses and other charges against income that did not use cash or working capital.

    The first of these, the cumulative effects of adopting *SFAS No. 106* in 1991 and *SFAS No. 112* in 1993 (see our comment 8), reduced net income in each of these two years, but had no effect on GE's cash flows. Therefore, GE adds this item back to income to derive operating cash flow.

    Depreciation expense reduces net income without using cash currently. Hence, GE adds this amount back to net income to derive cash provided by operations. The firm used cash some time in the past when it acquired the depreciable assets; see "Additions to property, plant, and equipment," at our comment 21, below.

    GE includes all earnings of GECS, which are $1,807 million in 1993, in income under the equity method. GECS declared dividends of $610 million in 1993. The income produced a larger investment balance on GE's balance sheet, while the dividend reduced the investment balance; see our comment 15. The difference between income and dividends from GECS, $1,197 million, provided no cash to GE and GE therefore subtracts it from net income to derive cash from operations.

    Income tax expense for each of the three the years exceeded the amount of income taxes payable. See the discussion at GE's Notes 9 and 23, and our comment 70. Because GE used less cash for income taxes than it reported as income tax expense, it must add the amount of expense not using cash to derive cash from operations.

⑲ The next seven lines show the increases and decreases in working capital accounts. The Statement of Cash Flows classifies cash flows into three types: operating activities, financing activities, and investment activities. *SFAS No. 95* requires that working capital items appear in the operating section, although one could argue that using cash to acquire inventory is an investing activity, just as is acquiring plant. Similarly, one could argue that saving cash by letting accounts payable increase is a financing item, just as is borrowing from a bank.

Increases in accounts receivable represent the amounts by which sales on account exceeded cash collections from customers. Conversely, decreases in accounts receivable represent the amount by which cash collections exceeded sales on account. Thus, we adjust net income, which includes sales, for this difference to derive cash flow.

Increases in inventories use cash, just as increases in property and plant do. Conversely, decreases in inventories provide funds.

Increases in accounts payable defer cash payments to future periods, decreasing the use of cash in this period. Conversely, decreases in accounts payable require cash payments.

⑳ Total cash produced by continuing operations appears after all adjustments to income. Operating cash flows from discontinued operations appear separately on the following line (see our comment 7).

㉑ The primary use of funds for most companies most of the time is the acquisition of new property, plant and equipment, for growth and to replace the old as it wears out. The amounts here will appear on the income statement in future periods as depreciation charges. GE uses cash when it acquires long-term assets, and its income decreases in later periods when it uses the assets.

㉒ The largest single equity of GECS is short-term borrowings (see the balance sheet on page 29). GE, correctly in our opinion, views this item as financing, not as operating.

㉓ GE shows separately cash provided by new long-term borrowings and cash used to reduce old long-term borrowings. Some companies show only the net effect, as GE does on the line above for "maturities 90 days or less." We prefer the separate disclosure, because the net amount provides no information about the amount of actual borrowings and repayments during the period.

㉔ GE demonstrates that the net cash flow ($89 in 1993) exactly explains the change in the Cash and equivalents account on the balance sheet.

Statement of Cash Flows

For the years ended December 31 (In millions)		General Electric Company and consolidated affiliates		
		1993	1992	1991
Cash flows from operating activities				
Net earnings	⑰	$ 4,315	$ 4,725	$ 2,636
Less earnings from discontinued operations		(753)	(420)	(451)
Adjustments to reconcile net earnings to cash provided from operating activities				
Cumulative effects of accounting changes	⑱	862	—	1,799
Depreciation, depletion and amortization		3,261	2,818	2,654
Earnings retained by GECS		—	—	—
Deferred income taxes		461	707	826
Decrease (increase) in GE current receivables	⑲	(571)	135	(215)
Decrease in GE inventories		750	820	378
Increase (decrease) in accounts payable		3,345	57	1,151
Increase in insurance reserves		1,479	703	725
Provision for losses on financing receivables		987	1,056	1,102
Net change in certain broker-dealer accounts		382	1,018	(1,548)
All other operating activities		(4,407)	(2,111)	(1,952)
Net cash from continuing operations	⑳	10,111	9,508	7,105
Net cash from discontinued operations		76	741	392
Cash provided from operating activities		10,187	10,249	7,497
Cash flows from investing activities				
Additions to property, plant and equipment	㉑	(4,739)	(4,824)	(4,870)
Dispositions of property, plant and equipment		1,155	1,793	1,090
Net increase in GECS financing receivables		(4,164)	(4,683)	(7,254)
Payments for principal businesses purchased		(2,090)	(2,013)	(3,769)
Proceeds from principal business dispositions		—	90	604
All other investing activities		(6,639)	(3,823)	(2,045)
Cash for investing activities — continuing operations		(16,477)	(13,460)	(16,244)
Cash from (used for) investing activities — discontinued operations		886	(93)	(117)
Cash used for investing activities		(15,591)	(13,553)	(16,361)
Cash flows from financing activities				
Net change in borrowings (maturities 90 days or less)	㉒	4,464	3,092	6,126
Newly issued debt (maturities more than 90 days)		15,468	13,084	15,374
Repayments and other reductions (maturities more than 90 days)	㉓	(11,853)	(9,008)	(10,158)
Disposition of GE shares from treasury (mainly for employee plans)		406	425	410
Purchase of GE shares for treasury		(770)	(1,206)	(1,112)
Dividends paid to share owners		(2,153)	(1,925)	(1,780)
All other financing activities		(69)	—	—
Cash provided from (used for) financing activities		5,493	4,462	8,860
Increase (decrease) in cash and equivalents during year		89	1,158	(4)
Cash and equivalents at beginning of year	㉔	3,129	1,971	1,975
Cash and equivalents at end of year		$ 3,218	$ 3,129	$ 1,971
Supplemental disclosure of cash flows information				
Cash paid during the year for interest		$ (6,689)	$ (6,477)	$ (7,145)
Cash paid during the year for income taxes		(1,644)	(1,033)	(1,244)

The notes to consolidated financial statements on pages 45-64 are an integral part of this statement.

	GE			GECS		
	1993	1992	1991	1993	1992	1991
	$ 4,315	$ 4,725	$ 2,636	$ 1,807	$ 1,499	$ 1,256
	(753)	(420)	(451)	—	—	—
	862	—	1,799	—	—	19
	1,631	1,483	1,429	1,630	1,335	1,225
	(1,197)	(999)	(925)	—	—	—
	120	675	271	341	32	555
	(625)	68	(109)	—	—	—
	750	820	378	—	—	—
	114	(43)	(203)	3,246	139	1,391
	—	—	—	1,479	703	725
	—	—	—	987	1,056	1,102
	—	—	—	382	1,018	(1,548)
	(16)	(1,736)	(1,199)	(4,419)	(439)	(754)
	5,201	4,573	3,626	5,453	5,343	3,971
	76	741	392	—	—	—
	5,277	5,314	4,018	5,453	5,343	3,971
	(1,588)	(1,445)	(2,126)	(3,151)	(3,379)	(2,744)
	55	46	61	1,100	1,747	1,029
	—	—	—	(4,164)	(4,683)	(7,254)
	—	—	(933)	(2,090)	(2,013)	(2,836)
	—	90	327	—	—	277
	298	(103)	(60)	(6,914)	(3,668)	(2,125)
	(1,235)	(1,412)	(2,731)	(15,219)	(11,996)	(13,653)
	886	(93)	(117)	—	—	—
	(349)	(1,505)	(2,848)	(15,219)	(11,996)	(13,653)
	46	(763)	483	4,462	3,895	5,641
	215	1,331	2,136	15,253	11,753	13,238
	(2,325)	(1,528)	(1,573)	(9,528)	(7,480)	(8,585)
	406	425	410	—	—	—
	(770)	(1,206)	(1,112)	—	—	—
	(2,153)	(1,925)	(1,780)	(610)	(500)	(350)
	—	—	—	(69)	—	—
	(4,581)	(3,666)	(1,436)	9,508	7,668	9,944
	347	143	(266)	(258)	1,015	262
	1,189	1,046	1,312	1,940	925	663
	$ 1,536	$ 1,189	$ 1,046	$ 1,682	$ 1,940	$ 925
	$ (473)	$ (570)	$ (761)	$ (6,216)	$ (5,907)	$ (6,384)
	(1,455)	(936)	(1,343)	(189)	(97)	99

In the supplemental consolidating data on this page, "GE" means the basis of consolidation as described in note 1 to the consolidated financial statements; "GECS" means General Electric Capital Services, Inc. and all of its affiliates and associated companies. Transactions between GE and GECS have been eliminated from the "General Electric Company and consolidated affiliates" columns on page 30.

Notes to Consolidated Financial Statements

Note 1 ㉕ *Summary of Significant Accounting Policies*

Consolidation. The consolidated financial statements represent the adding together of all affiliates — companies that General Electric directly or indirectly controls, either through majority ownership or otherwise. Results of associated companies — companies that are not controlled but are 20% to 50% owned — are included in the financial statements on a "one-line" basis.

Financial statement presentation. Financial data and related measurements are presented in the following categories.

■ **GE.** This represents the adding together of all affiliates other than General Electric Capital Services, Inc. ("GECS"), which is presented on a one-line basis.

■ **GECS.** This affiliate owns all of the common stock of General Electric Capital Corporation (GE Capital), Employers Reinsurance Corporation (ERC) and Kidder, Peabody Group Inc. (Kidder, Peabody). These affiliates and their respective affiliates are consolidated in the GECS columns and constitute its business.

■ **Consolidated.** These data represent the adding together of GE and GECS.

The effects of transactions among related companies within and between each of the above-mentioned groups are eliminated. Transactions between GE and GECS are not material.

Sales of goods and services. A sale is recorded when title passes to the customer or when services are performed in accordance with contracts.

GECS' revenues from operations ("earned income"). Income on all loans is recognized on the interest method. Accrual of interest income is suspended when collection of an account becomes doubtful, generally after the account becomes 90 days delinquent.

Financing lease income, which includes residual values and investment tax credits, is recorded on the interest method so as to produce a level yield on funds not yet recovered. Unguaranteed residual values included in lease income are based primarily on periodic independent appraisals of the values of leased assets remaining at expiration of the lease terms.

Operating lease income is recognized on a straight-line basis over the terms of underlying leases.

Origination, commitment and other nonrefundable fees related to fundings are deferred and recorded in earned income on the interest method. Commitment fees related to loans not expected to be funded and line-of-credit fees are deferred and recorded in earned income on a straight-line basis over the period to which the fees relate. Syndication fees are recorded in earned income at the time related services are performed unless significant contingencies exist.

Premiums on short-duration insurance contracts are reported as earned income over the terms of the related reinsurance treaties or insurance policies. In general, earned premiums are calculated on a pro rata basis or are determined based on reports received from reinsureds. Premium adjustments under retrospectively rated reinsurance contracts are recorded based on estimated losses and loss expenses, including both case and incurred-but-not-reported reserves. Revenues on long-duration insurance contracts are reported as earned when due. Premiums received under annuity contracts are not reported as revenues but as annuity benefits — a liability — and are adjusted according to terms of the respective policies.

Kidder, Peabody's proprietary securities and commodities transactions, unrealized gains and losses on open contractual commitments (principally financial futures), forward contracts on U.S. government and federal agency securities and when-issued securities are recorded on a trade-date basis. Customer transactions and related revenues and expenses, investment banking revenues from management fees, sales concessions and underwriting fees are recorded on a settlement-date basis. Advisory fees are recorded as revenues when services are substantially completed and the revenue is reasonably determinable.

Depreciation and amortization. The cost of most of GE's manufacturing plant and equipment is depreciated using an accelerated method based primarily on a sum-of-the-years digits formula. If manufacturing plant and equipment is subject to abnormal economic conditions or obsolescence, additional depreciation is provided.

The cost of GECS' equipment leased to others on operating leases is amortized, principally on a straight-line basis, to estimated net salvage value over the lease term or over the estimated economic life of the equipment. Depreciation of property and equipment for GECS' own use is recorded on either a sum-of-the-years digits formula or a straight-line basis over the lives of the assets.

Recognition of losses on financing receivables and investments. GE Capital maintains an allowance for losses on financing receivables at an amount that it believes is sufficient to provide adequate protection against future losses in the portfolio. When collateral is formally or substantively repossessed in satisfaction of a loan, the receivable is written down against the allowance for losses to estimated fair value and transferred to other assets. Subsequent to such transfer, these assets are carried at the lower of cost or estimated current fair value. This accounting has been employed principally for highly leveraged transactions (HLT) and real estate loans.

㉕ APB *Opinion No. 22* requires that all annual reports include a summary of significant accounting policies used, so the analyst can learn which accounting alternatives the company has chosen. Most firms provide this summary in the first footnote to their financial statements, as GE does.

㉖ GE explains its consolidation policy and three-entity presentation. See our comments 4, 15 and 16. The "one-line basis" is the *equity method* (see the Glossary).

㉗ Consolidated financial statements present information about a group of affiliated companies as if the group were one economic entity. Consequently, GE must eliminate from reported financial statements the gains or losses on sales of assets between companies in the consolidated group. GE postpones recognizing such gains or losses until one company of the consolidated group sells the assets to a buyer outside of the consolidated group.

㉘ GE uses the completed contract method of recognizing revenue on long-term construction projects. We know this, not because the language here is perfectly clear, but because we have asked GE about these words. See our comment 12.

㉙ See *effective interest method* and *amortized cost* in the Glossary.

㉚ GE is unusual among U.S. corporations in using accelerated depreciation for financial reporting. Most corporations use accelerated depreciation for tax reporting but less conservative methods in financial reporting. See *sum-of-the-years'-digits depreciation* in the Glossary.

㉛ See *allowance method* in the Glossary.

㉜ GECS holds large dollar values of marketable debt and equity securities, through its insurance subsidiaries and its investment banking subsidiary, the Kidder, Peabody Group Inc. In 1993, GE adopted *SFAS No. 115*, which requires these securities be classified into three categories: *trading, available for sale,* and *held to maturity* (see the Glossary, as well as GE's Notes 10 and 11, and our comment 56). In this portion of Note 1, GE describes the accounting required by *SFAS No. 115*.

㉝ GE uses the LIFO cost flow assumption for U.S. inventories. Most foreign governments do not allow LIFO for tax purposes, so GE gains no clear advantage from using LIFO outside the U.S. The company tells us it will not show an item of inventory on the balance sheet at an amount greater than net realizable value; we can deduce that it must be using a lower-of-cost-or-market valuation basis.

㉞ Goodwill results from GE's past acquisitions of other companies, in which it used purchase accounting. (See the Glossary under *purchase method* and *pooling-of-interests method*.) On the acquisition date, GE recorded the difference between the purchase price and the current value of the identifiable net assets acquired as an intangible asset called "goodwill." GE explains here that it amortizes goodwill over periods up to 40 years, the longest period allowed under APB *Opinion No. 17*. See GE's Note 16 on p. 54.

㉟ In Note 2, GE summarizes the sale of its Aerospace segment to Martin Marietta Corporation. See our comments 7, 11, and 20.

㊱ "Customer financing" is interest on receivables held by GE arising from some of its sales.

See note 8 for further information on GECS' allowance for losses on financing receivables.

Cash equivalents. Marketable securities with original maturities of three months or less are included in cash equivalents unless held for trading or investment.

③② *Investment and trading securities.* On December 31, 1993, the Company adopted Statement of Financial Accounting Standards (SFAS) No. 115, *Accounting for Certain Investments in Debt and Equity Securities,* which requires that investments in debt securities and marketable equity securities be designated as trading, held-to-maturity or available-for-sale. Trading securities are reported at fair value, with changes in fair value included in earnings. Investment securities include both available-for-sale and held-to-maturity securities. Available-for-sale securities are reported at fair value, with net unrealized gains and losses that would be available to share owners included in equity. Held-to-maturity debt securities are reported at amortized cost. See notes 10 and 11 for a discussion of the classification and reporting of these securities at December 31, 1992. For all investment securities, unrealized losses that are other than temporary are recognized in earnings.

Securities sold under agreements to repurchase (repurchase agreements) and securities purchased under agreements to resell (reverse repurchase agreements). Repurchase and reverse repurchase agreements are entered into by Kidder, Peabody and treated as financing transactions, carried at the contract amount at which the securities subsequently will be resold or reacquired. Repurchase agreements relate either to marketable securities, which are carried at market value, or to securities obtained pursuant to reverse repurchase agreements. It is Kidder, Peabody's policy to take possession of securities subject to reverse repurchase agreements, to monitor the market value of the underlying securities in relation to the related receivable, including accrued interest, and to obtain additional collateral when appropriate.

③③ *Inventories.* Virtually all of GE's U.S. inventories are stated on a last-in, first-out (LIFO) basis; other inventories are primarily stated on a first-in, first-out (FIFO) basis. None of the inventories exceed realizable values.

③④ *Intangible assets.* Goodwill is amortized over its estimated period of benefit and other intangible assets over their estimated lives. The amortization period does not exceed 40 years, and amortization is generally on a straight-line basis. Goodwill in excess of associated expected operating cash flows is considered to be impaired and is written down to fair value.

Deferred insurance acquisition costs. For the property and casualty business, deferred insurance acquisition costs are amortized pro rata over the contract periods in which the related premiums are earned. For the life insurance business, these costs are amortized over the premium-paying periods of the contracts in proportion either to anticipated premium income or to gross profit, as appropriate. For certain annuity contracts, such costs are amortized on the basis of anticipated gross profits. For other lines of business, acquisition costs are amortized over the life of the related insurance contracts. Deferred insurance acquisition costs are reviewed for recoverability; for short-duration contracts, anticipated investment income is considered in making recoverability evaluations.

Note 2 ㉟ Discontinued Operations

On April 2, 1993, General Electric Company transferred GE's Aerospace business segment, GE Government Services, Inc., and an operating component of GE that operated Knolls Atomic Power Laboratory under a contract with the U.S. Department of Energy to a new company controlled by the shareholders of Martin Marietta Corporation in a transaction valued at $3.3 billion. The transfer resulted in a gain of $678 million after taxes of $752 million. Net assets of discontinued operations at December 31, 1992, have been segregated in the Statement of Financial Position. Summary operating results of discontinued operations, excluding the above gain, are as follows.

(In millions)	1993	1992	1991
Revenues	$996	$5,231	$5,631
Earnings before income taxes	119	668	710
Provision for income taxes	44	248	259
Net earnings from discontinued operations	75	420	451

Note 3 GE Other Income

(In millions)	1993	1992	1991
Royalty and technical agreements	$371	$384	$394
Marketable securities and bank deposits	75	73	78
Associated companies	65	195	156
㊱ Customer financing	29	40	71
Other investments			
Dividends	50	18	3
Interest	21	22	18
Other sundry items	119	80	78
	$730	$812	$798

Note 4 GECS Revenues from Operations

(In millions)	1993	1992	1991
Time sales, loan, investment and other income	$11,999	$10,464	$ 9,790
Financing leases	2,315	2,151	1,836
Operating lease rentals	3,267	2,444	2,205
Premium and commission income of insurance affiliates	3,697	2,687	2,008
Commissions and fees of securities broker-dealer	859	694	560
	$22,137	$18,440	$16,399

Included in earned income from financing leases were gains on the sale of equipment at lease completion of $145 million in 1993, $126 million in 1992 and $147 million in 1991.

Noncancelable future rentals due from customers for equipment on operating leases as of December 31, 1993, totaled $6,133 million and are due as follows: $2,036 million in 1994; $1,455 million in 1995; $879 million in 1996; $458 million in 1997; $316 million in 1998; and $989 million thereafter.

Note 5 Supplemental Cost Details

Total expenditures for research and development were $1,955 million, $1,896 million and $1,866 million in 1993, 1992 and 1991, respectively. The Company-funded portion aggregated $1,297 million in 1993, $1,353 million in 1992 and $1,196 million in 1991.

Rental expense under operating leases was as follows.

(In millions)	1993	1992	1991
GE	$635	$683	$675
GECS	498	331	169

At December 31, 1993, minimum rental commitments under noncancelable operating leases aggregated $2,380 million and $3,579 million for GE and GECS, respectively. Amounts payable over the next five years are as follows.

(In millions)	1994	1995	1996	1997	1998
GE	$364	$274	$182	$144	$134
GECS	404	364	340	319	296

GE's selling, general and administrative expense totaled $5,124 million, $5,319 million and $5,422 million in 1993, 1992 and 1991, respectively.

Note 6 Pension and Other Retiree Benefits

GE and its affiliates sponsor a number of pension, retiree health and life insurance and other retiree benefit plans. Principal plans are discussed below; other plans are not significant individually or in the aggregate.

Effective January 1, 1991, the Company adopted SFAS No. 106, *Employers' Accounting for Postretirement Benefits Other Than Pensions,* using the immediate recognition transition option. The transition effect of this accounting change was a reduction in 1991 net earnings of $1,799 million ($2.07 per share).

Principal pension plans are the GE Pension Plan and the GE Supplementary Pension Plan.

The GE Pension Plan covers substantially all GE employees in the United States and approximately 45% of GECS employees. Generally, benefits are based on the greater of a formula recognizing career earnings or a formula recognizing length of service and final average earnings. Benefit provisions are subject to collective bargaining. At the end of 1993, the GE Pension Plan covered approximately 457,000 participants, including 143,000 employees, 139,000 former employees with vested rights to future benefits and 175,000 retirees and beneficiaries receiving benefits.

The GE Supplementary Pension Plan is an unfunded plan providing supplementary retirement benefits primarily to higher-level, longer-service U.S. employees.

Principal retiree benefit plans generally provide health and life insurance benefits to employees who retire under the GE Pension Plan with 10 or more years of service. Benefit provisions are subject to collective bargaining. At the end of 1993, these plans covered approximately 246,000 retirees and dependents.

Transfer of Aerospace businesses in 1993 resulted in associated transfers of GE Pension Plan assets of $1,169 million and projected benefit obligations of $979 million to new pension plans. The 1993 gain on transfer of discontinued operations included pension plan curtailment/settlement losses of $125 million before income taxes and retiree health and life plan curtailment/settlement gains of $245 million before income taxes.

(37) See *capital lease*, *direct financing lease* and *operating lease* in the Glossary.

(38) In these operating leases, GE acts as lessor. Although GE has an assured right to receive these payments and has already put the equipment in the hands of the users, it will not recognize revenue until it receives cash. Accounting views such operating leases as *executory contracts* (see the Glossary), not yet having generated revenue.

(39) *SFAS No. 2* requires GE to expense research and development (R & D) costs, and to disclose the costs incurred during the year for R & D. Since GE does not identify R & D costs separately on its income statement (they probably appear in "Other costs and expenses"), it reports them here. *SFAS No. 2* allows firms to capitalize reimbursable R & D costs they incur under contract. GE identifies the R & D costs that do not qualify for capitalization ($1,297 million in 1993) by stating that they are Company-funded.

(40) In these operating leases, GE acts as lessee. Although GE can use the leased equipment and must make future payments, it recognizes neither an asset nor liability. See the Glossary under *executory contracts*. *SFAS No. 13* requires companies with operating leases to report current rental expense and non-cancelable payable amounts for the next five years.

(41) These are *defined benefit plans*, in contrast to *defined contribution plans*; see the Glossary.

(42) GE uses these assumptions in computing its obligation and costs for pensions and other postretirement benefits. During 1993, GE reduced the discount rate it uses to compute the *projected benefit obligation* (see the Glossary) from 9.0 percent to 7.25 percent. GE also reduced its estimate of the rate at which wages and health care costs will increase in the future. GE expects the invested plan assets to earn a 9.5 percent rate of return on average.

(43) Pension cost comprises four pieces:

   (1) "Benefit cost for service during the year," sometimes called "current service costs," arises because employees have worked during the current year while covered by a defined benefit pension plan. GE's current service costs are $452 million for 1993.

   (2) "Interest cost on benefit obligation," $1,486 million, is the 1993 interest accumulation on the pension obligation for work performed in earlier years.

   (3) GE funds its pension plans with cash, which a pension plan trustee invests in assets such as debt and equity securities. The returns on those assets offset pension expense otherwise recorded. *SFAS No. 87* requires that the *expected* return on pension plan assets, not the actual return, offset pension expense. GE shows the actual return on plan assets, $3,221 million, then subtracts the excess of actual return over expected return, $1,066 million, so that the expected return, $2,155 (= $3,221 − $1,066) million, is part of pension cost. GE adds the "Unrecognized portion of return" to "Experience gains (losses)," an item which appears only in the notes (see comment 47 below).

   (4) GE amortizes three items, described below in our comment 47: the *SFAS No. 87* transition gain, Experience gains (losses), and Plan amendments. Amortization reduces GE's pension expense by $352 million in 1993.

(44) GE computes costs for postretirement benefits other than pensions in a manner similar to pension costs, which comment 43 describes.

(45) Federal law requires GE to fund its pension plan, i.e. to place assets with an independent trustee who will use them to satisfy obligations to employees in future. On its tax return, GE may deduct the amounts used to fund the pension plan only to the extent that the amounts satisfy legal funding requirements. Since 1987, GE's pension plan assets have exceeded the amount required by law, so the company has added no new funds and would receive no tax deduction if it did. No law requires non-pension postretirement benefits to be funded. Like most companies, GE funds these non-pension benefits only to the extent that it can deduct the amounts on its tax return.

Actuarial assumptions used during the past three years to determine costs and benefit obligations for principal plans are shown below.

Actuarial assumptions (42)

Determination of cost/income for the year	1993	1992	1991
Discount rate	8.5%	9.0%	9.0%
Compensation increases	5.5	6.0	6.0
Return on assets	9.5	9.5	9.5
Health care cost trend (a)	12.0	12.5	13.0
Determination of benefit obligation at year end			
Discount rate	7.25	9.0	9.0
Compensation increases	4.25	6.0	6.0
Health care cost trend	9.5(b)	12.0(a)	12.5(a)

(a) Gradually declining to 6.6% after 2049.
(b) Gradually declining to 5.0% after 2022.

Increasing the health care cost trend rates by one percentage point would increase the accumulated postretirement benefit obligation by $23 million and would increase annual aggregate service and interest costs by $3 million.

Gains and losses that occur because actual experience differs from actuarial assumptions are amortized over the average future service period of employees. Amounts allocable to prior service for plan amendments are amortized in a similar manner.

Employer costs for principal pension and retiree health and life insurance benefit plans follow.

Cost (income) for pension plans (43)

(In millions)	1993	1992	1991
Benefit cost for service during the year — net of employee contributions	$ 452	$ 494	$ 446
Interest cost on benefit obligation	1,486	1,502	1,400
Actual return on plan assets	(3,221)	(1,562)	(4,331)
Unrecognized portion of return	1,066	(584)	2,272
Amortization	(352)	(436)	(483)
Pension plan cost (income) (a)	$ (569)	$ (586)	$ (696)

(a) Pension plan cost (income) for continuing operations was $(555) million for 1993, $(494) million for 1992 and $(576) million for 1991.

Cost (income) for retiree health and life plans (44)

(In millions)	1993	1992	1991
Retiree health plans			
Benefit cost for service during the year	$ 49	$ 62	$ 65
Interest cost on benefit obligation	192	203	214
Actual return on plan assets	(3)	(4)	(9)
Unrecognized portion of return	1	—	5
Amortization	(26)	(40)	(33)
Retiree health plan cost	213	221	242
Retiree life plans			
Benefit cost for service during the year	21	24	23
Interest cost on benefit obligation	111	110	104
Actual return on plan assets	(152)	(78)	(129)
Unrecognized portion of return	42	(20)	39
Amortization	7	2	—
Retiree life plan cost	29	38	37
Total (a)	$242	$259	$279

(a) Retiree health and life plan cost for continuing operations was $224 million for 1993, $213 million for 1992 and $218 million for 1991.

Funding policy for the GE Pension Plan is to contribute (45) amounts sufficient to meet minimum funding requirements set forth in employee benefit and tax laws plus such additional amounts as GE may determine to be appropriate from time to time. GE has not made contributions since 1987 because the fully funded status of the GE Pension Plan precludes current tax deduction and because any Company contribution would require the Company to pay annual excise taxes. Subject to tax laws, the present value of future life insurance benefits for each eligible retiree is funded in the year of retirement. In general, retiree health benefits are paid as covered expenses are incurred.

The following table compares the market-related value of assets with the present value of benefit obligations, recognizing the effects of future compensation and service. The market-related value of assets is based on cost plus recognition of market appreciation and depreciation in the portfolio over five years, a method that reduces the short-term impact of market fluctuations.

Funded status of principal plans

(In millions)	1993	1992	1991
Pension plans			
Market-related value of assets	$24,532	$24,204	$23,192
Projected benefit obligation	20,796	17,999	17,355
Retiree health and life plans			
Market-related value of assets	1,252	1,220	1,124
Accumulated postretirement benefit obligation	4,120	3,743	3,675

Assets in trust consist mainly of common stock and fixed-income investments. GE common stock represents less than 2% of trust assets and is held in part in an indexed portfolio.

Schedules reconciling the benefit obligations for principal plans with GE's recorded liabilities in the Statement of Financial Position are shown on the following page.

(46) GE shows here that its pension plan assets exceed its projected benefit obligation, but the reverse is true for retiree health plans and life insurance plans.

(47) GE gradually amortizes three balances into pension, retiree health care and life plan expense (see item (4) in comment 43 above).

    (1)   When GE first adopted *SFAS No. 87*, its pension assets exceeded its liabilities. GE could have increased net income in the year of adoption with a "transition gain," but chose instead to defer the gain and amortize it gradually, reducing pension expense in future periods. The "*SFAS No. 87* transition gain" is the remaining unamortized portion of the initial net pension asset.

    (2)   "Experience gains (losses)" comprise differences between expected return on plan assets and actual return on plan assets (see item (3) in comment 43 above), along with changes in the actuarial assumptions used to compute the projected benefit obligation (see comment 42). In 1993, GE has unamortized experience gains in its pension plans, but it has unamortized experience losses in its other postretirement benefits. *SFAS No. 87* requires GE to amortize experience gains and losses only if the amount exceeds 10 percent of the larger of plan assets or the projected benefit obligation, measured at the beginning of the year. The experience losses in GE's retiree health plans exceed 10 percent of the related obligation (which GE reports on page 48 in the table marked "Funded status of principal plans"), so *SFAS No. 87* requires some amortization.

    (3)   Plan amendments, sometimes called "prior service costs," reflect changes in the projected obligation because GE amended the benefit plan, and the amendment applies retroactively to employees' past service. This can happen, for example, as a result of organized labor contract renegotiation. Prior to 1993, GE has amended its pension plan in a manner that increased the obligation (GE has "sweetened" the plan), and amended its retiree health plan in a way that reduced the obligation. GE amortizes these changes in the projected obligations gradually into expense.

(48) GE has several pension plans, whose results appear together in Note 6. At least one pension plan is overfunded at the end of 1993, with a prepaid pension balance of $3,840 million included on GE's balance sheet in "All other assets" (see Note 17 on p. 54). At least one pension plan is underfunded at year end 1993, with a liability of $496 million recorded on GE's balance sheet in "All other liabilities." Retiree health plans and life plans have liability balances of $2,499 and $11 million, respectively, in "All other liabilities."

(49) *SFAS No. 34* requires separate disclosure of amounts of interest capitalized into plant under construction.

(50) See *allowance method* in the Glossary, and GE's Note 1 near the callout for our comment 31.

Reconciliation of benefit obligation with recorded liability	Pension plans		Retiree health plans		Retiree life plans	
December 31 (In millions)	1993	1992	1993	1992	1993	1992
Benefit obligation	$ 20,796	$ 17,999	$2,586	$2,416	$ 1,534	$1,327
Fair value of trust assets	(27,193)	(26,466)	(13)	(32)	(1,317)	(1,221)
Unamortized balances						
SFAS No. 87 transition gain	1,077	1,231	—	—	—	—
Experience gains (losses)	2,371	4,939	(654)	(394)	(206)	(21)
Plan amendments	(395)	(518)	580	764	—	—
Recorded prepaid asset	3,840	3,310	—	—	—	—
Recorded liability	$ 496	$ 495	$2,499	$2,754	$ 11	$ 85

The portion of the projected benefit obligation representing the accumulated benefit obligation for pension plans was $19,890 million and $16,975 million at the end of 1993 and 1992, respectively. The vested benefit obligation for pension plans was $19,732 million and $16,799 million at the end of 1993 and 1992, respectively.

Details of the accumulated postretirement benefit obligation are shown below.

Accumulated postretirement benefit obligation December 31 (In millions)	1993	1992
Retiree health plans		
Retirees and dependents	$2,017	$1,789
Employees eligible to retire	119	137
Other employees	450	490
	$2,586	$2,416
Retiree life plans		
Retirees and dependents	$1,147	$ 907
Employees eligible to retire	79	83
Other employees	308	337
	$1,534	$1,327

Note 7 Interest and Other Financial Charges

GE. Interest capitalized, principally on major property, plant and equipment projects, was $21 million in 1993, $29 million in 1992 and $33 million in 1991.

GECS. Interest and discount expense reported in the Statement of Earnings is net of interest income on temporary investments of excess funds ($42 million, $48 million and $54 million in 1993, 1992 and 1991, respectively) and capitalized interest ($5 million, $6 million and $8 million in 1993, 1992 and 1991, respectively).

Note 8 GECS Allowance for Losses on Financing Receivables

GECS allowance for losses on financing receivables represented 2.63% of total financing receivables at year-end 1993 and 1992. The allowance for small-balance receivables is determined principally on the basis of actual experience during the preceding three years. Further allowances are provided to reflect management's judgment of additional loss potential. For other receivables, principally the larger loans and leases, the allowance for losses is determined primarily on the basis of management's judgment of net loss potential, including specific allowances for known troubled accounts. The table below shows the activity in the allowance for losses on financing receivables during each of the past three years.

(In millions)	1993	1992	1991
Balance at January 1	$ 1,607	$ 1,508	$ 1,360
Provisions charged to operations	987	1,056	1,102
Net transfers related to companies acquired or sold	126	52	135
Amounts written off — net	(990)	(1,009)	(1,089)
Balance at December 31	$ 1,730	$ 1,607	$ 1,508

All accounts or portions thereof deemed to be uncollectible or to require an excessive collection cost are written off to the allowance for losses. Small-balance accounts are progressively written down (from 10% when more than three months delinquent to 100% when 9-12 months delinquent) to record the balances at estimated realizable value. If at any time during that period an account is judged to be uncollectible, such as in the case of a bankruptcy, the uncollectible balance is written off. Large-balance accounts are reviewed at least quarterly, and those accounts that are more than three months delinquent are written down, if necessary, to record the balances at estimated realizable value. Amounts written off in 1993 were approximately 1.46% of average financing receivables outstanding during the year, compared with 1.58% and 1.87% of average financing receivables outstanding during 1992 and 1991, respectively.

(51) This schedule shows the details of income tax expense, which GE calls a "provision." The bottom line of the first schedule is the total expense reported on the statement of earnings, the sum of U.S. federal, foreign, and other income tax expenses. GE derives the income tax expense amounts by first reporting the amount of taxes payable, and then adjusting for *temporary differences* (see the Glossary, and GE's Note 23 on p. 57) and for the effect of the investment credit. Prior to its repeal by Congress, GE earned investment credits when it acquired new qualifying assets. Unlike most U.S. corporations, GE uses the more conservative deferral method of accounting for the investment credit, rather than the flow-through method. The deferral method recognizes the tax-reducing (income-increasing) effects of the investment credit over the lives of the assets producing the credit. GE and GECS recognized $24 million of investment credits during 1993. If GE had used the flow-through method, income tax expense would have been lower in some earlier years and larger in 1993 by $24 million.

(52) The SEC requires disclosure of pretax income disaggregated into domestic and foreign sources. (See the last paragraph of GE's Note 9, on page 50.) The analyst can thereby compute an effective foreign tax rate for 1993 of 50.4 percent (= $328/$651). Compare this with the overall effective rate discussed in our comment 53.

(53) The SEC requires companies to report in their notes how the reported income tax expense rate differs from the statutory U.S. federal tax rate of 35 percent (34 percent in 1992 and 1991). The 32.7 percent effective tax figure for 1993, which GE calls the "Actual income tax rate," results from dividing income tax expense of $2,151 million by pretax income, $6,575 million. Comment 54 explains the additions and subtractions to derive GE's actual effective income tax rate from the statutory income tax rate.

(54) The reasons that the effective tax rate (see comment 53) differs from the U.S. statutory rate include the following.

(1)   GE's 1993 income statement includes $1,807 million of *after-tax* income from GECS, using the equity method, yet it appears in GE's income statement before the income tax calculation. Since GE and GECS file a consolidated tax return, GE pays no further taxes on the income from GECS.

(2)   Because the corporate statutory tax rate increased from 34 to 35 percent in 1993, GE adjusts the deferred taxes it recorded in prior years for the new, higher rate expected to be in effect when it pays (or recovers) the taxes. (See GE's Note 23 and our comment 71.)

(3)   Amortization of goodwill acquired before August 11, 1993, is not tax-deductible. This *permanent difference* (see the Glossary) reduces shareholder net income, increasing the effective tax rate relative to the statutory rate.

(4)   Some of GECS's income, for example income on state and municipal bonds, is tax-exempt at the federal level — another permanent difference. This decreases the effective tax rate, relative to the statutory rate.

(5)   See the Glossary at *FSC*. The IRS exempts some income from Foreign Sales Corporations from tax, and taxes other such income at lower rates than the statutory rate.

(6)   To reduce the negative incentives created by taxing dividends paid by one corporation to another, Congress exempts between 70 and 80 percent of intercorporate dividends from income tax. See *double taxation* in the Glossary.

(55) *SFAS No. 115* became effective for GE's 1993 fiscal year. The standard requires firms to classify investments in debt and equity securities into three categories: trading, held-to-maturity and available-for-sale. Note 10 concerns *trading securities* (see the Glossary), which GECS holds primarily to generate short-term trading profits. Comment 56 on GE's Note 11 discusses *held-to-maturity* and *available-for-sale* securities. We infer from the title to Note 10 and the first line of Note 11 that GECS, not GE, holds all the trading securities. *SFAS No. 115* requires the firm to report trading securities at year-end market value, and to recognize both realized and unrealized gains and losses in net income. Note 10 discloses that in 1992, GECS classified equity securities held by its insurance affiliates as trading securities, but it reclassified them as available-for-sale when the FASB issued *SFAS No. 115* in 1993.

Note 9 Provision for Income Taxes

(In millions)	1993	1992	1991
GE			
Estimated amounts payable	$1,207	$ 697	$1,088
Deferred tax expense from temporary differences	120	762	311
Investment credit deferred (amortized) — net	(17)	(27)	(39)
	1,310	1,432	1,360
GECS			
Estimated amounts payable (recoverable)	507	374	(192)
Deferred tax expense from temporary differences	341	167	555
Investment credit deferred (amortized) — net	(7)	(5)	19
	841	536	382
Consolidated			
Estimated amounts payable	1,714	1,071	896
Deferred tax expense from temporary differences	461	929	866
Investment credit deferred (amortized) — net	(24)	(32)	(20)
	$2,151	$1,968	$1,742

GE includes GECS in filing a consolidated U.S. federal income tax return. GECS' provision for estimated taxes payable (recoverable) includes its effect on the consolidated return.

Estimated consolidated amounts payable includes amounts applicable to non-U.S. jurisdictions of $328 million, $294 million and $254 million in 1993, 1992 and 1991, respectively.

SFAS No. 109, *Accounting for Income Taxes*, was adopted effective January 1, 1992. The effect of adopting this new standard was not material.

Deferred income tax balances reflect the impact of temporary differences between the carrying amount of assets and liabilities and their tax bases and are stated at enacted tax rates expected to be in effect when taxes are actually paid or recovered. See note 23 for details.

Except for certain earnings that GE intends to reinvest indefinitely, provision has been made for the estimated U.S. federal income tax liabilities applicable to undistributed earnings of affiliates and associated companies.

Based on location (not tax jurisdiction) of the business providing goods and services, consolidated U.S. income before taxes was $5,924 million in 1993, $5,639 million in 1992 and $5,034 million in 1991. The corresponding amounts for non-U.S. based operations were $651 million in 1993, $634 million in 1992 and $692 million in 1991.

Reconciliation of U.S. federal statutory rate to actual tax rate	Consolidated			GE			GECS		
	1993	1992	1991	1993	1992	1991	1993	1992	1991
Statutory U.S. federal income tax rate	35.0%	34.0%	34.0%	35.0%	34.0%	34.0%	35.0%	34.0%	34.0%
Increase (reduction) in rate resulting from:									
Inclusion of after-tax earnings of GECS in before-tax earnings of GE	—	—	—	(11.0)	(8.9)	(8.1)	—	—	—
Rate increase — deferred taxes	1.5	—	—	(0.2)	—	—	4.3	—	—
Amortization of goodwill	1.5	1.3	1.4	1.1	0.9	1.0	1.2	1.4	1.6
Tax-exempt income	(2.8)	(2.6)	(2.9)	—	—	—	(6.8)	(8.1)	(10.1)
Foreign Sales Corporation tax benefits	(1.2)	(1.1)	(1.1)	(1.4)	(1.2)	(1.2)	—	—	—
Dividends received not fully taxable	(0.7)	(0.3)	(0.4)	(0.3)	—	—	(1.0)	(1.0)	(1.3)
All other — net	(0.6)	0.1	(0.6)	(0.4)	0.2	(0.3)	(0.9)	—	(1.1)
	(2.3)	(2.6)	(3.6)	(12.2)	(9.0)	(8.6)	(3.2)	(7.7)	(10.9)
Actual income tax rate	32.7%	31.4%	30.4%	22.8%	25.0%	25.4%	31.8%	26.3%	23.1%

Note 10 GECS Trading Securities

December 31 (In millions)	1993	1992
U.S. government and federal agency securities	$19,543	$16,172
Corporate stocks, bonds and non-U.S. securities	8,969	5,960
Mortgage loans	1,292	974
State and municipal securities	361	1,048
	$30,165	$24,154

The balance of GECS' trading securities at December 31, 1992, included investments in equity securities held by insurance affiliates at a fair value of $1,505 million, with unrealized pretax gains of $94 million (net of unrealized pretax losses of $37 million) included in equity. At December 31, 1993, equity securities held by insurance affiliates were classified as investment securities (see note 11).

A significant portion of GECS' trading securities at December 31, 1993, was pledged as collateral for bank loans and repurchase agreements in connection with securities broker-dealer operations.

(56) Prior to 1993, under *SFAS No. 12*, GE generally reported investments in equity securities at the lower of cost or market value, while it carried investments in debt securities at cost plus accrued interest, net of payments (See the Glossary at *amortized cost*.). *SFAS No. 115* allows GE to report *held-to-maturity* debt securities, those for which management has both the intent and ability to hold to maturity, at amortized cost. *Available-for-sale* securities comprise all debt securities that are not trading securities and not held-to-maturity securities, and all marketable equity securities, except equity shares for which the firm uses the equity method or consolidation. Under *SFAS No. 115*, GE reports available-for-sale securities at year-end market value, and records unrealized gains and losses in an owners' equity account separate from retained earnings. (See the Glossary at *held-to-maturity securities* and *available-for-sale securities*.) Note 11 records GE's transition from *SFAS No. 12* to *SFAS No. 115*, and tells us that GE carried its investment securities, all available-for-sale, at market value both years. GECS reported its investments at their cost of $11,224 million at December 31, 1992, but classified them as available-for-sale in 1993 and reported them at market value of $26,792. (Refer to the balance sheet columns labelled "GECS.")

(57) The SEC requires firms to report concentrations of credit risk arising because they sell to a small number of customers, in a narrow industry or in a limited geographic region. *SFAS No. 14* requires disclosure about customers whose purchases represent 10 percent or more of a firm's revenues. GE discloses here that its Aircraft engine accounts receivable are concentrated in one large customer, the U.S. government, and in one industry, airlines.

(58) GE has sold some accounts receivable, although it retains partial liability to the purchaser if customers default on their accounts. (See the Glossary under *factoring* and *recourse*.)

Note 11 Investment Securities

GE's investment securities were classified as available-for-sale at year-end 1993 and 1992. Carrying value was substantially the same as fair value at both year ends.

At December 31, 1993, GECS' investment securities were classified as available-for-sale and reported at fair value, including net unrealized gains of $1,261 million before taxes. At December 31, 1992, investment securities of $9,033 million were classified as available-for-sale and were reported at the lower of aggregate amortized cost or fair value. The balance of the 1992 investment securities portfolio was carried at amortized cost.

A summary of GECS' investment securities follows.

GECS investment securities

(In millions)	Amortized cost	Estimated fair value	Gross unrealized gains (a)	Gross unrealized losses (a)
December 31, 1993				
Corporate, non-U.S. and other	$11,448	$11,595	$ 206	$ (59)
State and municipal	8,859	9,636	786	(9)
Mortgage-backed	2,487	2,507	31	(11)
Equity	1,517	1,826	393	(84)
U.S. government and federal agency	1,220	1,228	15	(7)
	$25,531	$26,792	$1,431	$(170)
December 31, 1992				
Corporate, non-U.S. and other	$ 4,097	$ 4,167	$ 70	$ —
State and municipal	6,626	6,951	339	(14)
Mortgage-backed	246	252	7	(1)
U.S. government and federal agency	255	264	10	(1)
	$11,224	$11,634	$ 426	$ (16)

(a) December 31, 1992, amounts include gross unrealized gains and losses of $32 million and $5 million, respectively, on investment securities carried at amortized cost.

Contractual maturities of debt securities, other than mortgage-backed securities, at December 31, 1993, are shown below.

GECS contractual maturities
(excluding mortgage-backed securities)

(In millions)	Amortized cost	Estimated fair value
Due in		
1994	$ 2,665	$ 2,696
1995-1998	4,326	4,476
1999-2003	4,316	4,429
2004 and later	10,220	10,858

It is expected that actual maturities will differ from contractual maturities because borrowers have the right to call or prepay certain obligations, sometimes without call or prepayment penalties. Proceeds from sales of investment securities in 1993 were $6,112 million ($3,514 million in 1992 and $2,814 million in 1991). Gross realized gains were $173 million in 1993 ($171 million in 1992 and $106 million in 1991). Gross realized losses were $34 million in 1993 ($4 million in 1992 and $9 million in 1991).

Note 12 GE Current Receivables

December 31 (In millions)	1993	1992
Aircraft Engines	$1,860	$2,047
Appliances	456	446
Broadcasting	431	463
Industrial	1,161	1,150
Materials	1,060	719
Power Systems	2,083	1,389
Technical Products and Services	548	696
All Other	243	232
Corporate	889	498
	8,731	7,640
Less allowance for losses	(170)	(178)
	$8,561	$7,462

Of the total receivables balances at December 31, 1993 and 1992, $5,719 million and $5,284 million, respectively, were from sales of goods and services to customers, and $292 million and $170 million, respectively, were from transactions with associated companies.

Current receivables of $402 million at year-end 1993 and $256 million at year-end 1992 arose from sales, principally of aircraft engine goods and services, on open account to various agencies of the U.S. government, which is GE's largest single customer (about 8%, 9% and 10% of GE's sales of goods and services were to the U.S. government in 1993, 1992 and 1991, respectively). Current receivables from sales on open account of aircraft engine goods and services to airline industry customers were $418 million and $651 million at December 31, 1993 and 1992, respectively.

To reduce political and credit risks, certain long-term international medical equipment customer receivables are sold with partial credit recourse. Proceeds from such sales were $89 million, $71 million and $13 million in 1993, 1992 and 1991, respectively; balances outstanding were $146 million and $82 million at December 31, 1993 and 1992, respectively.

㊿ GE uses a LIFO cost flow assumption for inventories, but manages its inventories, as most sensible businesses do, on FIFO, using the older materials and finished goods before the newer. It keeps its records internally on a FIFO basis. The FIFO cost of 1993 year-end inventories is $5,453. GE makes an adjustment at year-end to convert the internal records to LIFO, by debiting Cost of Goods Sold (or Work in Process Inventory) and crediting Ending Inventory for $1,629 million. Some business analysts call this amount the "LIFO reserve," but we prefer GE's more descriptive caption. The numbers given for "Less revaluation to LIFO" allow the computation of pretax income had GE used FIFO, rather than LIFO. The IRS does not allow companies using LIFO for tax purposes to disclose in the financial statements what income would have been under FIFO. The SEC, however, requires the disclosure of beginning and ending inventories as they would have been under FIFO, if these amounts differ significantly from the LIFO amounts. The SEC's required disclosure allows the analyst to compute the income difference. As of December 31, 1993, *cumulative* pretax income is $1,629 million less than it would have been under FIFO. As of January 1, 1993, cumulative pretax income is $1,808 million less than it would have been under FIFO. This difference decreased by $179 (= $1,808 – $1,629) million during 1993. Hence, 1993 pretax income would have been $179 million smaller if GE had used FIFO. This calculation may be seen more clearly in the accompanying exhibit. Generally, FIFO leads to larger income than does LIFO. We explain the reasons for GE's smaller FIFO income in our comment 60.

INVENTORY DATA: GENERAL ELECTRIC, 1993
(For Authors' comment 59. Dollar amounts are in millions.)

	LIFO Cost-Flow Assumption (Actually Used)	+	Excess of FIFO over LIFO Amount	=	FIFO Cost-Flow Assumption (Hypothetical)
Beginning Inventory......................	$ 4,574[a]		$1,808		$ 6,382
Purchases[b]	21,856		0		21,856
Cost of Goods Available for Sale	$26,430		$1,808		$28,238
Less: Ending Inventory	3,824		1,629		5,453
Cost of Goods Sold	$22,606		$ 179		$22,785
Sales of Goods..........................	$29,509		$0		$29,509
Less: Cost of Goods Sold	22,606		179		22,785
Gross Margin on Sales	$ 6,903		($ 179)		$ 6,724

---

[a] Amounts shown in **boldface** appear in GE's financial statements and notes.
[b] Computation of Purchases:

Purchases	=	Cost of Goods Sold	+	Ending Inventory	–	Beginning Inventory
$21,856	=	$22,606	+	$3,824	–	$4,574

㉖ See the Glossary at *LIFO inventory layer*, particularly the last sentence. GE has decreased its inventory by selling more items than it acquired. Under LIFO, we assume that GE sold all the items it acquired in 1993, plus some items from beginning inventory. If GE had purchased sufficient amounts at year-end to avoid selling from old layers, these purchases would have cost more than the old layers assumed sold, cost of goods sold would have been higher and income for the period would have been lower. GE tells us that 1993 pretax income is $101 million larger because of the dips into old LIFO layers. The rest of the 1993 $179 million decrease in LIFO revaluation (and $179 million increase in pretax income) results from price declines.

㉖ GECS and its affiliates have a variety of long-term receivables, including loans, time sales and financing leases, which this note details.

㉖ GECS acts as the lessor in many equipment leases that provide financing to the equipment user, called *direct financing* and *leveraged leases* (see the Glossary). In these leases, GECS retains title to the leased equipment, but the equipment does not appear on its balance sheet. Instead, GECS records an "Investment in financing leases" equal to the discounted present value of the future payments receivable on the lease, plus the discounted present value of the expected residual value of the equipment after the lease term. For some of these leases, a third party provides some of the financing, while GE retains the "equity" interest.

Note *13* GE Inventories

December 31 (In millions)	1993	1992
Raw materials and work in process	$ 2,983	$ 3,598
Finished goods	2,314	2,596
Unbilled shipments	156	188
	5,453	6,382
Less revaluation to LIFO	(1,629)	(1,808)
	$ 3,824	$ 4,574

LIFO revaluations decreased $179 million in 1993 compared with decreases of $204 million and $141 million in 1992 and 1991, respectively. Included in these changes were decreases of $101 million, $183 million and $111 million (1993, 1992 and 1991, respectively) resulting from lower inventory levels. There were modest cost decreases in 1993, 1992 and 1991. At December 31, 1993, GE is obligated to acquire, under take-or-pay or similar arrangements, about $250 million per year of raw materials at market prices through 1998.

Note *14* GECS Financing Receivables (investment in time sales, loans and financing leases)

December 31 (In millions)	1993	1992
Time sales and loans		
Specialized financing	$17,138	$18,725
Consumer services	18,732	15,267
Mid-market financing	5,514	3,952
Equipment management	438	71
	41,822	38,015
Deferred income	(1,074)	(945)
Time sales and loans — net	40,748	37,070
Investment in financing leases		
Direct financing leases	22,063	20,890
Leveraged leases	2,867	3,035
Investment in financing leases	24,930	23,925
	65,678	60,995
Less allowance for losses	(1,730)	(1,607)
	$63,948	$59,388

Time sales and loans represents transactions in a variety of forms, including time sales, revolving charge and credit, mortgages, installment loans, intermediate-term loans and revolving loans secured by business assets. The portfolio includes time sales and loans carried at the principal amount on which finance charges are billed periodically, and time sales and loans acquired on a discount basis carried at gross book value, which includes finance charges. At year-end 1993 and 1992, specialized financing and consumer services loans included $11,887 million and $10,526 million, respectively, for commercial real estate loans and $3,293 million and $5,262 million, respectively, for highly leveraged transactions. Note 17 contains information on airline loans and leases.

At December 31, 1993, contractual maturities for time sales and loans over the next five years and after were: $16,287 million in 1994; $6,286 million in 1995; $4,350 million in 1996; $4,104 million in 1997; $3,112 million in 1998; and $7,683 million in 1999 and later — aggregating $41,822 million. Experience has shown that a substantial portion of receivables will be paid prior to contractual maturity. Accordingly, the maturities of time sales and loans are not to be regarded as forecasts of future cash collections.

Financing leases consists of direct financing and leveraged leases of aircraft, railroad rolling stock, autos, other transportation equipment, data processing equipment, medical equipment, and other manufacturing, power generation, mining and commercial equipment and facilities.

As the sole owner of assets under direct financing leases and as the equity participant in leveraged leases, GECS is taxed on total lease payments received and is entitled to tax deductions based on the cost of leased assets and tax deductions for interest paid to third-party participants. GECS generally is entitled to any investment tax credit on leased equipment and to any residual value of leased assets.

Investment in direct financing and leveraged leases represents unpaid rentals and estimated unguaranteed residual values of leased equipment, less related deferred income. Because GECS has no general obligation for principal and interest on notes and other instruments representing third-party participation related to leveraged leases, such notes and other instruments have not been included in liabilities but have been offset against the related rentals receivable. GECS' share of rentals receivable on leveraged leases is subordinate to the share of its other participants who also have a security interest in the leased equipment.

GECS' investment in financing leases is shown on the following page.

Ⓡ In Note 15, GE discloses the original cost of its property, plant and equipment. In addition to the equipment under financing leases described above in comment 62, GECS leases most of the equipment that appears on its balance sheet under *operating leases* (see the Glossary).

Ⓢ GE uses *accelerated depreciation* for most of its depreciable assets. GECS uses accelerated depreciation for its own property, plant and equipment, but *straight-line depreciation* for assets leased to others. (See GE's Note 1 on page 45 at the callout for our comment 30, and the Glossary.) If a firm depreciates an asset costing $1,000 on a straight-line basis in the amount of $100 per year and has accumulated depreciation of $400 at year-end, then the asset must be four (= $400/$100) years old. If we assume that GECS depreciates all its property, plant and equipment on a straight-line basis, then the analogous computation for GECS indicates that the assets are roughly 2.5 [= ($814 + $3,238)/$1,630] years old. This calculation uses depreciation expense, $1,630 million, from the Statement of Cash Flows on page 31. If GE used straight-line depreciation, the analogous computation indicates it spent the dollars on its assets roughly 7.9 (= $12,899/$1,631) years before the balance sheet date. Since GE uses accelerated depreciation, accumulated depreciation builds up at a faster rate than under straight-line depreciation, and we can conclude that GE spent dollars for plant on average less than 7.9 years prior to the end of 1993.

Ⓣ See GE's Note 1 at the callout for our comment 34.

Ⓤ See our comment 48.

Ⓥ The schedule at the top of the left-hand column of p. 55 in GE's Note 18 gives the details of its short-term borrowings. The schedule at the top of the right-hand column of the same page gives the details of its long-term borrowings. This paragraph helps the analyst to understand GE's intermediate-term borrowings. From these data, the analyst can estimate cash requirements for debt retirements over the next several years.

Ⓦ The borrower, GECS, can repay these long-term borrowings at any time and the lender can demand repayment at specified "option" times. At the option date, the lender may want to change the interest rate to then-current market conditions, and the borrower will agree to the new interest rate or will pay off the debt. The economic substance of such lending is, we think, short-term debt, not long-term debt, because the lender can require the debt be paid, even on a whim. Those who set GAAP, however, do not agree.

Ⓧ In Note 22, GE describes its adoption of *SFAS No. 112*, which requires that GE accrue postemployment, pre-retirement benefits like severance packages over an employee's service life, just as it accrues costs for pensions and postemployment medical benefits (see our comment 8). See GE's Note 6 and our accompanying comments for a description of the accounting for deferred employee benefits.

Investment in financing leases	Total financing leases		Direct financing leases		Leveraged leases	
December 31 (In millions)	1993	1992	1993	1992	1993	1992
Total minimum lease payments receivable	$38,080	$38,172	$26,584	$25,390	$11,496	$12,782
Less principal and interest on third-party nonrecourse debt	(8,398)	(9,446)	—	—	(8,398)	(9,446)
Rentals receivable	29,682	28,726	26,584	25,390	3,098	3,336
Estimated unguaranteed residual value of leased assets	4,490	4,352	3,323	3,115	1,167	1,237
Less deferred income (a)	(9,242)	(9,153)	(7,844)	(7,615)	(1,398)	(1,538)
Investment in financing leases (as shown on the previous page)	24,930	23,925	22,063	20,890	2,867	3,035
Less amounts to arrive at net investment						
Allowance for losses	(538)	(560)	(464)	(481)	(74)	(79)
Deferred taxes arising from financing leases	(4,917)	(4,553)	(2,157)	(1,986)	(2,760)	(2,567)
Net investment in financing leases	$19,475	$18,812	$19,442	$18,423	$ 33	$ 389

(a) Total financing lease deferred income is net of deferred initial direct costs of $83 million and $73 million for 1993 and 1992, respectively.

At December 31, 1993, contractual maturities for rentals receivable over the next five years and after were: $6,417 million in 1994; $5,426 million in 1995; $3,919 million in 1996; $2,570 million in 1997; $1,720 million in 1998 and $9,630 million in 1999 and later — aggregating $29,682 million. As with time sales and loans, experience has shown that a portion of receivables will be paid prior to contractual maturity and these amounts should not be regarded as forecasts of future cash flows.

Under arrangements with customers, GE Capital has committed to lend funds ($2,131 million and $1,794 million at December 31, 1993 and 1992, respectively) and has issued sundry financial guarantees and letters of credit ($1,863 million and $1,693 million at December 31, 1993 and 1992, respectively). The above commitments and guarantees exclude those related to commercial aircraft (see note 17). Note 21 discusses financial guaranties of insurance affiliates.

At December 31, 1993 and 1992, GE Capital was conditionally obligated to advance $2,244 million and $2,236 million, respectively, principally under performance-based standby lending commitments. GE Capital also was obligated for $2,946 million and $2,147 million at year-end 1993 and 1992, respectively, under standby liquidity facilities related to third-party commercial paper programs, although management believes that the prospects of being required to fund under such standby facilities are remote.

Nonearning consumer time sales and loans, primarily private-label credit card receivables, amounted to $391 million and $444 million at December 31, 1993 and 1992, respectively. A majority of these receivables were subject to various loss-sharing arrangements that provide full or partial recourse to the originating private-label entity. Nonearning and reduced earning receivables other than consumer time sales and loans were $509 million and $934 million at year-end 1993 and 1992, respectively. Earnings of $11 million and $30 million realized in 1993 and 1992, respectively, were $41 million and $75 million lower than would have been reported had these receivables earned income in accordance with their original terms.

(63)

Note 15 Property, Plant and Equipment (including equipment leased to others)

December 31 (In millions)	1993	1992
Original cost		
GE		
Land and improvements	$ 395	$ 375
Buildings, structures and related equipment	5,370	5,398
Machinery and equipment	15,420	14,936
Leasehold costs and manufacturing plant under construction	1,170	1,183
Other	86	86
	22,441	21,978
GECS		
Buildings and equipment	1,850	1,733
Equipment leased to others		
Aircraft	3,677	2,850
Marine shipping containers	2,985	2,584
Vehicles	3,568	2,274
Railroad rolling stock	1,498	1,478
Other	2,160	2,758
	15,738	13,677
	$38,179	$35,655
Accumulated depreciation, depletion and amortization		
GE	$12,899	$12,046
GECS		
Buildings and equipment	814	673
Equipment leased to others	3,238	2,549
	$16,951	$15,268

(64)

Included in GECS' equipment leased to others at year-end 1993 was $244 million of commercial aircraft off-lease ($94 million in 1992).

Current-year amortization of GECS' equipment leased to others was $1,395 million, $1,133 million and $1,055 million in 1993, 1992 and 1991, respectively.

Note 16 (85) Intangible Assets

December 31 (In millions)	1993	1992
GE		
Goodwill	$ 5,713	$5,873
Other intangibles	753	734
	6,466	6,607
GECS		
Goodwill	2,133	1,841
Other intangibles	1,765	1,062
	3,898	2,903
	$10,364	$9,510

GE's intangible assets are shown net of accumulated amortization of $1,760 million in 1993 and $1,476 million in 1992. GECS' intangible assets are net of accumulated amortization of $878 million in 1993 and $646 million in 1992.

Note 17 All Other Assets

December 31 (In millions)	1993	1992
GE		
Investments		
Associated companies (a)	$ 1,336	$ 1,301
Government and government- guaranteed securities	293	274
Other	1,639	390
	3,268	1,965
(66) Prepaid pension asset	3,840	3,310
Other	3,269	2,230
	10,377	7,505
GECS		
Investments		
Assets acquired for resale	8,141	3,388
Associated companies (b)	2,079	1,720
Other	1,756	2,216
	11,976	7,324
Deferred insurance acquisition costs	987	720
Foreclosed real estate properties	213	304
Other	1,121	848
	14,297	9,196
Eliminations	—	(76)
	$24,674	$16,625

(a) Includes advances of $131 million and $196 million at December 31, 1993 and 1992, respectively.
(b) Includes advances of $1,159 million and $687 million at December 31, 1993 and 1992, respectively.

In line with industry practice, sales of commercial jet aircraft engines often involve long-term customer financing commitments. In making such commitments, it is GE's general practice to require that it have, or be able to establish, a secured position in the aircraft being financed. Under such airline financing programs, GE had issued loans and guarantees (principally guarantees) amounting to $1,201 million at year-end 1993 and $974 million at year-end 1992; and it had entered into commitments totaling $1.4 billion and $2.3 billion at year-end 1993 and 1992, respectively, to provide financial assistance on future aircraft engine sales. Estimated fair values of the aircraft securing these receivables and guarantees exceeded the related account balances or guaranteed amounts at December 31, 1993. GECS acts as a lender and lessor to the commercial airline industry. At December 31, 1993 and 1992, the aggregate amount of such GECS loans, leases and equipment leased to others was $6,776 million and $5,978 million, respectively. In addition, GECS had issued financial guarantees and funding commitments of $450 million at December 31, 1993 ($645 million at year-end 1992) and had conditional commitments to purchase aircraft at a cost of $865 million. These purchase commitments are subject to the aircraft having been placed on lease under agreements, and with carriers, acceptable to GECS prior to delivery.

At year-end 1993, the National Broadcasting Company had $3,011 million of commitments to acquire broadcast material or the rights to broadcast television programs that require payments through the year 2000.

GECS' other investments included $75 million and $275 million at December 31, 1993 and 1992, respectively, of in-substance repossessions at the lower of cost or estimated fair value previously included in financing receivables. GECS' mortgage-servicing activities include the purchase and resale of mortgages. GECS had open commitments to purchase mortgages totaling $5,935 million and $2,963 million at December 31, 1993 and 1992, respectively, as well as open commitments to sell mortgages totaling $6,426 million and $1,777 million, respectively, at year-end 1993 and 1992. At December 31, 1993 and 1992, mortgages sold with full or partial recourse to GECS aggregated $2,526 million and $3,876 million, respectively.

Note *18* Borrowings

Short-term borrowings	1993		1992	
December 31 (In millions)	Amount	Average rate	Amount	Average rate
GE				
Commercial paper	$ 708	3.36%	$ 1,175	3.53%
Payable to banks (principally non-U.S.)	588	6.41	456	8.73
Notes to trust departments	102	3.03	269	3.14
Other (a)	993		1,548	
	2,391		3,448	
GECS				
Commercial paper	46,298	3.39	42,168	3.57
Payable to banks	4,957	3.59	4,516	4.20
Notes to trust departments	1,882	3.10	1,659	3.54
Other (a)	6,866		4,840	
	60,003		53,183	
Eliminations	(259)		(242)	
	$62,135		$56,389	

(a) Includes the current portion of long-term debt.

Confirmed credit lines of approximately $3.1 billion had been extended to GE by 40 banks at year-end 1993. Substantially all of GE's credit lines are available to GE Capital and GECS in addition to their own credit lines.

At year-end 1993, GE Capital had committed lines of credit aggregating $19.0 billion with 134 banks, including $6.0 billion of revolving credit agreements pursuant to which GE Capital has the right to borrow funds for periods exceeding one year. A total of $4.6 billion of GE Capital's credit lines is available for use by GECS; $1.8 billion is available for use by GE.

During 1993, neither GE nor GECS borrowed under any of these credit lines. Both compensate banks for credit facilities either in the form of fees or a combination of balances and fees as agreed to with each bank. Compensating balances and commitment fees were immaterial in each of the past three years.

Kidder, Peabody had established credit lines of $6.1 billion at December 31, 1993, including $3.1 billion available on an unsecured basis. Borrowings from banks were primarily unsecured demand obligations, at interest rates approximating broker call loan rates, to finance inventories of securities and to facilitate the securities settlement process.

Aggregate amounts of long-term borrowings that mature during the next five years, after deducting debt reacquired for sinking-fund needs, are as follows.

(In millions)	1994	1995	1996	1997	1998
GE	$ 819	$ 258	$ 627	$ 511	$ 584
GECS	6,421	6,204	4,868	2,971	3,566

Outstanding balances in long-term borrowings at December 31, 1993 and 1992, were as follows.

Long-term borrowings December 31 (In millions)	Weighted average interest rate	Maturities	1993	1992
GE				
Notes (a)	7.13%	1995-1998	$ 1,694	$ 2,298
Debentures/sinking-fund debentures	—	—	—	300
Deep discount notes	—	—	—	150
Industrial development/ pollution control bonds (a)	3.09	1995-2019	272	272
Other (a) (b)			447	400
			2,413	3,420
GECS				
Senior notes				
Notes (a) (c)	6.03	1995-2012	22,042	18,087
Zero coupon/deep discount notes	13.72	1995-2001	1,407	1,578
Reset or remarketed notes (d)	8.39	2007-2018	1,500	1,500
Floating rate notes (e)		1995-2053	521	496
Less unamortized discount/premium			(344)	(464)
			25,126	21,197
Subordinated notes (f)	8.12	2006-2012	759	760
			25,885	21,957
Eliminations			(28)	(1)
			$28,270	$25,376

(a) At December 31, 1993, GE and GECS had agreed with others to exchange currencies on principal amounts equivalent to U.S. $498 million and $8,101 million, respectively, and related interest payments. GE and GECS also had entered into interest rate swaps with others related to interest on $610 million and $13,224 million, respectively. At December 31, 1992, GE and GECS had agreed with others to exchange currencies on principal amounts equivalent to U.S. $1,224 million and $6,499 million, respectively, and related interest payments. GE and GECS also had entered into interest rate swaps with others relating to interest on $2,352 million and $8,549 million, respectively.

(b) Includes original issue premium and discount and a variety of obligations having various interest rates and maturities, including borrowings by parent operating components and all affiliate borrowings.

(c) At December 31, 1993 and 1992, counterparties held options under which GECS can be caused to execute interest rate swaps associated with interest payments through 1999 on $500 million and $625 million, respectively.

(d) Interest rates are reset at the end of the initial and each subsequent interest period. At each rate-reset date, GECS may redeem notes in whole or in part at its option. Current interest periods range from March 1994 to May 1996.

(e) The rate of interest payable on each note is a variable rate based on the commercial paper rate each month. Interest is payable either monthly or semiannually at the option of GECS.

(f) Includes $700 million at December 31, 1993 and 1992, guaranteed by GE.

Note 19 — GECS Securities Sold but Not Yet Purchased, at Market

December 31 (In millions)	1993	1992
U.S. government	$12,789	$ 9,570
Corporate stocks, bonds and non-U.S. securities	2,528	1,802
State and municipal securities	15	41
	$15,332	$11,413

Note 20 — GE All Other Current Costs and Expenses Accrued

At year-end 1993 and 1992, this account included taxes accrued of $1,664 million and $1,460 million, respectively, and compensation and benefit accruals (including the current portion of postretirement and postemployment benefit accruals) of $1,311 million and $1,000 million, respectively. Also included are amounts for product warranties, estimated costs on shipments billed to customers and a wide variety of sundry items.

Note 21 — Insurance Reserves and Annuity Benefits

Insurance reserves and annuity benefits represents policyholders' benefits, unearned premiums and provisions for policy losses in GECS' insurance and annuity businesses. The estimated liability for insurance losses and loss expenses consists of both case and incurred-but-not-reported reserves. Where experience is not sufficient, industry averages are used. Estimated amounts of salvage and subrogation recoverable on paid and unpaid losses are deducted from outstanding losses.

The liability for future policy benefits of the life insurance affiliates has been computed mainly by a net-level-premium method based on assumptions for investment yields, mortality and terminations that were appropriate at date of purchase or at the time the policies were developed, including provisions for adverse deviations.

Interest rates credited to annuity contracts in 1993 ranged from 3.7% to 9.7%. For most annuities, interest rates to be credited are redetermined by management on an annual basis.

SFAS No. 113, *Accounting and Reporting for Reinsurance of Short-Duration and Long-Duration Contracts,* was adopted during 1993. The principal effect of this Statement was to report reinsurance receivables and prepaid reinsurance premiums, a total of $1,818 million at December 31, 1993, as assets. Such amounts were reported as reductions of insurance reserves at the end of 1992.

Financial guaranties, principally by GE Capital's Financial Guaranty Insurance Company, were $101.4 billion and $81.3 billion at year-end 1993 and 1992, respectively, before reinsurance of $17.3 billion and $13.7 billion, respectively. Mortgage insurance risk in force of GE Capital's mortgage insurance operations aggregated $27.0 billion and $21.3 billion at December 31, 1993 and 1992, respectively.

Note 22 — GE All Other Liabilities (including postemployment benefits)

This account includes noncurrent compensation and benefit accruals at year-end 1993 and 1992 of $4,507 million and $3,743 million, respectively. Other noncurrent liabilities include amounts for product warranties, deferred incentive compensation, deferred income and a wide variety of sundry items.

The Company adopted SFAS No. 112, *Employers' Accounting for Postemployment Benefits,* effective as of January 1, 1993. This Statement requires that employers recognize over the service lives of employees the costs of postemployment benefits if certain conditions are met. The principal effect for GE was to change the method of accounting for severance benefits. Under the previous accounting policy, the total cost of severance benefits was expensed when the severance event occurred.

The cumulative effect of the accounting change as of January 1, 1993, amounted to $1,306 million before taxes ($862 million, or $1.01 per share, after taxes). Aside from the one-time effect of the adjustment, adoption of SFAS No. 112 was not material to 1993 earnings, and there was no 1993 cash flow impact.

⑦⓪ Under *SFAS No. 109*, deferred tax liabilities arise when a firm reports revenues to shareholders sooner, or reports expenses to shareholders later, than it reports those items to the IRS. Conversely, deferred tax assets arise when the firm reports revenues to shareholders later, or reports expenses to shareholders sooner, than it reports those items to the IRS. See the Glossary at *temporary differences*. This note shows the deferred tax assets and liabilities netted against each other for each reporting entity: GE, GECS and the consolidated company. The net consolidated position is a deferred tax liability of $5,109 million at December 31, 1993. GE (without GECS) has a net deferred tax asset, which GE reports on the balance sheet as a negative deferred tax liability. We believe GE uses this counterfactual placement of the net deferred tax asset in order to report the item uniformly for all three entities.

⑦① GE's deferred tax assets and liabilities arise primarily from four items: Provisions for expenses, Retiree insurance plans, GE pension and Depreciation. We discuss each of these in turn in this comment.

"Provisions for expenses" include bad debt expense and warranty expense. GE uses an *allowance method* (see the Glossary) to recognize bad debt expense and warranty expense for shareholder reporting, but the estimated expenses under the allowance method do not qualify as tax deductions. As we explain below, this generates a temporary difference between shareholder and tax net income, which causes GE to record a deferred tax asset. We illustrate the accounting with warranty costs; bad debt expense works similarly.

As GE sells products carrying warranties, it makes the following entry recognizing the estimated liability for future repairs and replacements:

Estimated Warranty Expense (Provision)	X	
Estimated Warranty Liability		X
Entry made in the period of sale for expected warranty costs.		

Later, when GE makes repairs and incurs warranty costs, the entry is:

Estimated Warranty Liability	Y	
Assets Used and Liabilities Incurred		Y
To recognize cost of actual repairs and replacements.		

The repair, and therefore the second entry, often occurs in a year subsequent to the year of sale. The cost of providing the warranty services does not become a tax deduction until GE actually makes the repair. This creates temporary differences: GE subtracts an expense on the financial statements in one year but deducts it on the tax return in a later year. The future tax effect of this temporary difference is the eventual benefit of deducting these accrued warranty costs on the tax return. Following *SFAS No. 109*, GE estimates the future benefit as the statutory tax rate (35 percent in 1993) times the difference between Estimated Warranty Liability and its "tax basis" — the amount of Warranty Liability that would be measured using tax accounting. In this case, the tax basis is zero because tax accounting never records an obligation prior to incurring costs. GE therefore estimates the future tax benefit as .35 times the balance in the Estimated Warranty Liability, and records this future benefit as a deferred tax asset.

Similarly, GE accrues expenses for "Retiree insurance plans" and "GE pension" when employees provide labor services (see GE's Note 6 and our comments 42 and 43), but tax rules allow deductions only when GE pays out benefits or provides legally-required funding (see our comment 45). The unfunded retiree insurance liability reported to shareholders has no (or little) tax basis. The deferred tax asset related to this liability is therefore approximately 35 percent times the liability, and represents the future benefit GE will receive when it deducts the insurance payments on its tax return in years following 1993.

In contrast, "GE pension" generates a deferred tax liability of $1,170 million, which means that cumulative pension tax deductions have exceeded cumulative pension expenses reported to shareholders, by an amount that can be computed as x (in millions) in the following:

$$\$1,170 = .35\,x$$
$$x = \$1,170/.35 = \$3,343$$

GE uses *MACRS depreciation* (see the Glossary) for tax purposes, as the law requires. This is an accelerated method based on reduced asset lives and declining-balance depreciation. GE also uses an accelerated method for shareholder reporting (see Note 1 at the callout for our comment 30), but the reduced lives of MACRS make it the more accelerated of the two methods. Since tax depreciation is faster than depreciation for shareholder reporting, the tax basis of GE's depreciable

Property, plant and equipment is smaller than its depreciated cost on the balance sheet. This difference between the tax basis and book value of these assets, multiplied by the statutory tax rate of 35 percent, is a deferred tax liability. It represents the future tax cost GE will incur when its depreciation expense reported to shareholders exceeds its depreciation tax deduction. Using the method applied above, we can compute that the tax basis of GE's depreciable Property, plant and equipment is smaller than the reported book value by $2,543 (= $890/.35). The tax basis of these assets is therefore $6,999 (= $9,542 – $2,543).

Notice that deferred tax "assets" and "liabilities" measure benefits to be received or costs to be incurred at some unspecified future time, which may be indefinitely far off. Nevertheless, GAAP require reporting *undiscounted* estimated amounts, among GE's resources and obligations. We believe that deferred taxes do not fit the usual definitions of *asset* and *liability* (see the Glossary) and GAAP should not report them in this way, but those who set GAAP disagree.

(72) See the Glossary at *minority interest* and our comment 5. Note 24 reveals that part of the minority interest in GECS's affiliates is in the form of *preferred shares* (see the Glossary), although the parent company, GE, reports no preferred stock on the consolidated balance sheet on page 28.

(73) APB *Opinion No. 12* requires the disclosure of all changes in owners' equity accounts.

(74) A company may recognize neither gain nor loss on transactions in its own shares (called *treasury shares*). GE's accounting is correct, but the use of the terms "gain" and "loss" may mislead. When GE reissues previously acquired treasury shares, the adjustment to achieve equal debits and credits is not to a gain or loss account (to appear on the income statement), but to the account "Other capital." If GE acquires treasury shares for an outlay of $1,000 and then reissues them for $1,200, then the entries would be:

Common Stock Held in Treasury	1,000	
Cash		1,000
To record acquisition of treasury shares.		

Cash	1,200	
Common Stock Held in Treasury		1,000
Other Capital		200
To record reissue of treasury shares for an amount greater than outlay to acquire them.		

If the firm receives proceeds on reissue of $800, not $1,200, then in the second entry it debits $200 to the "Other capital" account instead of crediting the account.

(75) *ARB No. 43* requires disclosure of the details of stock option plans and of the currently outstanding options. The FASB is currently considering new GAAP for these items. No issue ever on the FASB's agenda has been more controversial.

(76) At the end of 1993, the market price of a share of GE common stock is about $100. The average price of the 29,677,000 options exercisable at the end of 1993 is $72.99. Thus, if employees exercised all the options, the present owners' equity would be diluted approximately $802 million [= ($100.00 –$72.99) x 29,677,000] in comparison to the issue of new shares at the current market price.

(77) Note 28 discloses additional details of items that GE aggregates together on the Statement of Cash Flows on page 30.

Note 23 — Deferred Income Taxes ⑦⓪

Aggregate deferred tax amounts are summarized below.

December 31 (In millions)	1993	1992
Assets		
GE	$ 3,547	$ 2,864
GECS	2,204	1,810
	5,751	4,674
Liabilities		
GE	3,248	2,535
GECS	7,612	6,679
	10,860	9,214
Net deferred tax liability	$ 5,109	$ 4,540

Principal components of the net deferred tax liability balances are shown below for GE and GECS.

December 31 (In millions)	1993	1992
GE		
Provisions for expenses	$(2,219)	$(1,491)
Retiree insurance plans	(879)	(965)
GE pension	1,170	957
Depreciation	890	829
Other — net	739	341
	(299)	(329)
GECS		
Financing leases	4,917	4,553
Operating leases	966	811
Net unrealized gains on securities	437	19
Tax transfer leases	340	329
Provision for losses	(831)	(715)
Insurance reserves	(370)	(344)
AMT credit carryforwards	—	(200)
Other — net	(51)	416
	5,408	4,869
Net deferred tax liability	$ 5,109	$ 4,540

⑦①

Deferred taxes were determined under SFAS No. 109, *Accounting for Income Taxes,* which was adopted effective January 1, 1992.

Note 24 — Minority Interest in Equity of Consolidated Affiliates ⑦②

Minority interest in equity of consolidated GECS affiliates includes 8,750 shares of $100 par value variable cumulative preferred stock issued by GE Capital with a liquidation preference value of $875 million. Dividend rates on this preferred stock ranged from 2.33% to 2.79% during 1993 and from 2.44% to 3.49% during 1992.

Note 25 — Share Owners' Equity ⑦③

(In millions)	1993	1992	1991
Common stock issued			
Balance at January 1 and December 31	$ 584	$ 584	$ 584
Other capital			
Balance at January 1	$ 755	$ 938	$ 1,061
Currency translation adjustments	(279)	(209)	(175)
Unrealized gains on securities	812	30	45
Gains (losses) on treasury stock dispositions	110	(4)	7
Balance at December 31	$ 1,398	$ 755	$ 938
Retained earnings			
Balance at January 1	$26,527	$23,787	$22,959
Net earnings	4,315	4,725	2,636
Dividends declared	(2,229)	(1,985)	(1,808)
Balance at December 31	$28,613	$26,527	$23,787
Common stock held in treasury			
Balance at January 1	$ 4,407	$ 3,626	$ 2,924
Purchases	770	1,206	1,112
Dispositions	(406)	(425)	(410)
Balance at December 31	$ 4,771	$ 4,407	$ 3,626

⑦④ (beside "Gains (losses) on treasury stock dispositions")

Authorized shares of common stock (par value $0.63) total 1,100,000,000 shares. Common shares issued and outstanding are summarized in the table below.

Shares of GE common stock December 31 (In thousands)	1993	1992	1991
Issued	926,564	926,564	926,564
In treasury	(72,913)	(71,135)	(62,442)
Outstanding	853,651	855,429	864,122

The current Proxy Statement includes a proposal recommended by the Board of Directors on December 17, 1993, which, if approved by share owners, would (a) increase the number of authorized shares of common stock from 1,100,000,000 shares each with a par value of $0.63 to 2,200,000,000 shares each with a par value of $0.32 and

(b) split each unissued and issued common share, including shares held in treasury, into two shares of common stock each with a par value of $0.32.

GE has 50,000,000 authorized shares of preferred stock ($1.00 par value), but no such shares have been issued.

The effects of translating to U.S. dollars the financial statements of non-U.S. affiliates whose functional currency is the local currency are included in other capital. Asset and liability accounts are translated at year-end exchange rates, while revenues and expenses are translated at average rates for the period. The cumulative currency translation adjustment was a $246 million reduction of other capital at December 31, 1993, compared with cumulative additions to other capital of $33 million and $242 million at December 31, 1992 and 1991, respectively.

26

Note *Other Stock-Related Information* ⑦⑤

Stock option plans, stock appreciation rights (SARs), restricted stock and restricted stock units are described in the Company's current Proxy Statement. With certain restrictions, the Company can meet requirements for stock option shares from either unissued or treasury shares.

Stock option information		Average per share	
(Shares in thousands)	Shares subject to option	Option price	Market price
Balance at January 1, 1993	24,082	$64.37	$85.50
Options granted	8,790	91.80	91.80
Replacement options	441	57.19	57.19
Options exercised	(3,036)	56.65	95.14
Options terminated	(600)	73.67	—
⑦⑥ Balance at December 31, 1993	29,677	72.99	104.88

The replacement options replaced canceled SARs and have identical terms thereto. At December 31, 1993, there were 3,529,125 SARs exercisable at an average price of $75.32. There were 1,836,050 restricted stock shares and restricted stock units outstanding at December 31, 1993.

At December 31, 1993 and 1992, respectively, there were 8,069,046 and 8,755,078 shares available for grants of options, SARs, restricted stock and restricted stock units. Under the 1990 Long-Term Incentive Plan, 0.95% of the Company's issued common stock (including treasury shares) as of the first day of each calendar year during which the Plan is in effect become available for granting

awards in such year. Any unused portion, in addition to shares allocated to awards that are canceled or forfeited, is available for later years.

Outstanding options and rights expire on various dates through December 17, 2003. Restricted stock grants vest on various dates up to normal retirement of grantees.

27

Note *GECS' Broker-Dealer Positions*

December 31 (In millions)	1993	1992
Included in GECS' other receivables		
Securities failed to deliver	$2,315	$ 218
Deposits paid for securities borrowed	1,944	1,976
Clearing organizations and other	3,207	930
	$7,466	$3,124
Included in GECS' accounts payable		
Securities failed to receive	$1,701	$ 193
Deposits received for securities loaned	1,390	1,051
Clearing organizations and other	275	100
	$3,366	$1,344

Kidder, Peabody, in conducting its normal operations, employs a wide variety of financial instruments in order to balance its investment positions. Management believes that the most meaningful measures of these positions for a broker-dealer are the values at which the positions are presented in the Statement of Financial Position in accordance with securities industry practices.

The following required supplemental disclosures of gross contract terms are indicators of the nature and extent of such broker-dealer positions and are not intended to portray the much smaller credit or economic risk.

At December 31, 1993, open commitments to sell mortgage-backed securities amounted to $18,539 million ($17,191 million in 1992); open commitments to purchase mortgage-backed securities amounted to $14,637 million ($13,131 million in 1992); interest rate swap agreements were open for interest on $4,084 million ($6,038 million in 1992); commitments amounting to $10,837 million ($6,711 million in 1992) were open under options written to cover price changes in securities; the face amount of open interest rate futures and forward contracts for currencies as well as money market and other instruments amounted to $30,506 million ($10,936 million in 1992); contracts establishing limits on counterparty exposure to interest rates were outstanding for interest on $1,610 million ($2,722 million in 1992); and firm underwriting commitments for the purchase of stock or debt amounted to $3,311 million ($4,094 million in 1992).

Note 28 ⑦ Supplemental Cash Flows Information

Changes in operating assets and liabilities are net of acquisitions and dispositions of businesses. "Payments for principal businesses purchased" in the Statement of Cash Flows is net of cash acquired and includes debt assumed and immediately repaid in acquisitions.

"All other operating activities" in the Statement of Cash Flows consists principally of adjustments to current and noncurrent accruals of costs and expenses, amortization of premium and discount on debt, and adjustments to assets such as amortization of goodwill and intangibles.

The Statement of Cash Flows excludes certain noncash transactions that had no significant effects on the investing or financing activities of GE or GECS.

Certain supplemental information for GECS' cash flows is shown below.

For the years ended December 31 (In millions)	1993	1992	1991
Certain broker-dealer accounts			
Trading securities	$ (7,517)	$ (5,966)	$ (5,463)
Securities purchased under agreements to resell	(16,675)	(7,386)	4,006
Securities sold under agreements to repurchase	20,655	7,841	349
Securities sold but not yet purchased	3,919	6,529	(440)
	$ 382	$ 1,018	$ (1,548)
Financing receivables			
Increase in loans to customers	$ (30,002)	$ (27,069)	$ (25,030)
Principal collections from customers	27,571	25,136	25,289
Investment in equipment for financing leases	(7,204)	(7,758)	(8,829)
Principal collections on financing leases	6,812	5,338	3,726
Net change in credit card receivables	(1,341)	(330)	(2,410)
	$ (4,164)	$ (4,683)	$ (7,254)
All other investing activities			
Purchases of securities by insurance and annuity businesses	$ (10,488)	$ (6,865)	$ (6,002)
Dispositions and maturities of securities by insurance and annuity businesses	7,698	6,200	5,415
Other	(4,124)	(3,003)	(1,538)
	$ (6,914)	$ (3,668)	$ (2,125)
Newly issued debt having maturities more than 90 days			
Short-term (91-365 days)	$ 4,315	$ 4,456	$ 4,863
Long-term (over one year)	10,885	6,699	6,317
Long-term subordinated	—	450	250
Proceeds — nonrecourse, leveraged lease debt	53	148	1,808
	$ 15,253	$ 11,753	$ 13,238
Repayments and other reductions of debt having maturities more than 90 days			
Short-term (91-365 days)	$ (9,008)	$ (6,474)	$ (6,504)
Long-term (over one year)	(208)	(658)	(1,769)
Long-term subordinated	—	(76)	(32)
Principal payments — nonrecourse, leveraged lease debt	(312)	(272)	(280)
	$ (9,528)	$ (7,480)	$ (8,585)
All other financing activities			
Proceeds from sales of investment and annuity contracts	$ 509	$ —	$ —
Redemption of investment and annuity contracts	(578)	—	—
	$ (69)	$ —	$ —

(78) *SFAS No. 14* requires that the firm report revenues and assets for business *segments* (see the Glossary). The major difficulty in constructing useful segment reports results from the inability of accounting theory to provide a meaningful allocation of "corporate items" that are truly common or joint costs of running the entire corporation to the segments. GAAP requires allocating amounts to the various segments so that segment earnings add up to total corporate earnings. See *full costing* in the Glossary.

(79) Notes 30 and 31, not reproduced here, contain information on geographic segments (Note 30) and details about the determination of "fair values" for investment securities (Note 31).

(80) In 1976 the SEC defined a new class of footnotes with which the auditor is "associated" (to use the SEC's term), but which the auditor does not audit. The information here is in that class. During the year, GE (and other companies) must send quarterly (interim) financial statements to shareholders. The SEC requires companies to show in the annual statements the amounts of the interim earnings *after* all information for the year has become available. If differences exist, the company must explain why its interim reported numbers differ from the corresponding numbers later shown in the annual report.

Note **29** ⑦⑧ *Industry Segments*

(In millions)	Revenues For the years ended December 31								
	Total revenues			Intersegment revenues			External revenues		
	1993	1992	1991	1993	1992	1991	1993	1992	1991
GE									
Aircraft Engines	$ 6,580	$ 7,368	$ 7,777	$ 59	$ 57	$ 29	$ 6,521	$ 7,311	$ 7,748
Appliances	5,555	5,330	5,225	3	3	4	5,552	5,327	5,221
Broadcasting	3,102	3,363	3,121	—	—	1	3,102	3,363	3,120
Industrial	7,379	6,907	6,783	264	267	327	7,115	6,640	6,456
Materials	5,042	4,853	4,736	50	51	51	4,992	4,802	4,685
Power Systems	6,692	6,371	6,189	246	272	265	6,446	6,099	5,924
Technical Products and Services	4,174	4,674	4,686	18	68	99	4,156	4,606	4,587
All Other	2,043	1,749	1,545	—	—	—	2,043	1,749	1,545
Corporate items and eliminations	(208)	(361)	(468)	(640)	(718)	(776)	432	357	308
Total GE	40,359	40,254	39,594	—	—	—	40,359	40,254	39,594
GECS									
Financing	12,399	10,544	10,069	—	—	—	12,399	10,544	10,069
Specialty Insurance	4,862	3,863	2,989	—	—	—	4,862	3,863	2,989
Securities Broker-Dealer	4,861	4,022	3,346	—	—	—	4,861	4,022	3,346
All Other	15	11	(5)	—	—	—	15	11	(5)
Total GECS	22,137	18,440	16,399	—	—	—	22,137	18,440	16,399
Eliminations	(1,934)	(1,621)	(1,364)	—	—	—	(1,934)	(1,621)	(1,364)
Consolidated revenues	$60,562	$57,073	$54,629	$ —	$ —	$ —	$60,562	$57,073	$54,629

"All Other" GE revenues consists primarily of GECS' earnings.

(In millions)	Assets At December 31			Property, plant and equipment (including equipment leased to others) For the years ended December 31					
				Additions			Depreciation, depletion and amortization		
	1993	1992	1991	1993	1992	1991	1993	1992	1991
GE									
Aircraft Engines	$ 5,329	$ 6,153	$ 6,649	$ 208	$ 276	$ 371	$ 339	$ 294	$ 295
Appliances	2,193	2,248	2,503	132	126	118	131	105	106
Broadcasting	3,742	3,736	3,886	56	52	70	98	82	84
Industrial	4,909	4,983	4,824	379	299	320	310	282	262
Materials	8,181	8,081	8,340	376	255	784	417	393	369
Power Systems	4,408	3,614	3,450	251	245	267	185	159	144
Technical Products and Services	2,179	2,393	2,629	126	118	148	89	74	98
All Other	11,604	9,719	8,750	1	1	6	3	5	5
Corporate items and eliminations	8,589	7,148	6,119	59	73	80	59	89	66
Total GE	51,134	48,075	47,150	1,588	1,445	2,164	1,631	1,483	1,429
GECS									
Financing	106,854	82,207	74,554	3,352	4,761	3,688	1,545	1,259	1,161
Specialty Insurance	18,915	14,624	11,812	15	17	11	9	13	8
Securities Broker-Dealer	85,009	55,455	41,218	15	32	31	38	34	38
All Other	952	2,238	230	59	118	41	38	29	18
Total GECS	211,730	154,524	127,814	3,441	4,928	3,771	1,630	1,335	1,225
Eliminations	(11,358)	(9,723)	(8,456)	—	—	—	—	—	—
Consolidated totals	$251,506	$192,876	$166,508	$5,029	$6,373	$5,935	$3,261	$2,818	$2,654

"All Other" GE assets consists primarily of investment in GECS.

A description of industry segments for General Electric Company and consolidated affiliates follows.

▪ *Aircraft Engines.* Jet engines and replacement parts and repair services for all categories of commercial aircraft (short/medium, intermediate and long-range); a wide variety of military planes, including fighters, bombers, tankers and helicopters; and executive and commuter aircraft. Sold worldwide to airframe manufacturers, airlines and government agencies. Also, aircraft engine derivatives used as marine propulsion and industrial power sources.

▪ *Appliances.* Major appliances such as refrigerators, freezers, electric and gas ranges, dishwashers, clothes washers and dryers, microwave ovens and room air conditioning equipment. Sold primarily in North America, but also in global markets, under various GE and private-label brands. Distributed to retail outlets, mainly for the replacement market, and to building contractors and distributors for new installations.

▪ *Broadcasting.* Primarily the National Broadcasting Company (NBC). Principal businesses are furnishing of U.S. network television services to more than 200 affiliated stations, production of television programs, operation of six VHF television broadcasting stations, and investment and programming activities in cable television.

▪ *Industrial.* Lighting products (including a wide variety of lamps, wiring devices and quartz products); electrical distribution and control equipment; transportation systems products (including diesel-electric locomotives, transit propulsion equipment and motorized wheels for off-highway vehicles); electric motors and related products; a broad range of electrical and electronic industrial automation products; and GE Supply, a network of electrical supply houses. Markets are extremely varied. Products are sold to commercial and industrial end users, original equipment manufacturers, electrical distributors, retail outlets, railways and transit authorities. Increasingly, products are developed for and sold in global markets.

▪ *Materials.* High-performance engineered plastics used in applications such as automobiles and housings for computers and other business equipment; ABS resins; silicones; superabrasives such as man-made diamonds; and laminates. Sold worldwide to a diverse customer base consisting mainly of manufacturers.

▪ *Power Systems.* Products mainly for the generation, transmission and distribution of electricity, including related installation, engineering and repair services. Markets and competition are global. Steam turbine-generators are sold to electric utilities, to the U.S. Navy, and, for cogeneration, to industrial and other power customers. Marine steam turbines and propulsion gears are sold to the U.S. Navy. Gas turbines are sold principally as packaged power plants for electric utilities and for industrial cogeneration and mechanical drive applications. Power Systems also includes power delivery and control products, such as transformers, meters, relays, capacitors and arresters for the utility industry; nuclear reactors; and fuel and support services for GE's installed boiling water reactors.

▪ *Technical Products and Services.* Medical systems such as magnetic resonance (MR) and computed tomography (CT) scanners, x-ray, nuclear imaging, ultrasound and other diagnostic equipment sold worldwide to hospitals and medical facilities. This segment also includes a full range of computer-based information and data interchange services for internal use and external commercial and industrial customers.

▪ *GECS Financing.* Operations of GE Capital as follows:

Consumer services — private-label and bank credit card loans, time sales and revolving credit and inventory financing for retail merchants, auto leasing and inventory financing, mortgage servicing, and annuity and mutual fund sales.

Specialized financing — loans and financing leases for major capital assets, including aircraft, industrial facilities and equipment, and energy-related facilities; commercial and residential real estate loans and investments; and loans to and investments in highly leveraged management buyouts and corporate recapitalizations.

Equipment management — leases, loans and asset management services for portfolios of commercial and transportation equipment, including aircraft, trailers, auto fleets, modular space units, railroad rolling stock, data processing equipment, ocean-going containers and satellites.

Mid-market financing — loans and financing and operating leases for middle-market customers, including manufacturers, distributors and end users, for a variety of equipment, including data processing equipment, medical and diagnostic equipment, and equipment used in construction, manufacturing, office applications and telecommunications activities.

Very few of the products financed by GE Capital are manufactured by other GE segments.

▪ *GECS Specialty Insurance.* U.S. and international multiple-line property and casualty reinsurance and certain directly written specialty insurance; financial guaranty insurance, principally on municipal bonds and structured finance issues; private mortgage insurance; creditor insurance covering international customer loan repayments; and life reinsurance.

▪ *GECS Securities Broker-Dealer.* Kidder, Peabody, a full-service international investment bank and securities broker, member of the principal stock and commodities exchanges and a primary dealer in U.S. government securities. Offers services such as underwriting, sales and trading, advisory services on acquisitions and financings, research and asset management.

Note **32** ⑳ *Quarterly Information (unaudited)*

(Dollar amounts in millions; per-share amounts in dollars)	First quarter		Second quarter		Third quarter		Fourth quarter	
	1993	1992	1993	1992	1993	1992	1993	1992
Consolidated operations								
Earnings from continuing operations	$1,085	$ 964	$ 656	$1,130	$1,206	$ 996	$ 1,477	$ 1,215
Earnings from discontinued operations	75	94	—	86	—	114	—	126
Gain on transfer of discontinued operations	—	—	678	—	—	—	—	—
Accounting change	(862) (a)	—	—	—	—	—	—	—
Net earnings	$ 298	$1,058	$1,334	$1,216	$1,206	$1,110	$ 1,477	$ 1,341
Per share								
Earnings from continuing operations	$ 1.27	$ 1.12	$ 0.77	$ 1.32	$ 1.41	$ 1.17	$ 1.73	$ 1.42
Earnings from discontinued operations	0.09	0.11	0.79	0.10	—	0.13	—	0.15
Accounting change	(1.01) (a)	—	—	—	—	—	—	—
Net earnings	$ 0.35	$ 1.23	$ 1.56	$ 1.42	$ 1.41	$ 1.30	$ 1.73	$ 1.57
Selected data — continuing operations								
GE								
Sales of goods and services	$7,968	$7,996	$9,468	$9,513	$8,779	$9,242	$11,607	$11,192
Gross profit from sales	2,074	2,083	1,662	2,496	2,198	2,123	2,929	2,824
GECS								
Revenues from operations	4,763	4,301	5,129	4,493	5,919	4,761	6,326	4,885
Operating profit	644	517	583	484	833	542	588	492

(a) Reflects the cumulative effect to January 1, 1993, of the change in accounting for postemployment benefits (SFAS No. 112). As originally reported, net earnings for the first quarter were $1,160 million, or $1.36 per share.

For GE, gross profit from sales is sales of goods and services less cost of goods and services sold. For GECS, operating profit is income before taxes.

Second-quarter 1993 earnings from continuing operations were reduced by restructuring provisions of $678 million ($0.79 per share) after tax. Second-quarter gross profit from sales was reduced by restructuring provisions of $875 million before tax.

Earnings-per-share amounts for each quarter are required to be computed independently and, in 1992, did not equal the total year earnings-per-share amounts.

Balance Sheet for a Company Approaching Bankruptcy

On June 21, 1970, the Penn Central Company filed a bankruptcy petition for its major subsidiary, the Penn Central Transportation Company. On March 12, 1970, only three months before, Penn Central Transportation Company had issued its 1969 financial statements. The balance sheet and income statement from those statements appear here. They reinforce the point that analysis of the shareholders' equity section of a balance sheet need not indicate impending insolvency or bankruptcy.

At the end of 1969, Penn Central Transportation Company had retained earnings of almost half a billion dollars as a part of shareholders' equity of over $1.8 billion. Much of this equity, however, represented investments in track and roadbed—illiquid assets, for which there is no ready market. Penn Central could not sell these assets to raise funds. You can compute that at the end of 1968 and 1969, the Transportation Company had negative working capital; that is, current liabilities (as shown, plus debt due within one year) exceeded current assets. Working capital increased by about $18 million during 1969, but net quick assets—cash and receivables less current liabilities—decreased. The Company was in a less liquid position at the end of the year than at the start.

At the end of 1969, the Transportation Company had over $100 million of debt to repay during the following year. Although the Transportation Company had sufficient "net worth" to show almost half a billion dollars of retained earnings and almost two billion dollars of shareholders' equity, it did not have the funds to meet "only" a few hundred million dollars in current obligations. The company was approaching insolvency by the end of 1969, as can be discerned from these statements.

Like Penn Central Transportation Company, many bankrupt firms have positive net assets, or shareholder's equity, on the books at the time of bankruptcy.

Balance Sheet

Assets	December 31	1969	1968
Current Assets	Cash and temporary cash investments	$ 80,331,000	$ 46,915,000
	Accounts receivable and unbilled revenue ..	293,181,000	240,211,000
	Material and supplies, etc., at cost	104,303,000	88,692,000
	Total Current Assets	477,815,000	375,818,000
Noncurrent Assets	Investments and advances, at cost or less (notes 2 and 7)	1,139,038,000	1,217,796,000
	New Haven—net assets acquired, at cost (note 1)	—	127,544,000
	Properties (notes 3, 6, 7 and 12)		
	Road, structures, etc................	2,066,769,000	1,904,536,000
	Revenue equipment (rolling stock)......	1,662,759,000	1,745,448,000
	Other	96,051,000	90,541,000
		3,825,579,000	3,740,525,000
	Less accumulated depreciation and losses upon merger	902,731,000	992,036,000
	Total Properties—Net	2,922,848,000	2,748,489,000
	Deferred charges and sundry assets	56,939,000	43,703,000
	Total Assets	$4,596,640,000	$4,513,350,000

Liabilities and Shareholder's Equity

	December 31	1969	1968
Current Liabilities*	Notes payable (none to subsidiaries in 1969; $19,420,000 in 1968)	$ 102,048,000	$ 87,420,000
	Accounts payable and accrued expenses	396,407,000	356,519,000
	Total Current Liabilities (excluding debt due within one year)*	498,455,000	443,939,000
Long-Term Debt	Due within one year..................	106,058,000	76,716,000
	Due after one year	1,585,585,000	1,407,610,000
	Total Long-Term Debt (note 7)	1,691,643,000	1,484,326,000
Other	Estimated liabilities incurred upon merger (note 6)	101,935,000	119,346,000
	Casualty and other claims..............	90,667,000	81,803,000
	Amounts payable to subsidiary companies ..	167,711,000	122,582,000
	Other	240,857,000	231,015,000
	Total Other	601,170,000	554,746,000
Shareholder's Equity	Capital stock—$10 par value. Authorized 27,000,000 shares; issued 24,113,703 shares (1968—24,085,329) (note 8)	241,137,000	240,853,000
	Additional paid-in capital (note 8)........	1,068,730,000	1,068,257,000
	Retained earnings (note 13)	495,505,000	721,229,000
	Total Shareholder's Equity	1,805,372,000	2,030,339,000
	Total Liabilities and Shareholder's Equity	$4,596,640,000	$4,513,350,000

Statement of Earnings and Retained Earnings

Current Earnings	*Year ended December 31*	1969	1968
Income	Railway operating revenues	$1,651,978,000	$1,514,071,000
	Income from rental of properties, net	33,772,000	27,131,000
	Dividends and interest—consolidated		
	subsidiaries	66,324,000	40,155,000
	Dividends and interest—other	2,661,000	15,451,000
	Net gain on sales of properties and		
	investments.......................	12,587,000	35,437,000
	Income under tax allocation agreements		
	(note 5)..........................	21,543,000	19,038,000
	Total Income	1,788,865,000	1,651,283,000
Costs and Expenses	Railway operating expenses, excluding		
	items listed below	1,296,397,000	1,173,761,000
	Depreciation, including depreciation on		
	leased lines (note 3)	91,279,000	94,135,000
	Taxes, except Federal income	144,059,000	125,602,000
	Equipment and other rents, net (note 13)	183,802,000	169,292,000
	Interest on debt	96,764,000	68,787,000
	Guaranteed dividends and interest—		
	leased lines	26,173,000	26,315,000
	Miscellaneous, net	6,719,000	(1,454,000)
	Total Costs and Expenses	1,845,193,000	1,656,438,0001
Earnings (Loss)	From ordinary operations (note 13)	(56,328,000)	(5,155,000)
	Extraordinary item (loss on investment in long-		
	haul passenger service facilities) (note 12) ..	(126,000,000)	—
Net Earnings (Loss)	*For the year (notes 12 and 13)*.............	(182,328,000)	(5,155,000)
Retained Earnings			
	From prior years:		
	As previously reported	730,047,000	788,220,000
	Adjustment (note 13)................	(8,818,000)	(6,436,000)
		538,901,000	776,629,000
	Cash dividends	43,396,000	55,400,000
	Balance at end of year	$ 495,505,000	$ 721,229,000

Accounting Magic

Generally accepted accounting principles permit alternative treatments for certain accounting events. The treatment a company chooses affects the financial statements that the company issues. This section shows how alternative accounting treatments of identical events can lead to reported income figures that differ, perhaps surprisingly, from each other.[1]

The Scenario

On January 1, two companies start in business. The two companies engage in identical activities but account for them differently. Conservative Company chooses the accounting alternatives that will minimize its reported income while High Flyer Company chooses the alternatives that will maximize its reported income. Both companies choose, where permitted, accounting methods that will minimize income taxes. The following events occur during the year.

1. Both companies issue common stock to raise funds necessary to commence a merchandising business.
2. Both companies purchase $6,000,000 of equipment that they assume will have zero salvage value and useful life of 8 years.
3. Both companies make the following purchases of merchandise inventory:

Date	Units Purchased		Unit Price		Cost of Purchase
January 1	85,000	@	$60	=	$ 5,100,000
May 1	95,000	@	$63	=	5,985,000
September 1	100,000	@	$68	=	6,800,000
Total	280,000				$17,885,000

4. During the year, both companies sell 210,000 units at an average price of $100 each so that each realizes sales revenues of $21,000,000.
5. During the year, both companies have selling, general and administrative expenses, excluding officers' salaries, of $3,350,000.
6. At the end of the year, both companies give bonuses of $150,000 to officers for jobs well done in addition to the $350,000 paid to them during the year in salaries. Conservative Company pays cash bonuses of $150,000 while High Flyer Company awards options for purchasing shares of common stock to its officers. Comparable options have market value of $150,000.

[1]The idea and title for this example come from an article by Leonard Spacek, "Business Success Requires an Understanding of Unsolved Problems of Accounting and Financial Reporting," Arthur Andersen Pamphlet (September 25, 1959), pp. 19-28. Since the time Spacek prepared his illustration, generally accepted accounting principles have changed, but several of the alternatives we illustrate he illustrated, too.

Accounting Alternatives

At the end of the year both companies prepare financial statements. Both must decide how to report the various events that occurred during the year. The companies made the following decisions, all generally acceptable.

Inventory Cost Flow Assumption. During the year, both companies purchased more goods than they sold. Each company must make an assumption about the cost of goods sold it will show on the income statement and, simultaneously, about the cost of ending inventory it will show on the balance sheet. Conservative Company makes a last-in, first-out (LIFO) cost flow assumption while High Flyer Company makes a first-in, first-out (FIFO) assumption.

Because the beginning inventory is zero, the cost of goods available for sale by each company equals the purchases of $17,885,000 during the year. Both companies have 70,000 units in ending inventory. Conservative Company, using LIFO, reports a cost of goods sold of $13,685,000 (= $17,885,000 – 70,000 x $60) while High Flyer Company reports a cost of goods sold of $13,125,000 (= $17,885,000 – 70,000 x $68).

Income tax regulations require a company to use LIFO in its financial statements if it uses LIFO for its tax return. High Flyer wants to report high income, so does not use LIFO in its financial statements and, therefore, forgoes the savings in taxes from using LIFO on its tax returns.

Depreciation. Conservative Company depreciates its equipment using the double-declining-balance method on its financial statements while High Flyer Company uses the straight-line method. Conservative Company takes a full year of depreciation in the year it acquires equipment, while High Flyer Company uses a half-year convention under which it takes only one-half year of depreciation in the first year. (The modified accelerated cost recovery system, MACRS, used by both companies for income tax reporting effectively requires that both take one-half year of depreciation on their tax returns.) Conservative Company therefore reports depreciation expense of $1,500,000 (= 2 x 1/8 x $6,000,000) while High Flyer Company reports depreciation expense of $375,000 (= 1/8 x $6,000,000 x 1/2).

Officers' Bonuses. Conservative Company reports expense of $150,000 for the cash bonuses it pays, while High Flyer Company reports no expense for the stock options it granted. Generally accepted accounting principles do not allow the firm to show the fair market value of qualified stock options granted to employees as an expense.[2] If the employees exercise the options, but only then, High Flyer will record an accounting transaction. The entry will only record the cash the firm receives (i.e., the options' exercise price times the number of shares issued) as paid-in capital. High Flyer will never record compensation expense. In contrast, the IRS allows no deduction on the firm's tax return when the employee earns the options, but allows a compensation expense tax deduction when the employees exercise the options. The deductible amount is the difference between the exercise price of the options and the market value of the shares issued.

Published Income Statements

Income Tax Calculation. We assume a combined federal and state income tax rate of 40 percent. Both companies show deductions for MACRS depreciation of equipment on the income tax return different from the depreciation expense reported to shareholders. These are *temporary differences*. That is, in subsequent years, the companies may report on their tax returns amounts different in opposite directions from the amounts they report to shareholders. Consequently, each company reports deferred income taxes on its income statement and deferred tax assets or liabilities on its balance sheet.

High Flyer Company reports smaller depreciation on the income statement than the amount of depreciation claimed on the tax return and will have deferred tax credits on its balance sheet. (Most published annual reports reflect this situation for depreciation.) Conservative Company reports larger depreciation on the income statement than the amount it claims on the tax return and will have deferred tax assets on its balance sheet. (This phenomenon arises here because Conservative Company depreciates only one item of equipment and because the first-year conventions for tax reporting and financial reporting differ.) The following equation holds for both companies (dollar amounts are in thousands):

---

[2]In June 1993, the FASB issued an exposure draft of a proposed new standard that would require companies to show the estimated fair market value of employee stock options as an expense in the period when employees earn them. This has been the most-debated issue ever on the FASB's agenda, and the Board has not yet issued a final standard. After a period of public comment, the FASB delayed the effective date of the proposed standard, giving itself time to study the matter further.

Income Tax Expense	=	Income Tax Payable	+	Deferred Tax Credits	−	Deferred Tax Debits
Conservative Company:						
$786	=	$906	+	$0	−	$120
High Flyer Company:						
$1,520	=	$1,190	+	$330	−	$0

Deferred tax credits either increase a deferred tax liability or decrease a deferred tax asset, and the reverse is true of deferred tax debits. In this case, Conservative Company shows a deferred tax asset of $120,000, and High Flyer Company shows a deferred tax liability of $330,000.

The income statements for both companies appear below. As a result of its conservative treatment of accounting alternatives, Conservative Company reports net income and earnings per share about half of High Flyer Company's. Both companies used generally accepted accounting principles and each would receive a clean opinion from its auditor.

Accounting Magic Comparative Income Statements
For the Year Ending December 31
(Amounts in Thousands Except Per Share Amounts)

	Conservative Company		High Flyer Company	
	Financial Statement	Tax Return	Financial Statement	Tax Return
Sales Revenues	$21,000	$21,000	$21,000	$21,000
Expenses				
Cost of Goods Sold	$13,685	$13,685	$13,125	$13,125
Depreciation on Equipment.	1,500	1,200ᵃ	375	1,200ᵃ
Officers' Compensation:				
Salaries.	350	350	350	350
Cash Bonuses	150	150	—	—
Stock Options.	—	—	0	0
Other Selling, General and				
Administrative Expenses.	3,350	3,350	3,350	3,350
Expenses Before Income Taxes	$19,035	$18,735	$17,200	$18,025
Income Before Taxes	$ 1,965	$ 2,265	$ 3,800	$ 2,975
Income Tax Expenseᵇ.	786		1,520	
Net Income	$ 1,179		$ 2,280	
Earnings Per Share in Dollars (500,000 Shares Outstanding)	$ 2.36		$ 4.56	

ᵃAmounts based on MACRS, 5-year class; 20 percent of cost is deducted in the first year: .20 x $6,000 = $1,200.
ᵇComputation of Income Tax Expense:

Income Before Taxes	$ 1,965	$ 2,265	$ 3,800	$ 2,975
Income Tax Expense on Current Income (at 40 percent)	$ 786		$ 1,520	
Income Tax Currently Payable.		$ 906		$ 1,190
Income Taxes Deferred by the Timing Difference from Depreciation:				
Dr. = .40 x ($1,200 − $1,500)	$ (120)			
Cr. = .40 x ($1,200 − $375)			$ 330	

Comparisons of Cash Flows

Until the two companies paid their respective executive bonuses and income taxes, they were alike in all economically significant respects. Because of the difference in executives' bonuses—Conservative Company paid in cash, while High Flyer granted stock options with the same value—Conservative Company paid out $150,000 more cash than did High Flyer for this item. Because High Flyer Company wished to report higher net income, it paid $284,000 (= $1,190,000 − $906,000) more in income taxes than did Conservative Company. Thus, after tax payments, Conservative Company, in a real sense, is wealthier than is High Flyer. Overall, then, Conservative Company ends the year with $134,000 (= $284,000 − $150,000) more cash (or other net assets), than does High Flyer.

You might find it instructive to construct statements of cash flows for each of the two companies. You will find that Conservative Company generates $134,000 (= $284,000 tax savings − $150,000 higher bonus) more cash from operations than does High Flyer.

Managing Reported Earnings

The simple illustration for Conservative Company and High Flyer Company by no means exhausts the set of choices available to a firm to manage its earnings. Managing earnings refers to a process of taking deliberate steps within the constraints of generally accepted accounting principles to bring about a desired level of reported earnings. This section describes some of the techniques for managing earnings and offers arguments for and against an earnings management policy.

Techniques for managing earnings divide into three categories: (1) selection of accounting principles, (2) application of accounting principles, and (3) timing of asset acquisitions and dispositions. Next, we give some examples of actions in each of these categories.

Selection of Accounting Principles
1.   Revenue recognition—percentage of completion, completed contract, time of sale, installment.
2.   Inventory cost-flow assumption—FIFO, LIFO, weighted average.
3.   Depreciation method—straight-line, declining-balance, sum-of-the-years'–digits.
4.   Leases—operating, capital.
5.   Corporate acquisitions—purchase, pooling of interests.
6.   Mineral resource activities—successful-efforts costing, full costing.

Application of Accounting Principles
1.   Estimates of degree of completion of contracts on which the percentage-of-completion method is used.
2.   Estimates of service lives and salvage values of depreciable assets.
3.   Estimates of uncollectible rate on accounts receivable.
4.   Estimate of cost of warranty plans.
5.   Treatment of indirect costs as product costs versus period expenses.
6.   Classification of common stock investments as trading securities or as available-for-sale securities.
7.   Selection of actuarial cost basis for pension plan.
8.   Selection of interest rates for capitalized leases and for pension accounting.

Timing of Asset Acquisitions and Dispositions
1.   Timing of discretionary expenditures for research and development, advertising, and maintenance costs, which become expenses in the period when the firm incurs costs.
2.   Timing of the sale of property, plant, and equipment or of investments to accelerate or delay the recognition of a gain or loss.
3.   Accelerating or delaying shipments of merchandise to customers at the end of a period.

These lists are not exhaustive, but they indicate the variety of avenues available to management to manage earnings.

Arguments About Managing Earnings
Whether accounting magic matters to the reader of financial statements depends on the answers to two questions. First, do managers select accounting techniques strategically? Second, do managers or their firms gain anything by making strategic choices? Arguments on both sides of these questions, particularly the latter, vary both as to their underlying logic and to the evidence cited to support the position. We present the arguments here in as unbiased a manner as possible so that readers can make up their own minds.

Strategic Choices. Even if managers could make all accounting decisions with the sole objective of reporting economic reality faithfully, their choices would still be complex. Managers face conflicting goals and objectives when they make financial reporting decisions. For example, in choosing between LIFO and FIFO, a manager must decide what aspect of economic reality matters most. Nearly all firms manage their inventories internally using FIFO, and FIFO typically creates a more realistic balance sheet because the FIFO ending inventory amount reflects current costs. Managers cannot manipulate FIFO income with end-of-year purchases as they can LIFO, which may reassure investors. On the other hand, LIFO creates a more realistic income statement, because the LIFO cost of goods sold number reflects current costs. LIFO gives a tax savings to firms facing increasing input prices, as our example illustrates, which leaves investors with more wealth. Last and not at all least, LIFO results in lower net income when used by firms with increasing inventory costs, as our example illustrates.

The LIFO/FIFO decision is the only accounting choice that affects both the firm's current tax bill and reported earnings. Many anecdotes and some academic studies, however, support the argument that managers make accounting decisions with the intent or hope of reporting higher earnings. Aside from changes to LIFO, most of the voluntary (i.e., not mandated by changes in GAAP) accounting changes that firms make result in higher earnings. Firms that make these changes have lower sales and earnings growth than other firms, on average, prior to making a change. When a change in GAAP mandates an accounting change, firms whose earnings increase most as a result of the new GAAP are most likely to adopt the new method before the rules require them to do so.[3] While this evidence does not prove that managements make accounting choices for strategic reasons, it is suggestive.

Capital Market Efficiency. In one widely-accepted view, earnings management is futile because capital markets are efficient. When market prices adjust quickly, fully and in an unbiased manner to publicly available information, one cannot construct trading strategies based on observable data that consistently make money, and earnings management merely wastes valuable managerial time. Early theoretical and empirical studies provided support for the efficiency of capital markets.[4] For example, several studies examined the effects of changes in accounting methods on stock prices, and found that changes in accounting methods with no real or economic effects (that is, those that do not affect cash flows) appear to have little effect on stock prices.[5] Using information from the financial statements and notes, investors can distinguish changes with real effects from those without, and react accordingly.

Proponents of the view that capital markets are not fully efficient acknowledge this work but counter with two observations. First, the empirical work on market efficiency looks at average results for large numbers of firms. Since stock returns vary around these averages, in many cases the market has not priced securities efficiently for particular firms at particular times. Proponents of this view point to examples where the market prices of particular firms' shares decreased dramatically after analyses of the firms' (previously disclosed) accounting procedures appeared in the financial press.[6] Proponents of efficient capital markets counter that examples selected after the fact cannot disprove market efficiency, because trading opportunities require one to predict *future* stock prices.

[3]See Morton Pincus and Charles Wasley, "The Incidence of Accounting Changes and Characteristics of Firms Making Accounting Changes," *Accounting Horizons* (June 1994): 1-24, and the references listed therein.
[4]See Eugene F. Fama, "Efficient Capital Markets: A Review of Theory and Empirical Work," *Journal of Finance* (May 1970): 383-417; Nicholas J. Gonedes and Nicholas Dopuch, "Capital Market Equilibrium, Information-Production and Selecting Accounting Techniques: Theoretical Framework and Review of Empirical Work," *Studies on Financial Accounting Objectives: 1974*, Supplement to Vol. 12, *Journal of Accounting Research*: 48-129; and Robert S. Kaplan, "Information Content of Financial Accounting Numbers: A Survey of Empirical Evidence," in: *Symposium of Impact of Accounting Research in Financial Accounting and Disclosure on Accounting Practice*, ed. by T. Keller and R. Abdel-khalik (Durham: Duke University Press, 1978). See also Thomas R. Dyckman and Dale Morse, *Efficient Capital Markets and Accounting: A Critical Analysis*, 2nd ed. (Englewood Cliffs, N.J.: Prentice-Hall, 1986).
[5]See, for example, Ray Ball, "Changes in Accounting Techniques and Stock Prices," *Empirical Research in Accounting: Selected Studies, 1972*, Supplement to Vol. 10, *Journal of Accounting Research*: 1-38; Robert S. Kaplan and Richard Roll, "Investor Evaluation of Accounting Information: Some Empirical Evidence," *Journal of Business* (April 1972): 225-257; Shyam Sunder, "Relationship Between Accounting Changes and Stock Prices: Problems of Measurement and Some Empirical Evidence," *Empirical Research in Accounting: Selected Studies, 1973*, Supplement to Vol. 11, *Journal of Accounting Research*: 1-45.
[6]For several examples, see Abraham J. Briloff, *More Debits Than Credits* (New York: Harper & Row, 1976). For an analysis of these examples see George Foster, "Briloff and the Capital Market," *Journal of Accounting Research* (Spring 1979): 262-274.

The second observation is that later studies provide evidence that capital markets may not adjust fully to available information, even in aggregate.[7] Several recent studies document successful trading strategies for large portfolios of firms based on financial statement data, and suggest that stock prices reflect a naïve understanding of accounting information.

If capital markets are fully efficient, then earnings management cannot produce a capital market advantage. On the other hand, if capital markets are not efficient in all cases, then by managing earnings, firms may take advantage of inefficiencies and obtain capital at a lower cost than if they do not practice earnings management. In this case, investors do not necessarily allocate the economy's capital resources in a socially optimal way.

Management Incentives and Survival. Over sufficiently long time periods, net income equals cash-in minus cash-out. Some corporate managers acknowledge that, because of this eventual reckoning, earnings management will not benefit the firm in the long run. They point out, however, that the long run comprises a series of short-run periods during which shareholders, creditors, and boards of directors make decisions based in part on accounting data. (See *agency theory* in the Glossary.)

Financial contracts — like bond indenture agreements and executive compensation contracts — often use accounting earnings as triggers for transactions and, thereby, provide managers with incentives to manage the reported numbers in the short run. For example, bond covenants frequently contain financial ratio constraints (see the Glossary at *bond indenture* and *ratio*), which use reported accounting numbers. If an accounting change prevents violation of one of these constraints, the firm may avoid costly renegotiation with its creditors.[8] Likewise, corporate boards often link managers' bonus provisions to earnings performance. If managers can manipulate earnings numbers, they may be able to affect their own compensation.[9]

Corporate managers observe that, since other firms practice earnings management, their survival dictates that they do so as well. Shareholders, they argue, do not want to see wide, unexpected fluctuations in earnings from year to year. To smooth out these fluctuations and create the impression that management has operations under control, they continue, requires earnings management. In saying this, managers espouse the view that investors and creditors use accounting data naïvely, ignoring differences in accounting choices. Regardless of whether investors and creditors are naïve in using accounting numbers, if managers *believe* that it is true, then such managers have an incentive to manage earnings, and financial statement readers will find their accounting choices to be informative.

---

[7]See the papers published in *Current Studies on The Information Content of Accounting Earnings*, Supplement to Vol. 27, *Journal of Accounting Research*, especially Victor L. Bernard and Jacob K. Thomas, "Post-earnings-announcement Drift: Delayed Price Response or Risk Premium?" (1989): 1-36; Robert N. Freeman and Senyo Tse, "The Multiperiod Information Content of Accounting Earnings: Confirmations and Contradictions of Previous Earnings Reports," (1989): 49-79; and Jane A. Ou and Stephen H. Penman, "Accounting Measurement, Price-Earnings Ratio, and the Information Content of Security Prices," (1989): 111-144.

[8]See Messod D. Beneish and Eric Press, "Costs of Technical Violation of Accounting-Based Debt Covenants," *The Accounting Review* (April 1993): 233-257; and Amy Patricia Sweeney, "Debt-covenant Violations and Managers' Accounting Responses," *Journal of Accounting and Economics* (May 1994): 281-308.

[9]See Paul M. Healy, "The Effect of Bonus Schemes on Accounting Decisions," *Journal of Accounting and Economics* (April 1985): 85-107; and Paul M. Healy, Sok-Hyon Kang and Krishna Palepu, "The Effect of Accounting Procedure Changes on CEOs' Cash Salary and Bonus Compensation," *Journal of Accounting and Economics* (April 1987): 7-34. Interestingly, the latter paper finds that boards of directors appear not to adjust compensation formulas for accounting method changes.\

Accounting Pronouncements

The following list of accounting pronouncements contains most of the generally accepted accounting principles.

Committee on Accounting Procedure (1939-1959)

Accounting Research Bulletins (ARBs)

ARB No.

Accounting Terminology Bulletins (ATBs)

ATB No.

Accounting Principles Board (APB), (1959-1973)

APB Opinions

Opinion No.

APB Statements

Statement No.

Financial Accounting Standards Board (FASB), (1973 to present)

Statements of Financial Accounting Standards (SFASs)

SFAS No.

Statement of Financial Accounting Concepts

SFAC No.